# HOW THE CATHOLIC CHURCH BUILT WESTERN CIVILIZATION

# HOW THE CATHOLIC CHURCH BUILT WESTERN CIVILIZATION

Thomas E. Woods, Jr., Ph.D.

Since 1947
REGNERY
PUBLISHING, INC.
An Eagle Publishing Company • Washington, DC

Library of Congress Cataloging-in-Publication Data

Woods, Thomas E.
  How the Catholic Church built Western civilization / Thomas E. Woods, Jr.
    p. cm.
  Includes bibliographical references and index.
  ISBN 0-89526-038-7
  1. Catholic Church—Influence. 2. Civilization, Western. 3. Christianity and culture. 4. Catholic Church—History. I. Title.
  BX1795.C85W66 2005
  282'.09--dc22

                                                              2005007380


Published in the United States by

Regnery Publishing, Inc.
One Massachusetts Avenue, NW
Washington, DC 20001
www.regnery.com

Distributed to the trade by

National Book Network
Lanham, MD 20706

Printed on acid-free paper

Manufactured in the United States of America

10 9 8 7 6 5 4 3

Books are available in quantity for promotional or premium use. Write to Director of Special Sales, Regnery Publishing, Inc., One Massachusetts Avenue NW, Washington, DC 20001, for information on discounts and terms or call (202) 216-0600.

✢

*To our daughters, Regina and Veronica*

———————————

As this book went to press we learned that

POPE JOHN PAUL II,

pontiff of twenty-seven years,
had passed to his eternal reward.

The book is also dedicated to him,
for his heroic labors against Nazism and Communism
and on behalf of peace and innocent human life.

# CONTENTS

*Chapter One*

# The Indispensable Church

**P**hilip Jenkins, distinguished professor of history and religious studies at Pennsylvania State University, has called anti-Catholicism the one remaining acceptable prejudice in America. His assessment is difficult to dispute. In our media and popular culture, little is off-limits when it comes to ridiculing or parodying the Church. My own students, to the extent that they know anything at all about the Church, are typically familiar only with alleged Church "corruption," of which they heard ceaseless tales of varying credibility from their high school teachers. The story of Catholicism, as far as they know, is one of ignorance, repression, and stagnation. That Western civilization stands indebted to the Church for the university system, charitable work, international law, the sciences, important legal principles, and much else besides has not exactly been impressed upon them with terrific zeal. Western civilization owes far more to the Catholic Church than most people—Catholics included—often realize. The Church, in fact, built Western civilization.

Western civilization does not derive entirely from Catholicism, of course; one can scarcely deny the importance of ancient Greece and Rome or of the various Germanic tribes that succeeded the Roman Empire in the West as formative influences on our civilization. The Church repudiated none of these traditions, and in fact absorbed and learned from the best of them. What is striking, though, is how in popular culture the substantial—and essential—Catholic contribution has gone relatively unnoticed.

No serious Catholic would contend that churchmen were right in every decision they made. While Catholics believe that the Church will maintain the faith in its integrity until the end of time, that spiritual guarantee in no way implies that every action of the popes and the episcopate is beyond reproach. To the contrary, Catholics distinguish between the holiness of the Church as an institution guided by the Holy Spirit and the inevitable sinful nature of men, including the men who serve the Church.

Still, recent scholarship has definitively revised in the Church's favor some historical episodes traditionally cited as evidence of the Church's wickedness. For example, we now know that the Inquisition was not nearly as harsh as previously portrayed, and that the number of people brought before it was far smaller—by orders of magnitude—than the exaggerated accounts that were once accepted. This is not merely special pleading on the author's part, but the clearly stated conclusion of the best and most recent scholarship.[1]

The point is that in our present cultural milieu it is easy to forget—or not to learn in the first place—just how much our civilization owes to the Catholic Church. To be sure, most people recognize the influence of the Church in music, art, and architecture. The purpose of this book, however, is to demonstrate that the Church's influence on Western civilization goes well beyond these areas. With the exception of scholars of medieval Europe, most people believe that the thousand years prior to the Renaissance were a time of ignorance and intellectual repression in which vigorous debate and lively intellectual exchange did not occur, and that strict conformity was ruthlessly imposed on whatever scholarly community might be said to have existed. My students can hardly be blamed for believing this; after all, it is only what they were taught in school and in American popular culture.

Even some professional authors can still be found giving credence to this view. In the course of some research I came across a 2001 book called *Second Messiah* by Christopher Knight and Robert Lomas. These authors paint a picture of the Catholic Church and its influence on Western civilization that could not be more wrong. They get away with it thanks to the strong prejudice against the Middle Ages, as well as an overall lack of knowledge of the period, that exists among the public. For example, we read: "The establishment of the Romanised Christian era marked the beginning of the Dark Ages: the period of Western history when the lights went out on all learning, and superstition replaced knowledge. It lasted until the power of the Roman Church was undermined by the Reformation."[2] Again: "Everything that was good and proper was despised and all branches of human achievement were ignored in the name of Jesus Christ."[3]

Now, I realize that this is precisely what many readers were themselves taught in school, but there is scarcely a single historian to be found today who would view these comments with anything but amused contempt. The statements made in *Second Messiah* fly in the face of a century of scholarship, and Knight and Lomas, who are not trained historians, seem blissfully unaware that they are repeating tired old canards that not a single professional historian any longer believes. It must be frustrating to be a historian of medieval Europe: No matter how hard you work and how much evidence you produce to the contrary, just about everyone still believes that the entire period was intellectually and culturally barren, and that the Church bequeathed to the West nothing but repression.

Not mentioned by Knight and Lomas is that it was in "Dark Age" Europe that the university system, a gift of Western civilization to the world, was developed by the Catholic Church. Historians have marveled at the extent to which intellectual debate in those universities was free and unfettered. The exaltation of human reason and its capabilities, a commitment to rigorous and rational debate, a promotion of intellectual inquiry and scholarly exchange—all sponsored by the Church—provided the framework for the Scientific Revolution, which was unique to Western civilization.

For the last fifty years, virtually all historians of science—including A. C. Crombie, David Lindberg, Edward Grant, Stanley Jaki, Thomas Goldstein, and J. L. Heilbron—have concluded that the Scientific Revolution was indebted to the Church. The Catholic contribution to science went well beyond ideas—including theological ideas—to accomplished practicing scientists, many of whom were *priests*. For example, Father Nicholas Steno, a Lutheran convert who became a Catholic priest, is often identified as the father of geology. The father of Egyptology was Father Athanasius Kircher. The first person to measure the rate of acceleration of a freely falling body was yet another priest, Father Giambattista Riccioli. Father Roger Boscovich is often credited as the father of modern atomic theory. Jesuits so dominated the study of earthquakes that seismology became known as "the Jesuit science."

And that is far from all. Even though some thirty-five craters on the moon are named for Jesuit scientists and mathematicians, the Church's contributions to astronomy are all but unknown to the average educated American. Yet, as J. L. Heilbron of the University of California at Berkeley points out, "The Roman

Catholic Church gave more financial aid and social support to the study of astronomy for over six centuries, from the recovery of ancient learning during the late Middle Ages into the Enlightenment, than any other, and, probably, all other, institutions."[4] Still, the Church's true role in the development of modern science remains one of the best-kept secrets of modern history.

While the importance of the monastic tradition has been recognized to one degree or another in the standard narrative of Western history—everyone knows that the monks preserved the literary inheritance of the ancient world, not to mention literacy itself, in the aftermath of the fall of Rome—in this book, the reader will discover that the monks' contributions were in fact far greater. One can scarcely find a significant endeavor in the advancement of civilization during the early Middle Ages in which the monks did not play a major role. As one study described it, the monks gave "the whole of Europe . . . a network of model factories, centers for breeding livestock, centers of scholarship, spiritual fervor, the art of living . . . readiness for social action—in a word . . . advanced civilization that emerged from the chaotic waves of surrounding barbarity. Without any doubt, Saint Benedict [the most important architect of Western monasticism] was the Father of Europe. The Benedictines, his children, were the Fathers of European civilization."[5]

The development of the idea of international law, while at times tenuously associated with the ancient Stoics, is often attributed to the thinkers and rights theorists of the seventeenth and eighteenth centuries. In fact, however, the idea is first found in sixteenth-century Spanish universities, and it was Francisco de Vitoria, a Catholic priest and professor, who earned the title of father of international law. Faced with Spanish mistreatment of the natives of the New World, Vitoria and other Catholic philosophers and theologians began to speculate about human rights and the proper relations that ought to exist between nations. These Catholic thinkers originated the idea of international law as we understand it today.

Western law itself is very largely a gift of the Church. Canon law was the first modern legal system in Europe, proving that a sophisticated, coherent body of law could be assembled from the hodgepodge of frequently contradictory statutes, traditions, local customs, and the like with which both Church and state were faced in the Middle Ages. According to legal scholar Harold Berman, "[I]t was the church that first taught Western man what a modern legal system is like. The church first taught that conflicting customs, statutes, cases, and doctrines may be reconciled by analysis and synthesis."[6]

The idea of formulated "rights" comes from Western civilization. Specifically, it comes not from John Locke and Thomas Jefferson—as many might assume—but from the canon law of the Catholic Church. Other important legal principles associated with Western civilization can also be traced back to the Church's influence, as churchmen sought to introduce rational trial procedures and sophisticated legal concepts in place of the superstition-based trials by ordeal that had characterized the Germanic legal order.

According to old economic histories, modern economics comes from Adam Smith and other economic theorists of the eighteenth century. More recent studies, however, emphasize the importance of the economic thought of the Late Scholastics, particularly the Spanish Catholic theologians of the fifteenth and sixteenth centuries. Some, like the great twentieth-century economist Joseph Schumpeter, have even gone so far as to call these Catholic thinkers the founders of modern scientific economics.

Most people know about the charitable work of the Catholic Church, but what they often don't know is just how unique the Church's commitment to such work was. The ancient world affords us some examples of liberality toward the poor, but it is a liberality that seeks fame and recognition for the giver, and which tends to be indiscriminate rather than specifically focused on those in need. The poor were all too often treated with contempt, and the very idea of helping the destitute without any thought to reciprocity or personal gain was something foreign. Even W. E. H. Lecky, a nineteenth-century historian highly critical of the Church, admitted that the Church's commitment to the poor—both its spirit and its sheer scope—constituted something new in the Western world and represented a dramatic improvement over the standards of classical antiquity.

In all these areas the Church made an indelible imprint on the very heart of European civilization and was a profoundly significant force for good. A recent one-volume history of the Catholic Church was called *Triumph*—an entirely appropriate title for a history of an institution boasting so many heroic men and women and so many historic accomplishments. Yet relatively little of this information is found in the Western civilization textbooks the average student reads in high school and college. That, in large measure, is why this book was written. In many more ways than people now realize, the Catholic Church has shaped the kind of civilization we inhabit and the kind of people we are. Though the typical college textbook will not say so, the Catholic Church was the indispensable builder of Western civilization. Not only did the Church work to overturn the morally repugnant aspects of the ancient world—like infanticide and gladiatorial combats—but after Rome's fall, it was the Church that restored and advanced civilization. It began by tutoring the barbarians; and it is to the barbarians that we now turn.

*Chapter Two*

# A Light in the Darkness

T he term *"Dark Ages"* was once applied to the entire millennium separating the period of late antiquity from the Renaissance. Nowadays, there is widespread acknowledgment of the accomplishments of the High Middle Ages. As David Knowles points out, scholars have begun more and more to push the "Dark Age" designation back still further, excluding the eighth, ninth, and tenth centuries from that dubious distinction.

Still, there can be little doubt that the sixth and seventh centuries were marked by cultural and intellectual retrogression, in terms of education, literary output, and similar indicators. Was that the Church's fault? Historian Will Durant—an agnostic—defended the Church against this charge decades ago, placing blame for the decline not on the Church, which did everything it could to reverse it, but on the barbarian invasions of late antiquity. "The basic cause of cultural retrogression," Durant explained, "was not Christianity but barbarism; not religion but war. The human inundations ruined or impoverished cities, monasteries, libraries, schools, and made impossible the life of the scholar or the scientist. Perhaps the destruction would have been worse had not the Church maintained some measure of order in a crumbling civilization."[1]

By the late second century, a hodgepodge of Germanic tribes, moving westward from central Europe in what is referred to as the *Völkerwanderungen*, had begun to press on the Rhine and Danube frontiers. As time went on and Roman generals began devoting themselves to making and unmaking emperors instead of guarding the frontiers, the tribesmen began to pour in through the resulting gaps in the Roman defenses. These invasions hastened the collapse of Rome and presented the Church with an unprecedented challenge.

The impact of the barbarian incursions into Rome varied depending on the tribe. The Vandals were the most direct, sweeping through North Africa by violent conquest and sacking Rome itself in the mid–fifth century. Other peoples, however, were less hostile, often respecting Rome and classical culture. Thus even Alaric, the Goth who would sack Rome in 410, demanded after taking Athens that he be permitted to spend the day exploring the famed city, admiring its monuments, attending its theater, and having Plato's *Timaeus* read to him.[2] The Goths were admitted into the empire in 376 as they fled the ravaging Huns. By 378, in response to dreadful treatment at the hands of local officials, they revolted against Roman authority. A century later, Rome would be governed by Goths.

With political order severely disrupted around them and the division of the western Roman Empire into a patchwork of barbarian kingdoms a fait accompli, bishops, priests, and religious men set out to reestablish the groundwork of civilization on this most unlikely foundation. Indeed, the man we consider the father of Europe, Charlemagne, was not altogether free of the remnants of barbarian influence, yet he had been so persuaded of the beauty, truth, and superiority of the Catholic religion that he did everything possible to establish the new post-imperial Europe on the basis of Catholicism.

## The Barbarian Peoples

*The barbarians were rural or nomadic* peoples with no written literature and little political organization, aside from loyalty to a chief. According to some etymologies of the word, all the Romans could make out of these peoples' various languages was "bar, bar, bar"—hence "barbarian."

One of the great accomplishments of ancient Rome was the development of a sophisticated legal system, which would influence Europe for many centuries. In the barbarians' view, law was more about simply stopping a fight and keeping order than establishing justice. Thus, a person accused of a crime might be subjected to the ordeal by hot water, in which he had to reach into a pot of scalding water and retrieve a stone at the bottom. His arm would then be bandaged. Three days later, when the bandages were removed, the man was pronounced innocent if the wound had begun to heal and scabs were visible. If not, his guilt was established. Likewise, the ordeal by cold water consisted of tying the hands and feet of the accused and throwing him into a river. If he floated, he was pronounced guilty, since the divine principle in the water was thought to be rejecting him.

The barbarians were warrior peoples whose customs and conduct struck the Romans as savage. As Christopher Dawson put it, "The Church had to undertake the task of introducing the law of the Gospel and the ethics of the Sermon on the Mount among peoples who regarded homicide as the most honorable occupation and vengeance as synonymous with justice."

When the Visigoths sacked Rome in 410, Saint Jerome expressed a profound shock and sadness: "A terrible rumor has arrived from the West. Rome is besieged; the lives of the citizens have been redeemed by gold. Despoiled, they are again encircled, and are losing their lives after they have lost their riches. My voice cannot continue, sobs interrupt my dictation. The City is taken which took the whole world."[3] "See with what suddenness death has weighed the whole world," wrote Orientius at the invasion of Gaul in the first decade of the fifth century, "how many peoples the violence of war has struck down. Neither dense and savage forests nor high mountains, nor rivers rushing down through such rapids, nor citadels on remote heights nor cities protected by their walls, not the barrier of the sea nor the sad solitude of the desert, not holes in the ground nor caves under forbidding cliffs could escape from the barbarians' raids."[4]

The Franks, who had settled in Gaul (in the area of modern France), were the most significant of these barbarian peoples. Unlike many of the other barbarian groups, the Franks had not been converted to Arianism (the heresy that denied Christ's divinity), and thus the Church set her sights on them. It is a fact of missionary history that the Church has found it immensely easier to convert people directly from primitive paganism or animism than to convert them once they have adopted another faith like Arianism or Islam. When a man named Clovis became king of the Franks in 481, churchmen spotted their chance. Saint Remigius wrote the new king a congratulatory letter that reminded him of the benefits that would accrue to him were he to collaborate and cooperate with the episcopate. "Show deference towards your bishops," Saint Remigius boldly wrote, "always turn to them for advice. And, if you are in harmony with them, your land will prosper."

Historians have speculated that Clovis's marriage to the beautiful, pious, and Catholic Clotilda was inspired and arranged by the bishops, with an eye to converting her royal husband to the faith. Although political considerations doubtless played a role, Clovis was apparently moved by much of what he heard about the life of Christ. When told the story of the crucifixion, he is said to have exclaimed, "Oh, if only I had been there with my Franks!" It took a number of years, but Clovis would eventually be baptized. (The date is uncertain, but the traditionally accepted year is 496, and the French commemorated the 1,500th anniversary of the baptism of Clovis in 1996.) It would be another four hundred years before all the barbarian peoples of Western Europe had been converted, but the project was off to an auspicious start.

Saint Avitus, an important bishop in Gaul, recognized the significance of Clovis's conversion, telling the Frankish king, "Thanks to you this corner of the world shines with a great brilliance, and the light of a new star glitters in the West! In choosing for yourself, you choose for all. Your faith is our victory!"

Given the strong identification of the barbarian peoples with their kings, it was generally enough to convert the monarch, and the people would eventually follow. This was not always an easy or smooth process; in the centuries to come, Catholic priests from among the Franks would say Mass but also continue to offer sacrifice to the old nature gods.

For that reason, it was not enough simply to convert the barbarians; the Church had to continue to guide them, both to guarantee that the conversion had truly taken hold and to ensure that the faith would begin to transform their government and way of life. It has been said that recollections of these two tasks—conversion and ongoing guidance—are what primarily separate Saint Gregory of Tours's sixth-century *History of the Franks* from the Venerable Bede's eighth-century *Ecclesiastical History of the English People*. Saint Boniface, the great missionary, performed both tasks: In addition to making converts in Germany, in the 740s he also initiated the long overdue reform of the Frankish Church.

The Merovingian line of kings, to which Clovis belonged, lost its vigor throughout the sixth and seventh centuries. They were incompetent rulers, and they also fought—often viciously—among themselves; burning other family members alive was not unheard of. In the course of their various power struggles, they often traded power and land to Frankish aristocrats in exchange for support. As a result, they grew ever weaker. This weakening accelerated under the seventh-century Merovingian kings, whom historian Norman Cantor describes as a series of women, children, and mental defectives.

Unfortunately, the degeneration of the Merovingians affected the Church as well. She had made the terrible mistake of aligning herself so closely to the ruling family that, when the deterioration set in, it was impossible for her to escape its effects. "In gratitude for the exalted position which she owed to the Merovingians," explains a student of the period, "she [had] delivered herself almost entirely to them."[5] By the seventh century, the condition of the Frankish priesthood was increasingly desperate, so infected had it become by depravity and immorality. The state of the episcopate was hardly much better, as men vied with one another to take control of bishoprics that to them represented only secular power and wealth. The Frankish Church would ultimately be reformed from without at the hands of Irish and Anglo-Saxon missionaries, who had themselves received the Catholic faith from the Continent. Now, when the land of the Franks needed an infusion of faith, order, and civilization, it received these from Catholic missionaries.

Still, the papacy would turn to the Franks in the eighth century in its search for protection and for a partner in restoring Christian civilization. The papacy had enjoyed a special relationship with the later Roman emperors that continued after the collapse of the empire in the West, when the only remaining "Roman" authority was the eastern emperor in Constantinople (which had never succumbed to barbarian incursions). But that relationship became strained. For one thing, the eastern empire was fighting for its life against the Arabs and Persians in the seventh century and could hardly serve as the reliable source of protection and defense that the papacy desired. Worse still was that the emperors, as would become customary in the eastern empire, routinely intervened in the life of the Church in areas lying clearly beyond the state's competence.

It seemed to some churchmen that the time had come to begin to look elsewhere, to leave behind the Church's traditional reliance on the emperor and to find another political force with which it could forge a fruitful alliance.

## THE CAROLINGIAN RENAISSANCE

*The Church made the momentous* decision to turn its desire for protection and cooperation away from the emperors in Constantinople and toward the still semi-barbarian Franks, who had converted to Catholicism without passing through an Arian phase. In the eighth century, the Church blessed the official transfer of power from the Merovingian dynasty to the Carolingian family—the family of Charles Martel, who had famously defeated the Muslims at Tours in 732, and ultimately of Charles the Great or Charlemagne, who would become known as the father of Europe.

The Carolingians had profited from the decline of the Merovingians. They held what eventually became the hereditary position of mayor of the palace, similar to the role of prime minister. Far more skilled and sophisticated than the kings themselves, the Carolingian mayors of the palace performed more and more of the day-to-day governance of the kingdom of the Franks. By the mid–eighth century, the Carolingians, increasingly in possession of the *power* exercised by kings, sought to acquire the *title* of king. Pepin the Short, the mayor of the palace in 751, wrote to Pope Zachary I to inquire whether it was good that a man with no power was called king, while a man with power was deprived of that title. The pope, understanding full well what Pepin was driving at, replied that that was not a good situation, and that the names of things should correspond to reality. Thus did the pope, on the basis of his acknowledged spiritual authority, give his blessing to a change of dynasty in the kingdom of the Franks. The last Merovingian king quietly retired to a monastery.

The Church thus facilitated the peaceful transfer of power away from the decrepit Merovingians and into the hands of the Carolingians, with whom churchmen would work so closely in the ensuing years to restore the values of civilized life. Under the influence of the Church, this barbarian people would be transformed into civilization builders. Charlemagne (r. 768–814), perhaps the greatest Frank of them all, exemplified that ideal. (The Frankish realm, including the additions to it made by Charlemagne, extended by this time from the so-called Spanish March in the east through modern-day France, northern Italy, Switzerland, and much of Germany.) Although unable to write—though a popular legend, surely apocryphal, has him correcting biblical translations in the last year of his life—Charlemagne strongly encouraged education and the arts, calling upon the bishops to organize schools around their cathedrals. As historian Joseph Lynch explains, "The writing, book copying, artistic and architectural work, and thinking of the men trained in the cathedral and monastic schools stimulated a change in the quality and quantity of intellectual life."[6]

The result of this encouragement of education and the arts is known as the Carolingian Renaissance, which extended from the reign of Charlemagne through that of his son, Louis the Pious (r. 814–840). Perhaps the central intellectual figure of the Carolingian Renaissance was Alcuin, an Anglo-Saxon who had been educated at York by a pupil of the Venerable Bede, the great saint and ecclesiastical historian who was one of the great intellects of his day. Alcuin was the headmaster of the cathedral school at York and a deacon who would later serve as the abbot of the monastery of Saint Martin's at Tours. He was tapped by Charlemagne himself in 781 when the two met during Alcuin's brief trip to Italy. In addition to his knowledge of a variety of subjects, Alcuin also excelled as a teacher of Latin, having absorbed the successful techniques of his Irish and Anglo-Saxon predecessors. Teaching the Germanic people grammatically correct Latin—a difficult skill to acquire during the unsettled sixth and seventh centuries— was an essential element of the Carolingian Renaissance. Knowledge of Latin made possible both the study of the Latin Church fathers and the classical world of ancient Rome. In fact, the oldest surviving copies of most ancient Roman literature date back to the ninth century, when Carolingian scholars rescued them from oblivion. "People don't always realise," writes Kenneth Clark, "that only three or four antique manuscripts of the Latin authors are still in existence: our whole knowledge of ancient literature is due to the collecting and copying that began under Charlemagne, and almost any classical text that survived until the eighth century has survived until today."[7]

For the substance of Carolingian education, scholars looked to ancient Roman models, where they found the seven liberal arts. These were the *quadrivium* of astronomy, music, arithmetic, and geometry, and the *trivium* of logic, grammar, and rhetoric. Given the particular urgency of literary education, the *quadrivium* was often treated only superficially in the early years of this revival of schooling. But this was the groundwork on which future intellectual progress would be built.

Another achievement of the Carolingian Renaissance was an important innovation in writing known as "Carolingian minuscule." Previously, geographical isolation had contributed to the growth of a variety of scripts throughout Western Europe, such that it eventually became difficult for people to decipher what their counterparts elsewhere were saying.[8] The various scripts in use before the advent of Carolingian miniscule were difficult to read and time-consuming to write; there were no lowercase letters, punctuation, or blank spaces between words.

Fredegise, Alcuin's successor as abbot at Saint Martin's, played a definitive part in the development and introduction of Carolingian minuscule. Now Western Europe had a script that could be read and written with relative ease. The introduction of lowercase letters, spaces between words, and other measures intended to increase readability quickened both reading and writing. Two recent scholars describe its "unsurpassed grace and lucidity, which must have had a tremendous effect on the survival of classical literature by casting it in a form that all could read with both ease and pleasure."[9] "It would be no exaggeration," writes Philippe Wolff, "to link this development with that of printing itself as the two decisive steps in the growth of a civilization based on the written word."[10] Carolingian miniscule—developed by the monks of the Catholic Church—was crucial to building the literacy of Western civilization.

Historians of music often speak of the "anxiety of influence" suffered by composers so unfortunate as to follow geniuses and prodigies. A similar phenomenon is evident during the short-lived burst of activity of the Carolingian Renaissance. Thus Einhard, Charlemagne's biographer, clearly models his work after Suetonius's *Lives of the Caesars*, even lifting whole paragraphs from the ancient Roman's work. For how could he, a mere barbarian, hope to surpass the elegance and skill of such a rich and accomplished civilization?

And yet, despite their obvious disabilities, the Catholics of Charlemagne's day looked forward to the birth of a civilization still greater than ancient Greece or Rome. For as the great scholar Alcuin pointed out, they in the eighth and ninth centuries possessed something that the ancients had not: the Catholic faith. They modeled themselves after ancient Athens, but remained convinced that theirs would be a greater Athens because they possessed the pearl of great price of which their Greek predecessors, for all their accomplishments, could not boast. So excited was Alcuin that he could write in extravagant terms to Charlemagne about the heights of civilization that he believed were in reach:

> If many are infected by your aims, a new Athens will be created in France, nay, an Athens finer than the old, for ours, ennobled by the teachings of Christ, will surpass all the wisdom of the Academy. The old had only the disciplines of Plato for teacher and yet inspired by the seven liberal arts it still shone with splendor: but ours will be endowed besides with the sevenfold plenitude of the Holy Ghost and will outshine all the dignity of secular wisdom.[11]

The Carolingian Renaissance, though it suffered terrible blows at the hands of invading Vikings, Magyars, and Muslims in the ninth and tenth centuries, was never extinguished in spirit. Even in the darkest days of those invasions, the spirit of learning always remained alive in the monasteries, enough to make its full rebirth possible in more settled times. Of equal importance to the intellectual development of Western civilization was the contribution of the great Alcuin. Alcuin, writes David Knowles, who "insisted on the necessity of good copies of all the best models in the field of textbooks, and who had himself set up excellent scriptoria in many places," gave "a new impetus and technique to the copying of manuscripts; this continued without abatement at very many monasteries, more methodically and with a wider scope than before; and in the so-called Carolingian minuscule, which actually owed much to the script of Ireland and Northumbria, it had an instrument of great power. With Alcuin began the great age of the copying of Latin manuscripts, both patristic and classical, and this gradual accumulation of clearly (and more correctly) written books was of inestimable value when the more comprehensive revival came two centuries later."[12]

After Charlemagne's death, the initiative for the spread of learning would fall more and more to the Church. Local councils called for the opening of schools, as did a synod in Bavaria (798) as well as the councils of Chalons (813) and Aix (816).[13] Alcuin's friend Theodulf, who served as bishop of Orleans and abbot of Fleury, likewise called for the expansion of education: "In the villages and townships the priests shall open schools. If any of the faithful entrust their children to them to learn letters, let them not refuse to instruct these children in all charity. . . . [W]hen the priests undertake this task, let them ask no payment, and if they receive anything, let it be only the small gifts offered by the parents."[14]

The Church, as the educator of Europe, was the one light that survived repeated barbarian invasions. The barbarian invasions of the fourth and fifth centuries had ushered in a serious decline in those aspects of life with which we associate the very idea of civilization: cultural achievement, urban life, and the life of the mind. In the ninth and tenth centuries, Western Europe would fall victim to more waves of devastating attacks—this time from Vikings, Magyars, and Muslims. (For an idea of what these invasions were like, bear in mind that one of the better-known Viking warriors was named Thorfinn Skullsplitter.) The unfailing vision and determination of Catholic bishops, monks, priests, scholars and civil administrators saved Europe from a second collapse.[15] The seeds of learning sown by Alcuin sprouted in the Church, which again acted as a restoring influence on civilization. As one scholar writes, "There was but one tradition available for their use, and that flowed from the schools of the age quickened by Alcuin."[16]

After the decline of the Carolingian Empire, according to historian Christopher Dawson, the monks began the recovery of learning:

> [I]t was the great monasteries, especially those of Southern Germany, Saint Gall, Reichenau and Tegernsee, that were the only remaining islands of intellectual life amidst the returning flood of barbarism which once again threatened to submerge Western Christendom. For, though monasticism seems at first sight ill-adapted to withstand the material destructiveness of an age of lawlessness and war, it was an institution which possessed extraordinary recuperative power.[17]

The recuperative power of the monasteries meant that they could work quickly and dramatically to repair the devastation of invasion and political collapse.

*Ninety-nine out of a hundred monasteries could be burnt and the monks killed or driven out, and yet the whole tradition could be reconstituted from the one survivor,* and the desolate sites could be repeopled by fresh supplies of monks who would take up again the broken tradition, following the same rule, singing the same liturgy, reading the same books and thinking the same thoughts as their predecessors. In this way monasticism and the monastic culture came back to England and Normandy in the age of Saint Dunstan from Fleury and Ghent after more than a century of utter destruction; with the result that a century later the Norman and English monasteries were again among the leaders of Western culture.[18]

This preservation both of the West's classical heritage and of the accomplishments of the Carolingian Renaissance was no simple matter. Invading hordes had sacked many a monastery and set fire to libraries whose volumes were far more precious to the intellectual community of the time than modern readers, accustomed to an inexpensive and abundant supply of books, can readily appreciate. As Dawson rightly notes, it was the monks who kept the light of learning from being extinguished.

One of the brightest lights of the early stage of recovery was Gerbert of Aurillac, who later became Pope Sylvester II (r. 999–1003). Gerbert was certainly the most learned man in the Europe of his day. He was renowned for the breadth of his knowledge, which encompassed astronomy, Latin literature, mathematics, music, philosophy, and theology. His thirst for ancient manuscripts calls to mind the enthusiasm of the fifteenth century, when the Church offered rewards to humanist scholars who recovered ancient texts.

The details of Gerbert's life are not always clear, though important clues peek through some of his letters as well as the sometimes unreliable biographical sketch composed by Richer, a monk of the Order of Saint Remy, who was one of his best students. It is certain that beginning in the 970s he headed the episcopal school in Rheims—at which he had once been a student of advanced logic—where he was able to devote himself entirely to teaching and study. "The just man lives by faith," he would say, "but it is good that he should combine science with his faith."[19] Gerbert placed great emphasis on the cultivation of man's reasoning faculty, which God had not given him in vain. "The Divinity made a great gift to men in giving them faith while not denying them knowledge," Gerbert wrote. "[T]hose who do not possess it [knowledge] are called fools."[20]

In 997, the German king-emperor Otto III wrote to implore the assistance of the celebrated Gerbert. Urgently desiring knowledge, he turned to a future pope. "I am ignorant," he confessed, "and my education has been greatly neglected. Come and help me. Correct what has been ill done and advise me on the proper government of the Empire. Strip me of my Saxon boorishness and encourage the things I have inherited from my Greek forebears. Expound the book of arithmetic which you sent me." Gerbert happily acceded to the king's request. "Greek by birth and Roman by Empire," Gerbert assured him, "you may claim as it were by hereditary right the treasures of Greek and Roman wisdom. Surely in that there is something divine?"[21]

Gerbert's commitment to learning and his influence on subsequent teachers and thinkers were emblematic of Europe's recovery from over a century of invasions—a recovery that would have been impossible without the Church's guiding light. The work and intentions of the Church would bear their greatest fruit in the development of the university system, a topic that merits a chapter of its own, but first let us look at the seeds of learning planted by the monasteries.

*Chapter Three*

# How the Monks
# Saved Civilization

T*he monks played* a critical role in the development of Western civilization. But judging from Catholic monasticism's earliest practice, one would hardly have guessed the enormous impact on the outside world that it would come to exercise. This historical fact comes as less of a surprise when we recall Christ's words: "Seek ye first the kingdom of heaven, and all these things shall be added unto you." That, stated simply, is the history of the monks.

Early forms of monastic life are evident by the third century. By then, individual Catholic women committed themselves as consecrated virgins to lives of prayer and sacrifice, looking after the poor and the sick.[1] Nuns come from these early traditions.

Another source of Christian monasticism is found in Saint Paul of Thebes and more famously in Saint Anthony of Egypt (also known as Saint Anthony of the Desert), whose life spanned the mid-third century through the mid-fourth century. Saint Anthony's sister lived in a house of consecrated virgins. He became a hermit, retreating to the deserts of Egypt for the sake of his own spiritual perfection, though his great example led thousands to flock to him.

The hermit's characteristic feature was his retreat into remote solitude, so that he might renounce worldly things and concentrate intensely on his spiritual life. Hermits typically lived alone or in groups of two or three, finding shelter in caves or simple huts and supporting themselves on what they could produce in their small fields or through such tasks as basket-making. The lack of an authority to oversee their spiritual regimen led some of them to pursue unusual spiritual and penitential practices. According to Monsignor Philip Hughes, an accomplished historian of the Catholic Church, "There were hermits who hardly ever ate, or slept, others who stood without movement whole weeks together, or who had themselves sealed up in tombs and remained there for years, receiving only the least of poor nourishment through crevices in the masonry."[2]

Cenobitic monasticism (monks living together in monasteries), the kind with which most people are familiar, developed in part as a reaction against the life of the hermits and in recognition that men ought to live in community. This was the position of Saint Basil the Great, who played an important role in the development of Eastern monasticism. Still, the hermit life never entirely died out; a thousand years after Saint Paul of Thebes, a hermit was elected pope, taking the name Celestine V.

Eastern monasticism influenced the West in a number of ways: through the travels of Saint Athanasius, for example, and the writings of Saint John Cassian—a man of the West who possessed a wide knowledge of Eastern practice. But Western monasticism is most deeply indebted to one of its own: Saint Benedict of Nursia. Saint Benedict established twelve small communities of monks at Subiaco, thirty-eight miles from Rome, before heading fifty miles south to found Monte Cassino, the great monastery for which he is remembered. It was here, around 529, that he composed the famous Rule of Saint Benedict, the excellence of which was reflected in its all but universal adoption throughout Western Europe in the centuries that followed.

The moderation of Saint Benedict's Rule, as well as the structure and order it provided, facilitated its spread throughout Europe. Unlike the Irish monasteries, which were known for their extremes of self-denial (but which nevertheless attracted men in considerable numbers), Benedictine monasteries took for granted that the monk was to receive adequate food and sleep, even if during penitential seasons his regimen might grow more austere. The Benedictine monk typically lived at a material level comparable to that of a contemporary Italian peasant.

Each Benedictine house was independent of every other, and each had an abbot to oversee its affairs and good order. Monks had previously been free to wander from one place to another, but Saint Benedict envisioned a monastic lifestyle in which each remained attached to his own monastery.[3]

Saint Benedict also negated the worldly status of the prospective monk, whether his life had been one of great wealth or miserable servitude, for all were equal in Christ. The Benedictine abbot "shall make no distinction of persons in the monastery.... A freeborn man shall not be preferred to one coming from servitude, unless there be some other and reasonable cause. For whether we are bond or free, we are all one in Christ.... God is no respecter of persons."

A monk's purpose in retiring to a monastery was to cultivate a more disciplined spiritual life and, more specifically, to work out his salvation in an environment and under a regimen suitable to that purpose. His role in Western civilization would prove substantial. The monks' intention had not been to perform great tasks for European civilization, yet as time went on, they came to appreciate the task for which the times seemed to have called them.

During a period of great turmoil, the Benedictine tradition endured, and its houses remained oases of order and peace. It has been said of Monte Cassino, the motherhouse of the Benedictines, that her own history reflected that permanence. Sacked by the barbarian Lombards in 589, destroyed by the Saracens in 884, razed by an earthquake in 1349, pillaged by French troops in 1799, and wrecked by the bombs of World War II in 1944— Monte Cassino refused to disappear, as each time her monks returned to rebuild.[4]

Mere statistics can hardly do justice to the Benedictine achievement, but by the beginning of the fourteenth century, the order had supplied the Church with 24 popes, 200 cardinals, 7,000 archbishops, 15,000 bishops, and 1,500 canonized saints. At its height, the Benedictine order could boast 37,000 monasteries. And it was not merely their influence within the Church to which the statistics point; so exalted had the monastic ideal become throughout society that by the fourteenth century the order had already enrolled some twenty emperors, ten empresses, forty-seven kings, and fifty queens.[5] Thus a great many of Europe's most powerful would come to pursue the humble life and spiritual regimen of the Benedictine order. Even the various barbarian groups were attracted to the monastic life, and such figures as Carloman of the Franks and Rochis of the Lombards eventually pursued it themselves.[6]

## THE PRACTICAL ARTS

*Although most educated people* think of the medieval monasteries' scholarly and cultural pursuits as their contribution to Western civilization, we should not overlook the monks' important cultivation of what might be called the practical arts. Agriculture is a particularly significant example. In the early twentieth century, Henry Goodell, president of what was then the Massachusetts Agricultural College, celebrated "the work of these grand old monks during a period of fifteen hundred years. They saved agriculture when nobody else could save it. They practiced it under a new life and new conditions when no one else dared undertake it."[7] Testimony on this point is considerable. "We owe the agricultural restoration of a great part of Europe to the monks," observes another expert. "Wherever they came," adds still another, "they converted the wilderness into a cultivated country; they pursued the breeding of cattle and agriculture, labored with their own hands, drained morasses, and cleared away forests. By them Germany was rendered a fruitful country." Another historian records that "every Benedictine monastery was an agricultural college for the whole region in which it was located."[8] Even the nineteenth-century French statesman and historian François Guizot, who was not especially sympathetic to the Catholic Church, observed: "The Benedictine monks were the agriculturists of Europe; they cleared it on a large scale, associating agriculture with preaching."[9]

Manual labor, expressly called for in the Rule of Saint Benedict, played a central role in the monastic life. Although the Rule was known for its moderation and its aversion to exaggerated penances, we often find the monks freely embracing work that was difficult and unattractive, since for them such tasks were channels of grace and opportunities for mortification of the flesh. This was certainly true in the clearing and reclaiming of land. The prevailing view of swamps was that they were sources of pestilence utterly without value. But the monks thrived in such locations and embraced the challenges that came with them. Before long, they managed to dike and drain the swamp and turn what had once been a source of disease and filth into fertile agricultural land.[10]

Montalembert, the great nineteenth-century historian of the monks, paid tribute to their great agricultural work. "It is impossible to forget," he wrote, "the use they made of so many vast districts (holding as they did one-fifth of all the land in England), uncultivated and uninhabited, covered with forests or surrounded by marshes." That was indeed the character of much of the land that the monks occupied, partly because they chose the most secluded and inaccessible sites to reinforce the communal solitude of their life and partly because this was land that lay donors could more easily give the monks.[11] Although they cleared forests that stood in the way of human habitation and use, they were also careful to plant trees and conserve forests when possible.[12]

A particularly vivid example of the monks' salutary influence on their physical surroundings comes from the fen district of Southampton, England. An expert describes what the area would have looked like in the seventh century, before the founding of Thorney Abbey:

> It was nothing but a vast morass. The fens in the seventh century were probably like the forests at the mouth of the Mississippi or the swamp shores of the Carolinas. It was a labyrinth of black, wandering streams; broad lagoons, morasses submerged every spring-tide; vast beds of reed and sedge and fern; vast copses of willow, alder and gray poplar, rooted in the floating peat, which was swallowing up slowly, all-devouring, yet all-preserving, the forests of fir and oak, ash and poplar, hazel and yew, which had once grown in that low, rank soil. Trees torn down by flood and storm floated and lodged in rafts, damming the waters back upon the land. Streams bewildered in the forests changed their channels, mingling silt and sand with the black soil of the peat. Nature left to herself ran into wild riot and chaos more and more, till the whole fen became one dismal swamp.[13]

Five centuries later, this is how William of Malmesbury (c. 1096–1143) described the area:

> It is a counterfeit of Paradise, where the gentleness and purity of heaven appear already to be reflected. In the midst of the fens rise groves of trees which seem to touch the stars with their tall and slender tops; the charmed eye wanders over a sea of verdant herbage, the foot which treads the wide meadows meets with no obstacle in its path. Not an inch of land as far as the eye can reach lies uncultivated. Here the soil is hidden by fruit trees; there by vines stretched upon the ground or trailed on trellises. Nature and art rival each other, the one supplying all that the other forgets to produce. O deep and pleasant solitude! Thou hast been given by God to the monks, so that their mortal life may daily bring them nearer to heaven.[14]

Wherever they went, the monks introduced crops, industries, or production methods with which the people had not been previously familiar. Here they would introduce the rearing of cattle and horses, there the brewing of beer or the raising of bees or fruit. In Sweden, the corn trade owed its existence to the monks; in Parma, it was cheese making; in Ireland, salmon fisheries—and, in a great many places, the finest vineyards. Monks stored up the waters from springs in order to distribute them in times of drought. In fact, it was the monks of the monasteries of Saint Laurent and Saint Martin who, spying the waters of springs that were distributing themselves uselessly over the meadows of Saint Gervais and Belleville, directed them to Paris. In Lombardy, the peasants learned irrigation from the monks, which contributed mightily to making that area so well known throughout Europe for its fertility and riches. The monks were also the first to work toward improving cattle breeds, rather than leaving the process to chance.[15]

In many cases, the monks' good example inspired others, particularly the great respect and honor they showed toward manual labor in general and agriculture in particular. "Agriculture had sunk to a low ebb," according to one scholar. "Marshes covered once fertile fields, and the men who should have tilled the land spurned the plow as degrading." But when the monks emerged from their cells to dig ditches and to plow fields, "the effort was magical. Men once more turned back to a noble but despised industry."[16] Pope Saint Gregory the Great (590–604) tells us a revealing story about the abbot Equitius, a sixth-century missionary of noted eloquence. When a papal envoy came to his monastery looking for him, the envoy went immediately to the scriptorium, expecting to find him among the copyists. But he was not there. The calligraphers explained simply, "He is down there in the valley, cutting hay."[17]

The monks also pioneered in the production of wine, which they used both for the celebration of Holy Mass and for ordinary consumption, which the Rule of Saint Benedict expressly permitted. In addition, the discovery of champagne can be traced to Dom Perignon of Saint Peter's Abbey, Hautvilliers-on-the-Marne. He was appointed cellarer of the abbey in 1688, and developed champagne through experimentation with blending wines. The fundamental principles he established continue to govern the manufacture of champagne even today.[18]

Although perhaps not as glamorous as some of the monks' intellectual contributions, these crucial tasks were very nearly as important to building and preserving the civilization of the West. It would be difficult to find any group anywhere in the world whose contributions were as varied, as significant, and as indispensable as those of the Catholic monks of the West during a time of general turmoil and despair.

The monks were also important architects of medieval technology. The Cistercians, a reform-minded Benedictine order established at Cîteaux in 1098, are especially well known for their technological sophistication. Thanks to the great network of communication that existed between the various monasteries, technological information was able to spread rapidly. Thus we find very similar water-powered systems at monasteries that were at great distances from each other, even thousands of miles away.[19] "These monasteries," a scholar writes, "were the most economically effective units that had ever existed in Europe, and perhaps in the world, before that time."[20]

The Cistercian monastery of Clairvaux in France leaves us a twelfth-century report about its use of waterpower that reveals the surprising extent to which machinery had become central to European life. The Cistercian monastic community generally ran its own factory. The monks used waterpower for crushing wheat, sieving flour, fulling cloth, and tanning.[21] And as Jean Gimpel points out in his book *The Medieval Machine*, this twelfth-century report could have been written 742 times, since that was the number of Cistercian monasteries in Europe in the twelfth century. The same level of technological achievement could have been observed in practically all of them.[22]

Although the world of classical antiquity had not adopted mechanization for industrial use on any considerable scale, the medieval world did so on an enormous scale, a fact symbolized and reflected in the Cistercians' use of waterpower:

> Entering the Abbey under the boundary wall [writes a twelfth-century source], which like a janitor allows it to pass, the stream first hurls itself impetuously at the mill where in a welter of movement it strains itself, first to crush the wheat beneath the weight

of the millstones, then to shake the fine sieve which separates flour from bran. Already it has reached the next building; it replenishes the vats and surrenders itself to the flames which heat it up to prepare beer for the monks, their liquor when the vines reward the wine-growers' toil with a barren crop. The stream does not yet consider itself discharged. The fullers established near the mill beckon to it. In the mill it had been occupied in preparing food for the brethren; it is therefore only right that it should now look to their clothing. It never shrinks back or refuses to do anything that is asked for. One by one it lifts and drops the heavy pestles, the fullers' great wooden hammers... and spares, thus, the monks' great fatigues.... How many horses would be worn out, how many men would have weary arms if this graceful river, to whom we owe our clothes and food, did not labor for us.

When it has spun the shaft as fast as any wheel can move, it disappears in a foaming frenzy; one might say it had itself been ground in the mill. Leaving it here it enters the tannery, where in preparing the leather for the shoes of the monks it exercises as much exertion as diligence; then it dissolves in a host of streamlets and proceeds along its appointed course to the duties laid down for it, looking out all the time for affairs requiring its attention whatever they might be, such as cooking, sieving, turning, grinding, watering, or washing, never refusing its assistance in any task. At last, in case it receives any reward for work which it has not done, it carries away the waste and leaves everywhere spotless.[23]


## THE MONKS AS TECHNICAL ADVISERS

*The Cistercians were also known* for their skill in metallurgy. "In their rapid expansion throughout Europe," writes Jean Gimpel, the Cistercians must have "played a role in the diffusion of new techniques, for the high level of their agricultural technology was matched by their industrial technology. Every monastery had a model factory, often as large as the church and only several feet away, and waterpower drove the machinery of the various industries located on its floor."[24] At times iron ore deposits were donated to the monks, nearly always along with the forges used to extract the iron, and at other times they purchased the deposits and forges. Although they needed iron for their own use, Cistercian monasteries would come in time to offer their surplus for sale; in fact, from the mid-thirteenth through the seventeenth century, the Cistercians were the leading iron producers in the Champagne region of France. Ever eager to increase the efficiency of their monasteries, the Cistercians used the slag from their furnaces as fertilizer, as its concentration of phosphates made it particularly useful for this purpose.[25]

Such achievements were part of a broader phenomenon of technological achievement on the part of the monks. As Gimpel observes, "The Middle Ages introduced machinery into Europe on a scale no civilization had previously known."[26] And the monks, according to another study, were "the skillful and unpaid technical advisers of the third world of their times—that is to say, Europe after the invasion of the barbarians."[27] It goes on:

> In effect, whether it be the mining of salt, lead, iron, alum, or gypsum, or metallurgy, quarrying marble, running cutler's shops and glassworks, or forging metal plates, also known as firebacks, there was no activity at all in which the monks did not display creativity and a fertile spirit of research. Utilizing their labor force, they instructed and trained it to perfection. Monastic know-how [would] spread throughout Europe.[28]

Monastic accomplishments ranged from interesting curiosities to the intensely practical. In the early eleventh century, for instance, a monk named Eilmer flew more than 600 feet with a glider; people remembered this feat for the next three centuries.[29] Centuries later, Father Francesco Lana-Terzi, not a monk but a Jesuit priest, pursued the subject of flight more systematically, earning the honor of being called the father of aviation. His 1670 book *Prodromo alla Arte Maestra* was the first to describe the geometry and physics of a flying vessel.[30]

The monks also counted skillful clock-makers among them. The first clock of which we have any record was built by the future Pope Sylvester II for the German town of Magdeburg, around the year 996. Much more sophisticated clocks were built by later monks. Peter Lightfoot, a fourteenth-century monk of Glastonbury, built one of the oldest clocks still in existence, which now sits, in excellent condition, in London's Science Museum.

Richard of Wallingford, a fourteenth-century abbot of the Benedictine abbey of Saint Albans (and one of the initiators of Western trigonometry), is well known for the large astronomical clock he designed for that monastery. It has been said that a clock that equaled it in technological sophistication did not appear for at least two centuries. The magnificent clock, a marvel for its time, no longer survives, perhaps having perished amid Henry VIII's sixteenth-century monastic confiscations. However, Richard's notes on the clock's design have permitted scholars to build a model and even a full-scale reconstruction. In addition to timekeeping, the clock could accurately predict lunar eclipses.

Archaeologists are still discovering the extent of monastic skills and technological cleverness. In the late 1990s, University of Bradford archeometallurgist Gerry McDonnell found evidence near Rievaulx Abbey in North Yorkshire, England, of a degree of technological sophistication that pointed ahead to the great machines of the eighteenth-century Industrial Revolution. (Rievaulx Abbey was one of the monasteries that King Henry VIII ordered closed in the 1530s as part of his confiscation of Church properties.) In exploring the debris of Rievaulx and Laskill (an outstation about four miles from the monastery), McDonnell found that the monks had built a furnace to extract iron from ore.

The typical such furnace of the sixteenth century had advanced relatively little over its ancient counterpart and was noticeably inefficient by modern standards. The slag, or byproduct, of these primitive furnaces contained a substantial concentration of iron, since the furnaces could not reach temperatures high enough to extract all the iron from the ore. The slag that McDonnell discovered at Laskill, however, was low in iron content, similar to slag produced by a modern blast furnace.

McDonnell believes that the monks were on the verge of building dedicated furnaces for the large-scale production of cast iron—perhaps the key ingredient that ushered in the industrial age—and that the furnace at Laskill had been a prototype of such a furnace. "One of the key things is that the Cistercians had a regular meeting of abbots every year and they had the means of sharing technological advances across Europe," he said. "The break-up of the monasteries broke up this network of technology transfer." The monks "had the potential to move to blast furnaces that produced nothing but cast iron. They were poised to do it on a large scale, but by breaking up the virtual monopoly, Henry VIII effectively broke up that potential."[31]

Had it not been for a greedy king's suppression of the English monasteries, therefore, the monks appear to have been on the verge of ushering in the industrial era and its related explosion in wealth, population, and life expectancy figures. That development would instead have to wait two and a half more centuries.

## CHARITABLE WORKS

*We shall look at the Church's* charitable works in more detail in a separate chapter. For now we may simply note that Benedict's Rule called for the monks to dispense alms and hospitality. According to the Rule, "All guests who come shall be received as though they were Christ." Monasteries served as gratuitous inns, providing a safe and peaceful resting place for foreign travelers, pilgrims, and the poor. An old historian of the Norman abbey of Bec wrote: "Let them ask Spaniards or Burgundians, or any foreigners whatever, how they have been received at Bec. They will answer that the door of the monastery is always open to all, and that its bread is free to the whole world."[32] Here was the spirit of Christ at work, giving shelter and comfort to strangers of all kinds.

In some cases, the monks were even known to make efforts to track down poor souls who, lost or alone after dark, found themselves in need of emergency shelter. At Aubrac, for example, where a monastic hospital had been established amid the mountains of the Rouergue in the late sixteenth century, a special bell rang every night to call to any wandering traveler or to anyone overtaken by the intimidating forest darkness. The people dubbed it "the bell of the wanderers."[33]

In a similar vein, it was not unusual for monks living near the sea to establish contrivances for warning sailors of perilous obstacles or for nearby monasteries to make provision for shipwrecked men in need of lodging. It has been said that the city of Copenhagen owes its origin to a monastery established by its founder, Bishop Absalon, which catered to the needs of the shipwrecked.

In Scotland, at Arbroath, the abbots fixed a floating bell on a notoriously treacherous rock on the Forfarshire coast. Depending on the tide, the rock could be scarcely visible, and many a sailor had been frightened at the prospect of striking it. The waves caused the bell to sound, thereby warning sailors of danger ahead. To this day, the rock is known as "Bell Rock."[34] Such examples constituted only a small part of the concern that monks showed for the people who lived in their environs; they also contributed to the building or repair of bridges, roads, and other such features of the medieval infrastructure.

The monastic contribution with which many people are familiar is the copying of manuscripts, both sacred and profane. This task, and those who carried it out, were accorded special honor. A Carthusian prior wrote, "Diligently labor at this work, this ought to be the special work of enclosed Carthusians.... This work in a certain sense is an immortal work, if one may say it, not passing away, but ever remaining; a work, so to speak, that is not a work; a work which above all others is most proper for educated religious men."[35]

## THE WRITTEN WORD

*Honored as it was, the copyist's task* was difficult and demanding. Inscribed on one monastic manuscript are the words, "He who does not know how to write imagines it to be no labor; but though three fingers only hold the pen, the whole body grows weary." The monks often had to work through the most punishing cold. A monastic copyist, imploring our sympathy upon completing a copy of Saint Jerome's commentary on the Book of Daniel, wrote: "Good readers who may use this work, do not, I pray you, forget him who copied it: it was a poor brother named

Louis, who, while he transcribed this volume, brought from a foreign country, endured the cold, and was obliged to finish in the night what he was not able to write by daylight. But Thou, Lord, wilt be to him the full recompense of his labors."[36]

In the sixth century, a retired Roman senator named Cassiodorus had an early vision of the cultural role that the monastery was to play. Sometime around the middle of the century, he established the monastery of Vivarium in southern Italy, providing it with a very fine library—indeed, the only sixth-century library of which scholars are aware—and emphasizing the importance of copying manuscripts. Some important Christian manuscripts from Vivarium appear to have made their way to the Lateran Library and into the possession of the popes.[37]

Surprisingly, it is not to Vivarium, but to other monastic libraries and scriptoria (the rooms set aside for the copying of texts) that we owe the great bulk of ancient Latin literature that survives today. When these works weren't saved and transcribed by the monks, we owe their survival to the libraries and schools associated with the great medieval cathedrals.[38] Thus, when the Church was not making original contributions of her own, she was preserving books and documents that were of seminal importance to the civilization she was to save.

Describing the holdings at his library at York, the great Alcuin—the polyglot theologian who worked closely with Charlemagne to restore study and scholarship in west-central Europe—mentioned works by Aristotle, Cicero, Lucan, Pliny, Statius, Trogus Pompeius, and Virgil. In his correspondence he quotes still other classical authors, including Ovid, Horace, and Terence.[39] Alcuin was far from alone in his familiarity with and appreciation for the ancient writers. Lupus (c. 805–862), the abbot of Ferrieres, can be found quoting Cicero, Horace, Martial,

Suetonius, and Virgil. Abbo of Fleury (c. 950–1004), who served as abbot of the monastery of Fleury, demonstrates particular familiarity with Horace, Sallust, Terence, and Virgil. Desiderius, described as the greatest of the abbots of Monte Cassino after Benedict himself and who became Pope (Blessed) Victor III in 1086, specifically oversaw the transcription of Horace and Seneca, as well as Cicero's *De Natura Deorum* and Ovid's *Fasti.*[40] His friend Archbishop Alfano, who had also been a monk of Monte Cassino, possessed a similar fluency in the works of the ancient writers, frequently quoting from Apuleius, Aristotle, Cicero, Plato, Varro, and Virgil, and imitating Ovid and Horace in his verse. Saint Anselm, while abbot of Bec, commended Virgil and other classical writers to his students, though he wished them to put aside morally objectionable passages.[41]

The great Gerbert of Aurillac, who later became Pope Sylvester II, did not confine himself to teaching logic; he also brought to his students an appreciation of Horace, Juvenal, Lucan, Persius, Terence, Statius, and Virgil. We hear of lectures being delivered on the classical authors at places like Saint Alban's and Paderborne. A school exercise composed by Saint Hildebert survives in which he had pieced together excerpts from Cicero, Horace, Juvenal, Persius, Seneca, Terence, and others; John Henry Cardinal Newman, the nineteenth century's great convert from Anglicanism and an accomplished historian in his own right, suggests that Saint Hildebert knew Horace practically by heart.[42] The fact is, the Church cherished, preserved, studied, and taught the works of the ancients, which would otherwise have been lost.

Certain monasteries might be known for their skill in particular branches of knowledge. Thus, for example, lectures in medicine were given by the monks of Saint Benignus at Dijon, the monastery of Saint Gall had a school of painting and engraving, and lectures in Greek, Hebrew, and Arabic could be heard at certain German monasteries.[43]

Monks often supplemented their education by attending one or more of the monastic schools established during the Carolingian Renaissance and beyond. Abbo of Fleury, having mastered the disciplines taught at his own house, went to study philosophy and astronomy at Paris and Rheims. We hear similar stories about Archbishop Raban of Mainz, Saint Wolfgang, and Gerbert (Pope Sylvester II).[44]

In the eleventh century, the mother monastery of the Benedictine tradition, Monte Cassino, enjoyed a cultural revival, called "the most dramatic single event in the history of Latin scholarship in the eleventh century."[45] In addition to its outpouring of artistic and intellectual endeavor, Monte Cassino renewed its interest in the texts of classical antiquity:

> At one swoop a number of texts were recovered which might otherwise have been lost for ever; to this one monastery in this one period we owe the preservation of the later *Annals* and *Histories* of Tacitus (Plate XIV), the *Golden Ass* of Apuleius, the *Dialogues* of Seneca, Varro's *De lingua latina*, Frontinus' *De aquis*, and thirty-odd lines of Juvenal's sixth satire that are not to be found in any other manuscript.[46]

In addition to their careful preservation of the works of the classical world and of the Church fathers, both of which are central to Western civilization, the monks performed another work of immeasurable importance in their capacity as copyists: their preservation of the Bible.[47] Without their devotion to this crucial task and the numerous copies they produced, it is not clear how the Bible would have survived the onslaught of the barbarians. The monks often embellished the Gospels with beautiful artistic decoration, as in the famous Lindau and Lindisfarne Gospels—works of art as well as faith.

Throughout the history of monasticism we find abundant evidence of the devotion of monks to their books. Saint Benedict Biscop, for example, who established the monastery of Wearmouth in England, searched far and wide for volumes for his monastic library, embarking on five sea voyages for the purpose (and coming back each time with a sizable cargo).[48] Lupus asked a fellow abbot for an opportunity to copy Suetonius' *Lives of the Caesars*, and implored another friend to bring him Sallust's accounts of the Catilinarian and Jugurthan Wars, the *Verrines* of Cicero, and any other volume that might be of interest. He asked to borrow Cicero's *De Rhetorica* from another friend, and appealed to the pope for a copy of Cicero's *De Oratore*, Quintilian's *Institutions*, and other texts. Gerbert possessed a like enthusiasm for books, offering to assist another abbot in completing incomplete copies of Cicero and the philosopher Demosthenes, and seeking copies of Cicero's *Verrines* and *De Republica*.[49] We read that Saint Maieul of Cluny always had a book in his hand when he traveled on horseback, so devoted was he to reading. Likewise, Halinard, who served as abbot of Saint Benignus at Dijon before becoming Archbishop of Lyons, followed the same practice, recounting his particular fondness for the philosophers of antiquity.[50] "Without study and without books," said a monk of Muri, "the life of a monk is nothing." Saint Hugh of Lincoln, while prior at Witham, the first Carthusian house in England, spoke similarly: "Our books are our delight and our wealth in time of peace, our offensive and defensive arms in time of war, our food when we are hungry, and our medicine when we are sick."[51] Western civilization's admiration for the written word and for the classics comes to us from the Catholic Church that preserved both through the barbarian invasions.

Although the extent of the practice varied over the centuries, monks were teachers. Saint John Chrysostom tells us that already in his day (c. 347–407) it was customary for people in Antioch to send their sons to be educated by the monks. Saint Benedict instructed the sons of Roman nobles.[52] Saint Boniface established a school in every monastery he founded in Germany, and in England Saint Augustine and his monks set up schools wherever they went.[53] Saint Patrick is given credit for encouraging Irish scholarship, and the Irish monasteries would develop into important centers of learning, dispensing instruction to monks and laymen alike.[54]

Most education for those who would not profess monastic vows, however, would take place in other settings, and eventually in the cathedral schools established under Charlemagne. But even if the monasteries' contribution to education had been merely to teach their own how to read and write, that would have been no small accomplishment. When the Mycenaean Greeks suffered a catastrophe in the twelfth century B.C.—an invasion by the Dorians, say some scholars—the result was three centuries of complete illiteracy known as the Greek Dark Ages. Writing simply disappeared amid the chaos and disorder. But the monks' commitment to reading, writing, and education ensured that the same terrible fate that had befallen the Mycenaean Greeks would not be visited upon Europeans after the fall of the Roman Empire. This time, thanks to the monks, literacy would survive political and social catastrophe.

Monks did more than simply preserve literacy. Even an unsympathetic scholar could write of monastic education: "They studied the songs of heathen poets and the writings of historians and philosophers. Monasteries and monastic schools blossomed forth, and each settlement became a center of religious life as well as of education."[55] Another unsympathetic chronicler wrote of the monks, "They not only established the schools, and were the schoolmasters in them, but also laid the foundations for the universities. They were the thinkers and philosophers of the day and shaped the political and religious thought. To them, both collectively and individually, was due the continuity of thought and civilization of the ancient world with the later Middle Ages and with the modern period."[56]

This treatment of the monks' contributions barely scratches the surface of an immense subject. In the 1860s and 1870s, when the Comte de Montalembert wrote a six-volume history of the monks of the West, he complained at times of his inability to provide anything more than a cursory overview of great figures and deeds, and could only refer his readers to the references in his footnotes. The monastic contribution to Western civilization, as we have seen, is immense. Among other things, the monks taught metallurgy, introduced new crops, copied ancient texts, preserved literacy, pioneered in technology, invented champagne, improved the European landscape, provided for wanderers of every stripe, and looked after the lost and shipwrecked. Who else in the history of Western civilization can boast such a record? The Church that gave the West its monks also created the university, as we will see in the next chapter.

*Chapter Four*

# The Church
# and the University

*lthough many college* students today couldn't locate the Middle Ages on a historical timeline, they are nevertheless sure that the period was one of ignorance, superstition, and intellectual repression. Nothing could be further from the truth—it is to the Middle Ages that we owe one of Western civilization's greatest—unique—intellectual contributions to the world: the university system.

The university was an utterly new phenomenon in European history. Nothing like it had existed in ancient Greece or Rome.[1] The institution that we recognize today, with its faculties, courses of study, examinations, and degrees, as well as the distinction between undergraduate and graduate study, comes to us directly from the medieval world. The Church developed the university system because, according to historian Lowrie Daly, it was "the only institution in Europe that showed consistent interest in the preservation and cultivation of knowledge."[2]

We cannot give exact dates for the appearance of universities at Paris and Bologna, Oxford and Cambridge, since they evolved over a period of time—the former beginning as cathedral schools and the latter as informal gatherings of masters and students. But we may safely say that they began taking form during the latter half of the twelfth century.

In order to identify a particular medieval school as a university, we look for certain characteristic features. A university possessed a core of required texts, on which professors would lecture while adding their own insights. A university was also characterized by well-defined academic programs lasting a more or less fixed number of years, as well as by the granting of degrees. The granting of a degree, since it entitled the recipient to be called *master*, amounted to admitting new people to the teaching guild, just as a master craftsman was admitted to the guild of his own profession. Although the universities often struggled with outside authorities for self-government, they generally attained it, as well as legal recognition as corporations.[3]

Aside from the Church's intellectual role in fostering the universities, the papacy played a central role in establishing and encouraging them. Naturally, the granting of a charter to a university was one indication of this papal role. Eighty-one universities had been established by the time of the Reformation. Of these, thirty-three possessed a papal charter, fifteen a royal or imperial one, twenty possessed both, and thirteen had none.[4] In addition, it was the accepted view that a university could not award degrees without the approbation of pope, king, or emperor. Pope Innocent IV officially granted this privilege to Oxford University in 1254. The pope (in fact) and the emperor (in theory) possessed authority over all of Christendom, and for this reason it was to them that a university typically had to turn for the right to issue degrees. Equipped with the approval of one or the other of these universal figures, the university's degrees would be respected throughout all of Christendom. Degrees awarded only by the approval of national monarchs, on the other hand, were considered valid only in the kingdom in which they were issued.[5]

In certain cases, including the universities at Bologna, Oxford, and Paris, the master's degree entitled the bearer to teach anywhere in the world (*ius ubique docendi*). We first see this in Pope Gregory IX's 1233 document pertaining to the University of Toulouse, which became a model for the future. By the end of the thirteenth century, the *ius ubique docendi* had become "the juridical hallmark of a university."[6] Theoretically, such scholars could freely join other faculties in Western Europe, though in practice each institution preferred to examine the candidate before admitting him.[7] Still, this privilege, conferred by the popes, played a significant role in encouraging the dissemination of knowledge and fostering the idea of an international scholarly community.

## TOWN AND GOWN

*The papal role in the university* system extended to a great many other matters. A glance at the history of the medieval university reveals that conflicts between the university and the people or government of the area were not uncommon. Local townsmen were frequently ambivalent toward university students; on one hand, the university was a boon for local merchants and for economic activity in general, since the students brought money to spend, but on the other, university students could be irresponsible and unruly. As a modern commentator puts it, inhabitants of medieval university towns loved the money but hated the students. As a result, students and their professors were often heard to complain that they were "abused by the locals, treated roughly by the police, denied what we would call due process of law and cheated over rent, food and books."[8]

In this atmosphere, the Church provided special protection to university students by offering them what was known as benefit of clergy. Clergymen in medieval Europe enjoyed special legal status: It was an extraordinarily serious crime to lay a hand on them, and they had the right to have their cases heard in an ecclesiastical rather than a secular court. University students, as actual or potential clerical candidates, would also enjoy these privileges. Secular rulers often extended similar protections: In 1200, Philip Augustus of France granted and confirmed such privileges to students of the University of Paris, permitting them to have their cases heard in what would certainly be a more sympathetic court than that of the local town.[9]

The popes intervened on the university's behalf on numerous occasions, as when Pope Honorius III (1216–1227) sided with the scholars at Bologna in 1220 against infringements on their liberties. When the chancellor of Paris insisted on an oath of loyalty to himself personally, Pope Innocent III (1198–1216) intervened. In 1231, when local diocesan officials encroached on the institutional autonomy of the university, Pope Gregory IX issued the bull *Parens Scientiarum* on behalf of the masters of Paris. In this document, he effectively granted the University of Paris the right to self-government, whereby it could make its own rules pertaining to courses and studies. The pope also granted the university a separate papal jurisdiction, emancipating it from diocesan interference. "With this document," writes one scholar, "the university comes of age and appears in legal history as a fully formed intellectual corporation for the advancement and training of scholars."[10] The papacy, writes another, "has to be considered a major force in shaping the autonomy of the Paris guild [i.e., the organized body of scholars at Paris]."[11]

In that same document, the pope tried to establish a just and peaceful environment for the university by granting a privilege known as *cessatio*—the right to suspend lectures and go on a general strike if its members were abused. Just cause included "refusal of the right to fix ceiling prices for lodgings, an injury or mutilation of a student for which suitable satisfaction had not been given within fifteen days, [or] the unlawful imprisonment of a student."[12]

It became common for universities to bring their grievances to the pope in Rome.[13] On several occasions, the pope even intervened to force university authorities to pay professors their salaries; Popes Boniface VIII, Clement V, Clement VI, and Gregory IX all had to take such measures.[14] Little wonder, then, that one historian has declared that the universities' "most consistent and greatest protector was the Pope of Rome. He it was who granted, increased, and protected their privileged status in a world of often conflicting jurisdictions."[15]

When the university system was still young, therefore, the popes were its most consistent protectors and the authority to which students and faculty alike regularly had recourse. The Church granted charters, protected the university's rights, sided with scholars against obnoxious interference by overbearing authorities, built an international academic community with the *ius ubique docendi* privilege, and (as we shall see) permitted and fostered the kind of robust and largely unfettered scholarly debate and discussion that we associate with the university. In the universities and elsewhere, no other institution did more to promote the dissemination of knowledge than the Catholic Church.

Medieval universities differed in certain major respects from their modern counterparts. In its earliest stage, the university lacked buildings or campuses of its own. The university was its faculty and students, not a particular locale. Lectures were delivered not in campus lecture halls but in cathedrals or in private halls of various kinds. Neither were there libraries. Significant collections of books would have been difficult to acquire even if the universities had possessed real estate of their own; some estimates have it that a typical volume occupied six to eight months of a scribe's labor. (Thus even the great monastic collections were, by modern standards, rather scant and unimpressive.) Books that were absolutely necessary for students were typically rented rather than purchased.

Apparently, many medieval university students came from families of modest backgrounds, though the well-to-do were prominently represented as well. Most of the students of arts (broadly conceived) were from fourteen to twenty years of age. A great many attended university in order to prepare themselves for a career. For that reason, it is hardly surprising that the most common course of study was law. These students were also joined by many men in holy orders who either desired simply to become more knowledgeable or who had been sponsored by an ecclesiastical superior.[16]

The more established the universities became, the more traumatic it would be to the life of the town if a university chose to relocate. And it was not uncommon for such relocation to occur, particularly since universities in their early stages were not bound to a particular locale by their own buildings and campus. Thus the University of Padua originated from the movement of scholars away from Bologna in 1222. To keep them from seceding, secular authorities were prepared to offer these institutions a variety of attractive grants and privileges.[17]

What was studied at these great institutions? The seven liberal arts, for starters, along with civil and canon law, natural philosophy, medicine, and theology. As the universities took shape in the twelfth century, they were the happy beneficiaries of the fruits of what some scholars have called the renaissance of the twelfth century.[18] Massive translation efforts brought forth many of the great works of the ancient world that had been lost to Western scholarship for too many centuries, including the geometry of Euclid; the logic, metaphysics, natural philosophy, and ethics of Aristotle; and the medical work of Galen. Legal studies began to flourish as well, particularly at Bologna, when the *Digest*, the key component of the sixth-century emperor Justinian's *Corpus Juris Civilis* (a compendium of Roman law, much admired from its origins to the present day), was rediscovered.

## ACADEMIC LIFE

*The distinction between undergraduate* and graduate education was made in the early universities more or less as it is today. And as today, some places were especially known for academic distinction in particular subject areas—Bologna thus became renowned for the graduate study of law, as did Paris for theology and the arts.

The undergraduate, or artist (that is, a student of the liberal arts), attended lectures, took part in occasional disputations in class, and attended the formal disputations of others. His masters typically lectured on an important text, often drawn from classical antiquity. Alongside their commentaries on these ancient texts, professors gradually began to include a series of questions to be resolved through logical argument. Over time, the questions essentially displaced the commentaries. Here was the origin of the question method of scholastic argument, of the kind found in Saint Thomas Aquinas's *Summa Theologiae*.

Such questions were also posed in what was known as the ordinary disputation. The master would assign students to argue one or the other side of a question. When their interaction had ceased, it was then up to the master to "determine," or resolve, the question. To obtain the Bachelor of Arts degree, a student was expected to determine a question by himself to the satisfaction of the faculty. (Before being permitted to do so, however, he had to prove that he possessed adequate preparation and was fit to be evaluated.) This kind of emphasis on careful argument, on marshaling a persuasive case for each side of a question, and on resolving a dispute by means of rational tools sounds like the opposite of the intellectual life that most people associate with medieval man. But that was how the degree-granting process operated.

Once the student had "determined" a question, he was awarded the Bachelor of Arts degree. The process would typically take four to five years. At that point, the student could simply declare his education completed, as most bachelors of arts do today, and look for remunerative work (even as a teacher, perhaps in some of the lesser schools of Europe) or decide to continue his studies and pursue a graduate degree. The so-called master's degree, to which satisfactory completion of his graduate study entitled him, would render him qualified to teach within the university system.

The prospective master had to demonstrate competence within the canon of important works of Western civilization. This was before he petitioned for his license to teach, or licentiate, which was awarded between the bachelor's and master's degrees, and was part of the process not only for future teachers but for those seeking desirable posts in civil or ecclesiastical service. We get some idea of the advanced student's background from this

modern historian's overview of texts with which that student was
expected to be familiar:

> After his bachelorship, and before he petitioned for his license
> to teach, the student must have "heard at Paris or in another
> university" the following Aristotelian works: *Physics*, *On Gen-
> eration and Corruption*, *On the Heavens*, and the *Parva Natu-
> ralia*; namely, the treatises of Aristotle *On Sense and Sensation*,
> *On Waking and Sleeping*, *On Memory and Remembering*, *On
> the Length and Shortness of Life*. He must also have heard (or
> have plans to hear) *On the Metaphysics*, and have attended
> lectures on the mathematical books. [Historian Hastings]
> Rashdall, when speaking of the Oxford curriculum, gives the
> following list of works, to be read by the bachelor between the
> period of his determination and his inception (mastership):
> books on the liberal arts: in grammar, Priscian; in rhetoric,
> Aristotle's *Rhetoric* (three terms), or the *Topics* of Boethius
> (bk. iv.), or Cicero's *Nova Rhetorica* or Ovid's *Metamorphoses*
> or *Poetria Virgilii*; in logic, Aristotle's *De Interpretatione*
> (three terms) or Boethius' *Topics* (bks. 1-3) or the *Prior Ana-
> lytics* or *Topics* (Aristotle); in arithmetic and in music,
> Boethius; in geometry, Euclid, Alhacen, or Vitellio, *Perspec-
> tiva*; in astronomy, *Theorica Planetarum* (two terms), or
> Ptolemy, *Almagesta*. In natural philosophy the additional
> works are: the *Physics* or *On the Heavens* (three terms) or *On
> the Properties of the Elements* or the *Meteorics* or *On Vegeta-
> bles and Plants* or *On the Soul* or *On Animals* or any of the
> *Parva Naturalia*; in moral philosophy, the *Ethics* or *Economics*
> or *Politics* of Aristotle for three terms, and in metaphysics, the
> *Metaphysics* for two terms or for three terms if the candidate
> had not determined.[19]

The process for acquiring the licentiate defies ready generalization, but it consisted of another demonstration of knowledge and a commitment to certain principles of university life. Once this process was complete, the license was officially awarded. At Ste. Geneviève, the person to be licensed knelt in front of the vice-chancellor, who said:

> I, by the authority vested in me by the apostles Peter and Paul, give you the license for lecturing, reading, disputing, and determining and for exercising other scholastic and magisterial acts both in the faculty of arts at Paris and elsewhere, in the name of the Father and of the Son and of the Holy Ghost, Amen.[20]

The precise length of time that typically passed between reception of the licentiate and reception of the master's degree (which apparently required knowledge of a wider array of books) is difficult to determine, but one reasonable estimate is that it ranged between six months and three years. One candidate, who had perhaps already read all the required books, is recorded as having received both distinctions on the same day.[21]

Contrary to the general impression that theological presuppositions colored all of their investigations, medieval scholars by and large respected the autonomy of what was referred to as natural philosophy (a branch of study that concerned itself with the functioning of the physical world and particularly with change and motion in that world). Seeking natural explanations for natural phenomena, they kept their studies separate from theology. Natural philosophers in the arts faculties, writes Edward Grant in *God and Reason in the Middle Ages*, "were expected to refrain from introducing theology and matters of faith into natural philosophy."[22]

This respect for the autonomy of natural philosophy from the-ology held true also among theologians who wrote about the physical sciences. Albertus Magnus, Saint Thomas Aquinas's great teacher, was asked by his Dominican brothers to write a book on physics that would help them to understand the physical works of Aristotle. Lest they expect him in this book to intermin-gle theological ideas with natural philosophy, however, Albertus explicitly rejected that idea, explaining that theological ideas belonged in theological treatises, not in physical ones.

The medieval study of logic provides additional testimony to the medievals' commitment to rational thought. "Through their high-powered logic courses," writes Grant, "medieval students were made aware of the subtleties of language and the pitfalls of argumentation. Thus were the importance and utility of reason given heavy emphasis in a university education." Edith Sylla, a specialist in thirteenth- and fourteenth-century natural philoso-phy, logic, and theology, writes that we ought to "wonder at the level of logical sophistication that advanced undergraduates in fourteenth-century Oxford must have attained."[23]

Naturally, scholars took their lead from Aristotle, a logical genius, but they also composed logic texts of their own. Who wrote the most famous of these? A future pope, Peter of Spain (John XXI), in the 1230s. His *Summulae logicales* became the standard text for hundreds of years and would go through some 166 editions by the seventeenth century.

## THE AGE OF SCHOLASTICISM

*Had the Middle Ages really been* a time when all questions were to be resolved by mere appeals to authority, this commitment to the study of formal logic would make no sense. Rather, the commitment to the discipline of logic reveals a civilization that aimed to understand and to persuade. To that end, educated men wanted students to be able to detect logical fallacies and to be able to form logically sound arguments.

This was the age of Scholasticism. It is difficult to arrive at a satisfactory definition of Scholasticism that would apply to all the thinkers to whom the label has been affixed. At one level, Scholasticism was the term assigned to the scholarly work done in the schools—that is, in the universities of Europe. The term is less helpfully used to describe the *content* of the thought of the intellectuals to which it refers than it is to identify the *method* that they used. The Scholastics, by and large, were committed to the use of reason as an indispensable tool in theological and philosophical study, and to dialectic—the juxtaposition of opposing positions, followed by a resolution of the matter at hand by recourse to both reason and authority—as the method of pursuing issues of intellectual interest. As the tradition matured, it became common for Scholastic treatises to follow a set pattern: posing a question, considering arguments on both sides, giving the writer's own view, and answering objections.

Perhaps the earliest of the Scholastics was Saint Anselm (1033–1109). Anselm, who served as abbot of the monastery of Bec and later as archbishop of Canterbury, differed from most other Scholastics in that he did not hold a formal academic post. But he shared what became the characteristic Scholastic interest in using reason to explore philosophical and theological questions. For instance, his *Cur Deus Homo* examines from a rational point of view why it was appropriate and fitting for God to have become man.

In philosophical circles, however, Saint Anselm is better known for his rational proof for the existence of God. Known as the ontological argument, Anselm's line of reasoning has stimulated and intrigued even those who have disagreed with it. For Anselm, the existence of God was logically implied in the very definition of God. Just as a thorough knowledge and understanding of the idea of nine implied that its square root was three, so did a thorough understanding of the idea of God imply that such a being must exist.[24] Anselm posits as a working definition of God "that than which nothing greater can be conceived." (For the sake of simplicity we shall modify Anselm's formulation to "the greatest conceivable being.") The greatest conceivable being must possess every perfection, else it would not be the greatest conceivable being. Now existence is a perfection, said Anselm, for it is better to exist than not to exist. But suppose God existed only in people's minds and did not exist in reality. That is to say, suppose that this greatest conceivable being existed only as an idea in our minds, and had no existence in the extramental world (the world outside our minds). Then it would *not* be the greatest conceivable being, since we could conceive of a greater one: one that existed both in our minds *and* in reality. Thus the very notion of "the greatest conceivable being" immediately implies the existence of such a being, for without existence in the real world this would not be the greatest conceivable being.

Subsequent philosophers, including Saint Thomas Aquinas, have generally not been persuaded by Anselm's proof—although a minority of philosophers have insisted that Anselm was correct—but over the course of the next five centuries and beyond, a great many philosophers felt compelled to reckon with the saint's arguments. More significant even than the centuries-long reverberations of Anselm's argument is its commitment to the use of reason, which later Scholastics pursued to even greater effect.

Another important early Scholastic was Peter Abelard (1079–1142), a much-admired teacher who spent ten years of his career teaching at the cathedral school at Paris. In *Sic et Non* (*Yes and No*, c. 1120) Abelard assembled a list of apparent contradictions, citing passages from the early Church fathers and from the Bible itself. Whatever the solution would prove to be in each case, it was the task of human reason—and, more specifically, of Abelard's students—to resolve these intellectual difficulties.

The prologue to *Sic et Non* contains a beautiful testimony to the importance of intellectual activity and the zeal with which it should be pursued:

> I present here a collection of statements of the Holy Fathers in the order in which I have remembered them. The discrepancies which these texts seem to contain raise certain questions which should present a challenge to my young readers to summon up all their zeal to establish the truth and in doing so to gain increased perspicacity. For the prime source of wisdom has been defined as continuous and penetrating inquiry. The most brilliant of all philosophers, Aristotle, encouraged his students to undertake this task with every ounce of their curiosity.... [H]e says: "It is foolish to make confident statements about these matters if one does not devote a lot of time to them. It is useful practice to question every detail." By raising questions we begin to enquire, and by enquiring we attain the truth, and, as the Truth has in fact said: "Seek, and ye shall find; knock, and it shall be opened unto you." He demonstrated this to us by His own moral example when He was found at the age of twelve "sitting in the midst of the doctors both hearing them and asking them questions." He who is the Light itself, the full and perfect wisdom of God, desired by His questioning to give His disciples an example before He became a model for teachers

in His preaching. When, therefore, I adduce passages from the scriptures it should spur and incite my readers to enquire into the truth and the greater the authority of these passages, the more earnest this enquiry should be.[25]

Although his work on the Trinity earned him ecclesiastical censure, Abelard was very much in keeping with the intellectual vitality of his day, and he shared its confidence in the powers of man's God-given reason. Abelard was a faithful son of the Church; modern scholars reject the suggestion that he was a thoroughgoing rationalist of the eighteenth-century variety who would have used reason to try to undermine the faith. His work was always aimed at building up and providing additional support for the great edifice of truth that the Church possessed. He once said that he did not "wish to be a philosopher if it meant rebelling against [the Apostle] Paul, nor an Aristotle if it meant cutting [himself] off from Christ."[26] Heretics, he said, used arguments from reason to assault the faith, and thus it was most fitting and appropriate for the Church's faithful to make use of reason in defense of the faith.[27]

Although Abelard raised some eyebrows in his day, his use of reason to reckon with theological issues would be taken up by later Scholastics, culminating in the following century with Saint Thomas Aquinas. In the shorter run, something of Abelard's influence is evident in the case of Peter Lombard (c. 1100–1160), who may have been his student. Peter Lombard, who served a brief term as archbishop of Paris, wrote the *Sentences*—which, next to the Bible, became the central textbook for students of theology for the next five centuries. The book is a systematic exposition of the Catholic faith, including discussion of everything from God's attributes to such topics as sin, grace, the Incarnation, redemption, the virtues, the sacraments and the Four Last

Things (death, judgment, heaven, and hell). Significantly, it sought to combine a reliance on authority with a willingness to employ reason in the explanation of theological points.[28]

The greatest of the Scholastics, and indeed one of the great intellects of all time, was Saint Thomas Aquinas (1225–1274). His towering achievement, the *Summa Theologiae*, raised and answered thousands of questions in theology and philosophy, ranging from the theology of the sacraments to the justice of war to whether all vices should be criminalized (Saint Thomas said no). He showed that Aristotle, whom he and many of his contemporaries considered the best of secular thought, could be readily harmonized with Church teaching.

The Scholastics discussed a great many issues of significance, but in the cases of Anselm and Aquinas I have chosen to focus on the existence of God, perhaps the classic example of the use of reason in defense of the faith. (The existence of God belonged to that category of knowledge that Saint Thomas believed could be known through reason as well as by divine revelation.) We have already seen Anselm's argument; Aquinas, for his part, developed five ways for demonstrating God's existence in his *Summa Theologiae*, and described them at greater length in the *Summa Contra Gentiles*. To give the reader some idea of the character and depth of Scholastic argument, we shall consider Aquinas's approach to this question by looking at what is technically referred to as his argument from efficient causality, borrowing a bit from the argument from contingency and necessity.[29]

Saint Thomas's views are best understood if we begin with thought experiments from the secular world. Suppose you want to purchase a pound of turkey at the deli counter. Upon arrival there, you find that you must take a number before you can place your order. Just as you are about to take a number, however, you find that you are required to take a number before you can take a number. And just as you are about to take that number, you find that you must first take yet another number. Thus you must take a number to take a number to take a number to be able to place your order at the deli counter.

Suppose further that the series of numbers you are required to take is infinite. Every single time you are about to take a number, you discover that there exists a prior number you must first take before you can take the next number. You will never get to the deli counter under such conditions. From now until the end of time you will be forever taking numbers.

Now if you were to come across someone in the grocery store walking around with half a pound of roast beef that he had purchased at the deli counter, you would instantly know that the series of numbers must in fact not go on forever. We have seen that with an infinite series of numbers no one could ever reach the deli counter. But the person with the roast beef must somehow have managed to get to the counter. Thus the series cannot be infinite.

Consider another example. Suppose you wish to register for a college course, and you therefore pay a visit to the registrar, Mr. Smith. Mr. Smith tells you that in order to register for that particular course, you must see Mr. Jones. Mr. Jones, in turn, instructs you to see Mr. Young. Mr. Young sends you to Mr. Brown. If this series went on infinitely—if there were *always* another person you had to see before you could register—it is abundantly clear that you would never be able to register for the course.

These examples may appear quite remote from the question of God's existence, but they are not; Saint Thomas's proof is in a certain way analogous to them both. He begins with the idea that every effect requires a cause, and that nothing that exists in the physical world is the cause of its own existence. This is known as the principle of sufficient reason. When we encounter a table, for example, we know perfectly well that it did not come into existence spontaneously. It owes its existence to something else: a builder and previously existing raw materials.

An existing thing Z owes its existence to some cause Y. But Y itself, not being self-existing, is also in need of a cause. Y owes its own existence to cause X. But now X must be accounted for. X owes its existence to cause W. We are faced, as with the examples of the deli counter and the college course, with the difficulties posed by an infinite series.

In this case, we are faced with the following problem: Every cause of a given effect itself demands a cause in order to account for its own existence; this cause in turn requires a cause, and so on. If we have an infinite series on our hands, in which each cause itself requires a cause, then *nothing could ever have come into existence.*

Saint Thomas explains that there must, therefore, be an Uncaused Cause—a cause that is not itself in need of a cause. This first cause can therefore begin the sequence of causes. This first cause, Saint Thomas says, is God. God is the one self-existing being whose existence is part of His very essence. No human being must exist; there was a time before each one came into existence, and the world will continue to exist after each one perishes. Existence is not part of the essence of any human being. But God is different. He cannot not exist. And He depends on nothing prior to Himself in order to account for His existence.

This kind of philosophical rigor characterized the intellectual life of the early universities. Little wonder that the popes and other churchmen ranked the universities among the great jewels of Christian civilization. It was typical to hear the University of Paris described as the "new Athens"[30]—a designation that calls to mind the ambitions of the great Alcuin from the Carolingian period of several centuries earlier, who sought through his own educational efforts to establish a new Athens in the kingdom of the Franks. Pope Innocent IV (1243–1254) described the universities as "rivers of science which water and make fertile the soil of the universal Church," and Pope Alexander IV (1254–1261) called them "lanterns shining in the house of God." And the popes deserved no small share of the credit for the growth and success of the university system. "Thanks to the repeated intervention of the papacy," writes historian Henri Daniel-Rops, "higher education was enabled to extend its boundaries; the Church, in fact, was the matrix that produced the university, the nest whence it took flight."[31]

As a matter of fact, among the most important medieval contributions to modern science was the essentially free inquiry of the university system, where scholars could debate and discuss propositions, and in which the utility of human reason was taken for granted. Contrary to the grossly inaccurate picture of the Middle Ages that passes for common knowledge today, medieval intellectual life made indispensable contributions to Western civilization. "[S]cholars of the later Middle Ages," concludes David Lindberg in *The Beginnings of Western Science* (1992), "created a broad intellectual tradition, in the absence of which subsequent progress in natural philosophy [the natural sciences, essentially] would have been inconceivable."[32]

Christopher Dawson, one of the great historians of the twentieth century, observed that from the days of the earliest universities "the higher studies were dominated by the technique of logical discussion—the *quaestio* and the public disputation which so largely determined the *form* of medieval philosophy even in its greatest representatives. 'Nothing,' says Robert of Sorbonne, 'is known perfectly which has not been masticated by the teeth of disputation,' and the tendency to submit every question, from the most obvious to the most abstruse, to this process of mastication not only encouraged readiness of wit and exactness of thought but above all developed that spirit of criticism and methodic doubt to which Western culture and science have owed so much."[33]

Historian of science Edward Grant concurs with this judgment:

> What made it possible for Western civilization to develop science and the social sciences in a way that no other civilization had ever done before? The answer, I am convinced, lies in a pervasive and deep-seated spirit of inquiry that was a natural consequence of the emphasis on reason that began in the Middle Ages. With the exception of revealed truths, reason was enthroned in medieval universities as the ultimate arbiter for most intellectual arguments and controversies. It was quite natural for scholars immersed in a university environment to employ reason to probe into subject areas that had not been explored before, as well as to discuss possibilities that had not previously been seriously entertained.[34]

The creation of the university, the commitment to reason and rational argument, and the overall spirit of inquiry that characterized medieval intellectual life amounted to "a gift from the Latin Middle Ages to the modern world... though it is a gift that may never be acknowledged. Perhaps it will always retain the status it has had for the past four centuries as the best-kept secret of Western civilization."[35] It was a gift of the civilization whose center was the Catholic Church.

*Chapter Five*

# The Church and Science

**W**as it just a coincidence that modern science developed in a largely Catholic milieu, or was there something about Catholicism itself that enabled the success of science? Even to raise the question is to transgress the boundaries of fashionable opinion. Yet more and more scholars have begun to ask it, and their answers may come as a surprise.

This is no small matter. The Catholic Church's alleged hostility toward science may be her greatest debit in the popular mind. The one-sided version of the Galileo affair with which most people are familiar is very largely to blame for the widespread belief that the Church has obstructed the advance of scientific inquiry. But even if the Galileo incident had been every bit as bad as people think it was, John Henry Cardinal Newman, the celebrated nineteenth-century convert from Anglicanism, found it revealing that this is practically the only example that ever comes to mind.

The controversy centered around the work of Polish astronomer Nicholas Copernicus (1473–1543). Some modern treatments of Copernicus have gone so far as to call him a priest, but although he was named a canon of the chapter of Frauenburg in the late 1490s, there is no direct evidence that he ever took higher orders. One indication that he may have received priestly ordination comes from the decision of Poland's King Sigismund in 1537 to name him one of four possible candidates to a vacant episcopal seat. Whatever his clerical status, Copernicus had come from a religious family, all of whom belonged to the Third Order of Saint Dominic, which extended to the laity the opportunity to partake in Dominican spirituality and tradition.[1]

As a scientist, he was a figure of no small renown in ecclesiastical circles. He was consulted by the Fifth Lateran Council (1512–1517) on the subject of calendar reform. In 1531, Copernicus prepared an outline of his astronomy for the benefit of his friends. It attracted considerable attention; Pope Clement VII even called on Johann Albert Widmanstadt to deliver a public lecture at the Vatican on the subject. The pope left very favorably impressed by what he had heard.[2]

Meanwhile, churchmen and academic colleagues alike implored Copernicus to publish his work for general circulation. Thus at the urging of friends, including several prelates, Copernicus finally relented and published *Six Books on the Revolutions of the Celestial Orbits*, which he dedicated to Pope Paul III, in 1543. Copernicus retained much of the conventional astronomy of his day, which was overwhelmingly indebted to Aristotle and above all to Ptolemy (87–150 A.D.), a brilliant Greek astronomer who posited a geocentric universe. Copernican astronomy shared with its Greek precursors such features as perfectly spherical heavenly bodies, circular orbits, and constant planetary speed. The significant difference that Copernicus introduced was that he placed the sun, rather than Earth, at the center of the system.

This heliocentric model posited a moving Earth orbiting the sun just as the other planets did.

Although viciously attacked by Protestants for its alleged opposition to Holy Scripture, the Copernican system was subject to no formal Catholic censure until the Galileo case. Galileo Galilei (1564–1642), in addition to his work in physics, made some important astronomical observations with his telescope that helped to undermine aspects of the Ptolemaic system. He saw mountains on the moon, thus undermining the ancient certainty that the heavenly bodies were perfect spheres. He discovered four moons orbiting Jupiter, demonstrating not only the presence of celestial phenomena of which Ptolemy and the ancients had been unaware, but also that a planet moving in its orbit would not leave its smaller satellites behind. (One of the arguments against the motion of the Earth had been that the moon would be left behind.) Galileo's discovery of the phases of Venus was yet another piece of evidence in favor of the Copernican system.

Initially, Galileo and his work were welcomed and celebrated by prominent churchmen. In late 1610, Father Christopher Clavius wrote to tell Galileo that his fellow Jesuit astronomers had confirmed the discoveries he had made through his telescope. When Galileo went to Rome the following year he was greeted with enthusiasm by religious and secular figures alike. He wrote to a friend, "I have been received and shown favor by many illustrious cardinals, prelates, and princes of this city." He enjoyed a long audience with Pope Paul V, and the Jesuits of the Roman College held a day of activities in honor of his achievements. Galileo was delighted: Before an audience of cardinals, scholars, and secular leaders, students of Father Christopher Grienberger and Father Clavius spoke about the great astronomer's discoveries.

These were scholars of considerable distinction. Father Grienberger, who personally verified Galileo's discovery of Jupiter's moons, was an accomplished astronomer who had invented the equatorial mount, which rotated a telescope about an axis parallel to Earth's. He also contributed to the development of the refracting telescope in use today.[3]

Father Clavius, one of the great mathematicians of his day, had headed the commission that yielded the Gregorian calendar (which went into effect in 1582), which resolved the inaccuracies that had plagued the old Julian calendar. His calculations regarding the length of the solar year and the number of days necessary to keep the calendar in line with the solar year—ninety-seven leap days every four hundred years, he explained—were so precise that scholars to this day remain stumped as to how he did it.[4]

Everything seemed to be in Galileo's favor. When in 1612 he published his *Letters on the Sunspots*, in which he espoused the Copernican system for the first time in print, one of the many enthusiastic letters of congratulation came from none other than Cardinal Maffeo Barberini, who later became Pope Urban VIII.[5]

The Church had no objection to the use of the Copernican system as an elegant theoretical model whose literal truth was far from established, but which accounted for celestial phenomena more reliably than any other system. There was thought to be no harm in presenting and using it as a hypothetical system. Galileo, on the other hand, believed the Copernican system to be literally true rather than merely a hypothesis that yielded accurate predictions. But he lacked anything approaching adequate evidence to support his belief. Thus, for example, he argued that the movement of the tides constituted proof of the earth's motion, a suggestion that scientists now find quaintly risible. He could not answer the geocentrists' objection, which dated all the way back to Aristotle, that if the earth moved then parallax shifts should be evident in our observations of the stars, but they were not. In the absence of strict scientific proof, Galileo nevertheless insisted on the literal truth of the Copernican system and refused to accept a compromise whereby Copernicanism would be taught as a hypothesis until persuasive evidence could be produced on its behalf. When he took the additional step of suggesting that apparent scriptural verses to the contrary had to be reinterpreted, he was viewed as having usurped the authority of the theologians.

Jerome Langford, among the most judicious modern scholars of the subject, provides a useful summary of Galileo's position at this point:

> Galileo was convinced that he had the truth. But objectively he had no proof with which to win the allegiance of open-minded men. It is a complete injustice to contend, as some historians do, that no one would listen to his arguments, that he never had a chance. The Jesuit astronomers had confirmed his discoveries; they [waited] eagerly for further proof so that they could abandon Tycho's system[6] and come out solidly in favor of Copernicanism. Many influential churchmen believed that Galileo might be right, but they had to wait for more proof.

"Obviously it is not entirely accurate to picture Galileo as an innocent victim of the world's prejudice and ignorance," Langford adds. "Part of the blame for the events which follow must be traced to Galileo himself. He refused the compromise, then entered the debate without sufficient proof and on the theologians' home grounds."[7]

It was Galileo's insistence on the *literal truth* of Copernicanism that caused the difficulty, since on the surface the heliocentric model appeared to contradict certain passages of Scripture.

The Church, sensitive to Protestant charges that Catholics did not pay proper regard to the Bible, hesitated to permit the suggestion that the literal meaning of Scripture—which at times appeared to imply a motionless Earth—should be set aside in order to accommodate an unproven scientific theory.[8] Yet even here the Church was not altogether inflexible. As Cardinal Robert Bellarmine famously remarked at the time:

> If there were a real proof that the sun is in the center of the universe, that the earth is in the third heaven, and that the sun does not go round the earth but the earth round the sun, then we should have to proceed with great circumspection in explaining passages of Scripture which appear to teach the contrary, and rather admit that we did not understand them than declare an opinion to be false which is proved to be true. But as for myself, I shall not believe that there are such proofs until they are shown to me.[9]

Bellarmine's theoretical openness to new interpretations of Scripture in light of additions to the sum total of human knowledge was nothing new. Saint Albert the Great had held a similar view. "It very often happens," he once wrote, "that there is some question as to the earth or the sky, or the other elements of this world, respecting which one who is not a Christian has knowledge derived from most certain reasoning or observation, and it is very disgraceful and mischievous, and of all things to be carefully avoided, that a Christian speaking of such matters as being according to the Christian Scriptures, should be heard by an unbeliever talking such nonsense that the unbeliever, perceiving him to be as wide from the mark as east from west, can hardly restrain himself from laughing."[10] Saint Thomas Aquinas had likewise warned of the certain consequences of holding to a particular interpretation of Scripture after there had arisen serious grounds for believing it not the correct one:

> First, the truth of Scripture must be held inviolable. Secondly, when there are different ways of explaining a Scriptural text, no particular explanation should be held so rigidly that, if convincing arguments show it to be false, anyone dare to insist that it still is the definitive sense of the text. Otherwise unbelievers will scorn Sacred Scripture, and the way to faith will be closed to them.[11]

Nevertheless, in 1616, after Galileo had publicly and persistently taught the Copernican system, Church authorities told him that he must cease to teach the Copernican theory as true, though he remained free to treat it as a hypothesis. Galileo agreed, and continued on with his work.

In 1624, he made another trip to Rome, where once again he was received with great enthusiasm, and where influential cardinals were eager to discuss scientific questions with him. Pope Urban VIII presented him with several impressive gifts, including two medals and a statement urging further patronage for his work. The pope spoke of Galileo as a man "whose fame shines in the sky and is spread over the whole world." Urban VIII told the astronomer that the Church had never declared Copernicanism to be heretical, and that the Church would never do so.

Galileo's *Dialogue on the Great World Systems*, published in 1632, was written at the urging of the pope, but it ignored the instruction to treat Copernicanism as a hypothesis rather than as established truth. Years later, Father Grienberger allegedly remarked that had Galileo treated his conclusions as hypotheses, the great astronomer could have written anything he wished.[12] Unfortunately for Galileo, in 1633 he was declared suspected of heresy and was ordered to desist from publishing

on Copernicanism. Galileo did go on to produce still more good
and important work, particularly his *Discourses Concerning
Two New Sciences* (1635). But this unwise censure of Galileo
has tainted the Church's reputation.

It is important, however, not to overstate what took place. As
J. L. Heilbron explains:

> Informed contemporaries appreciated that the reference to
> heresy in connection with Galileo or Copernicus had no gen-
> eral or theological significance. Gassendi, in 1642, observed
> that the decision of the cardinals, though important for the
> faithful, did not amount to an article of faith; Riccioli, in 1651,
> that heliocentrism was not a heresy; Mengoli, in 1675, that
> interpretations of Scripture can only bind Catholics if agreed
> to at a general council; and Baldigiani, in 1678, that everyone
> knew all that.[13]

The fact is, Catholic scientists were essentially permitted to
carry on their research unhindered as long as they treated the
motion of the earth as a hypothesis (as the 1616 decree of the
Holy Office had called for). A 1633 decree did so further, excluding all mention of the earth's motion from scholarly discussion.
But because Catholic scientists like Father Roger Boscovich continued to use the idea of a moving earth in their work, scholars
speculate that the 1633 decree was likely "aimed personally at
Galileo Galilei" and not at Catholic scientists as a whole.[14]

Certainly the condemnation of Galileo, even when understood
in its proper context rather than in the exaggerated and sensa-
tional accounts so common in the media, proved to be an embar-
rassment to the Church, establishing the myth that the Church is
hostile to science.

# GOD "ORDERED ALL THINGS
# BY MEASURE, NUMBER, WEIGHT"

*Ever since the work of historian* Pierre Duhem in the early twentieth century, the accelerating trend among historians of science has been to underline the Church's crucial role in the development of science. Unfortunately, little of this academic work has penetrated popular consciousness. This is not unusual. Most people, for example, still believe that the Industrial Revolution drastically reduced the workers' living standards, when in fact the average standard of living actually rose.[15] So too the Church's true role in the development of modern science remains something of a secret to the general public.

Father Stanley Jaki is a prizewinning historian of science—with doctorates in theology and physics—whose scholarship has helped give Catholicism and Scholasticism their due in the development of Western science. Jaki's many books have advanced the provocative claim that far from hindering the development of science, Christian ideas helped to make it possible.

Jaki places great significance on the fact that the Christian tradition, from its Old Testament prehistory through the High Middle Ages and beyond, conceives of God—and, by extension, His creation—as rational and orderly. Throughout the Bible, the regularity of natural phenomena is described as a reflection of God's goodness, beauty, and order. For if the Lord "has imposed an order on the magnificent works of his wisdom," that is only because "He is from everlasting to everlasting" (Sir. 42:21). "The world," writes Jaki, summing up the testimony of the Old Testament, "being the handiwork of a supremely reasonable Person, is endowed with lawfulness and purpose." This lawfulness is evident all around us. "The regular return of seasons, the unfailing course of stars, the music of the spheres, the movement of the forces of nature according to fixed ordinances, are all the results of the One who alone can be trusted unconditionally." The same holds for Jeremiah's citation of the faithful recurrence of harvests as a demonstration of God's goodness, or the parallel he draws "between Yahweh's unfailing love and the eternal ordinances by which Yahweh set the course of stars and the tides of the sea."[16]

Jaki directs our attention to Wisdom 11:21, in which God is said to have "ordered all things by measure, number, weight."[17] This point, according to Jaki, not only lent support to Christians in late antiquity who upheld the rationality of the universe, but also inspired Christians a millennium later who, at the beginnings of modern science, had embarked on quantitative inquiry as a way of understanding the universe.

This point may appear so obvious as to be of little interest. But the idea of a rational, orderly universe—enormously fruitful and indeed indispensable for the progress of science—has eluded entire civilizations. One of Jaki's central theses is that it was not coincidental that the birth of science as a self-perpetuating field of intellectual endeavor should have occurred in a Catholic milieu. Certain fundamental Christian ideas, he suggests, have been indispensable in the emergence of scientific thought. Non-Christian cultures, on the other hand, did not possess the same philosophical tools, and indeed were burdened by conceptual frameworks that hindered the development of science. In *Science and Creation*, Jaki extends this thesis to seven great cultures: Arabic, Babylonian, Chinese, Egyptian, Greek, Hindu, and Maya. In these cultures, Jaki explains, science suffered a "stillbirth."

Such stillbirths can be accounted for by each of these cultures' conceptions of the universe and their lack of belief in a transcendent Creator who endowed His creation with consistent physical laws. To the contrary, they conceived of the universe as a huge organism dominated by a pantheon of deities and destined to go through endless cycles of birth, death, and rebirth. This made the development of science impossible. The animism that characterized ancient cultures, which conceived of the divine as immanent in created things, hindered the growth of science by making the idea of constant natural laws foreign. Created things had minds and wills of their own—an idea that all but precluded the possibility of thinking of them as behaving according to regular, fixed patterns.

The Christian doctrine of the Incarnation militates strongly against such thinking. Christ is the *monogenes,* or "only begotten," Son of God. Within the Greco-Roman worldview, on the other hand, "the universe was the 'monogenes' or 'only begotten' emanation from a divine principle not really different from the universe itself."[18] Christianity, since it reposed the divine strictly in Christ and in a Holy Trinity that transcended the world, avoided any kind of pantheism and allowed Christians to view the universe as a realm of order and predictability.

Jaki does not deny that these cultures made some impressive technological contributions. His point is that we do not see the flowering of *formal and sustained scientific inquiry* emerging from this work. This is why another recent treatment of the subject could argue that "the earlier technical innovations of Greco-Roman times, of Islam, of imperial China, let alone those achieved in prehistoric times, do not constitute science and are better described as lore, skills, wisdom, techniques, crafts, technologies, engineering, learning, or simply knowledge."[19]

Ancient Babylonia is an instructive example. Babylonian cosmogony was supremely unsuited to the development of science, and in fact positively discouraged it. The Babylonians perceived the natural order as so fundamentally uncertain that only an annual ceremony of expiation could hope to prevent total cosmic disorder. Here again we have a civilization that had distinguished itself in watching the heavens, gathering astronomical data, and developing the rudiments of algebra. But living in that kind of spiritual and philosophical milieu, they could hardly have been expected to direct these practical gifts toward the development of what we could seriously refer to as science.[20] It is of more than passing significance, on the other hand, that in Christian creation, as described in Genesis, the chaos is completely subject to the sovereignty of God.[21]

Similar cultural factors tended to inhibit science in China. Oddly enough, it was a Marxist historian, Joseph Needham, who really got to the bottom of this failure. In his view, the culprit was the religious and philosophical framework in which Chinese thinkers operated. Such a conclusion is all the more stunning given Needham's Marxist ideology, which should have preferred some kind of economic or materialist explanation for the stillbirth of science in China. Chinese intellectuals, he argued, were unable to believe in the idea of laws of nature. This inability stemmed from the fact that "the conception of a divine celestial lawgiver imposing ordinances on non-human Nature never developed." "It was not that there was no order in nature for the Chinese," Needham went on,

> but rather that it was not an order ordained by a rational personal being, and hence there was no conviction that rational personal beings would be able to spell out in their lesser earthly languages the divine code of laws which he had decreed aforetime. The Taoists, indeed, would have scorned such an idea as being too naïve for the subtlety and complexity of the universe as they intuited it.[22]

Particularly challenging is the case of ancient Greece, which made such impressive strides in the application of human reason to the study of various disciplines. Of all the ancient cultures analyzed by Jaki, the Greeks came closest to—but ultimately fell well short of—the development of modern science. The Greeks assigned conscious purposes to the material actors of the cosmos; thus Aristotle explained the circular motion of celestial bodies in terms of their affection for such a pattern. Jaki has argued that in order for science to progress, it was up to the Scholastics of the High Middle Ages to carry out the *depersonalization* of nature, so that, for instance, the explanation for falling stones was not said to be their innate love for the center of the earth.

A great deal of scholarly attention has been devoted to the scientific contributions of Muslim scholars, particularly in such branches of study as medicine and optics. In addition, the translation by Arab scholars of ancient Greek classics led to their dissemination throughout the Western world in the twelfth century—a profoundly important part of Western intellectual history. The fact is, however, that the contributions of Muslim scientists typically occurred in spite of Islam rather than because of it. Orthodox Islamic scholars absolutely rejected any conception of the universe that involved consistent physical laws, because the absolute autonomy of Allah could not be restricted by natural laws.[23] Apparent natural laws were nothing more than mere *habits*, so to speak, of Allah, and might be discontinued at any time.[24]

Catholicism admits the possibility of miracles and acknowledges the role of the supernatural, but the very idea of a miracle suggests that the event in question is *unusual*, and of course it is only against the backdrop of an orderly natural world that a miracle can be recognized in the first place. Moreover, the mainstream of Christian thought has never portrayed God as fundamentally arbitrary; it was accepted that nature operates according to fixed and intelligible patterns. This is what Saint Anselm meant when he spoke of the distinction between God's ordered power (*potentia ordinata*) and His absolute power (*potentia absoluta*). According to Saint Anselm, since God has chosen to reveal to us something of His nature, of the moral order, and of His plan of redemption, He has thereby bound Himself to behave in a certain way and can be trusted to keep His promise.[25]

By the thirteenth and fourteenth centuries this distinction had taken significant root.[26] It is true that a figure like William of Ockham eventually emphasized God's absolute will to a degree that was unhelpful in the development of science, but overall the fundamental order of the universe was taken for granted in Christian thought.

Saint Thomas Aquinas, in fact, struck an important balance between God's freedom to create any kind of universe He wanted and His consistency in governing the universe He did create. As Father Jaki explains, the Thomistic Catholic view was that it was important to find out precisely what kind of universe God created and so avoid abstract thinking about how the universe *must* be. God's complete creative freedom means it did not *have* to be any particular way. It is by means of experience—a key ingredient of the scientific method—that we come to know the nature of the universe that God chose to create. And we can come to know it because it is rational, predictable, and intelligible.[27]

This approach avoids two potential errors. First, it cautions against speculation about the physical universe that is divorced from experience, of a kind in which the ancients frequently engaged. A priori arguments claiming that the universe "must" be this or that way, or that "it is fitting" that the universe should be this or that way, are thereby dealt a profoundly important blow. Aristotle claimed that an object that was twice as heavy as another object would fall twice as fast if both were dropped from the same height. Simple introspection led him to that conclusion, but it is not true, as anyone can easily verify. Yet although Aristotle collected much empirical data over the course of his various investigations, he persisted in believing that natural philosophy could be based on purely rational, as opposed to strictly empirical, investigation. For him, the eternal universe was a *necessary* universe, and its physical principles could be attained through an intellectual process divorced from experience.[28]

Second, it implies that the universe that God created is intelligible and orderly, since although God possesses the raw power to bring about randomness and lawlessness in the physical world, it would be inconsistent with His orderliness and rationality to behave in such a manner. It was precisely this sense of the rationality and predictability of the physical world that gave early modern scientists the philosophical confidence to engage in scientific study in the first place. As one scholar puts it, "It was only in such a conceptual matrix that science could experience the kind of viable birth which is followed by sustained growth."[29]

This point finds surprising support in the work of Friedrich Nietzsche, one of the nineteenth century's greatest critics of Christianity. "Strictly speaking," argued Nietzsche, "there is no such thing as science 'without any presuppositions'...a philosophy, a 'faith,' must always be there first, so that science can acquire from it a direction, a meaning, a limit, a method, a right to exist.... It is still a *metaphysical faith* that underlies our faith in science."[30]

Jaki's thesis that Christian theology sustained scientific enterprise in the West can also be applied to how Western scholars resolved important questions concerning motion, projectiles, and impetus. For the ancient Greeks, the natural state of all bodies was rest. Motion, therefore, demanded explanation, and Aristotle's attempt at providing one proved especially influential.

According to him, earth, water, and air—three of the four elements of which the terrestrial world was said to be composed—possessed a natural tendency toward the center of the earth. When an object was dropped from a tree and plunged to the ground, it was simply acting according to its nature in seeking the center of the earth (impeded in reaching that ultimate destination, of course, by the ground). Fire, on the other hand, tended to move to some point above us, though well within the sublunary region (that is, the region beneath the moon).[31]

Aristotle spoke of natural motion and violent motion. Natural motion was exemplified by rising flames and falling balls—in other words, cases in which the thing in motion sought its natural place of rest. The classic example of violent motion, on the other hand, involved projectiles, as when a ball is thrown in the air, against its natural tendency toward the center of the earth.

Accounting for the motion of projectiles was particularly difficult for Aristotle. If someone throws a ball, Aristotle's theory seems to suggest that it should drop to the ground at the instant it leaves the person's hand, since its nature is to move toward the earth. The ball's motion would make sense only if it never left the person's hand; if it were pushed along by someone carrying it, this externally applied force would explain its movement. But when that force is removed, Aristotle seems unable to account for the motion of the ball through the air. He attempted to solve this dilemma by suggesting that as the projectile flew through the air there indeed *was* a force pushing it at each moment: vibrations in the medium in which the object traveled.

An essential ingredient in the transition from ancient to modern physics, therefore, was the introduction of the concept of inertia, the resistance of an object to a change in its state of motion. In the eighteenth century, Isaac Newton described the concept in his first law of motion, according to which bodies at rest tend to stay at rest and bodies in motion tend to stay in motion.

Modern scholars have begun to acknowledge the importance of medieval precedents in the development of the idea of inertial motion. Of particular importance was the work of Jean Buridan, a fourteenth-century professor at the Sorbonne. Like any Catholic, Buridan was compelled by his religious beliefs to reject the Aristotelian idea that the universe itself was eternal. Instead, Buridan maintained that the universe had been created by God at a particular moment, out of nothing. And if the universe itself was not eternal, then the celestial motion whose eternity Aristotle also posited had to be conceived of in some other way. In other words, if the *planets* had begun to exist at a particular moment in time, then *planetary motion* must also have begun at a particular moment in time.

What Buridan sought to discover was how the celestial bodies, once created, could have begun to move and remained in motion in the absence of a continuing force propelling them. His answer was that God had *imparted* the motion to the celestial bodies upon creating them, and that this motion had never dissipated because the celestial bodies, moving in outer space, encountered no friction. Since these moving bodies encountered no counter-vailing force that could slow or stop their motion, they continued to move. Here, in a nutshell, are the ideas of momentum and iner-tial motion.[32] While Buridan never entirely escaped from the con-fines of Aristotelian physics, and his conception of impetus remained encumbered by some of the misconceptions of antiq-uity, this was a profound theoretical advance.[33]

It is important to keep in mind the theological context and religious milieu in which Buridan reached this conclusion, since the absence of such a context within the great ancient cultures helps to account for their failure to develop the idea of inertial motion. As Jaki has explained, all of those cultures were pagan, and therefore held to the belief that the universe and its motions were eternal, with neither a beginning nor an end. On the other hand, as Jaki explains, once the belief in creation *ex nihilo* had become "a widely shared cultural consensus during the Christian Middle Ages, it became almost natural that there should arise the idea of inertial motion."[34]

These questions continued to be discussed over the centuries, but within the enormous corpus of writings that lie between Buridan and Descartes, endorsements of Buridan's idea far out-number rejections. A solid consensus developed around Buridan's idea. "Insofar as that broad creedal or theological consensus is the work of Christianity," Jaki contends, "science is not Western, but Christian."[35]

Successors of Buridan and Nicholas Oresme were not espe-cially known for their eagerness to acknowledge their intellectual debts. Isaac Newton, for example, devoted considerable time in his old age to erasing the name of Descartes from his notebooks, in order to conceal the latter's influence. Descartes, likewise, did not disclose his own indebtedness to the medieval theory of impe-tus so central to his own position.[36] Copernicus referred to impe-tus theory in his own work, though again without citing sources. It is quite likely that he learned of the theory while studying at the University of Cracow, where he could easily have obtained manuscript copies of the relevant commentaries of Buridan and Oresme.[37]

What is clear, however, is that this critical insight, a direct result of Buridan's Catholic faith, had a profound effect on West-ern science. Newton's first law represents the culmination of this important line of thought. "Insofar as science is a quantitative study of things in motion and the first law of Newton is the basis of other laws," Jaki concludes, "one may indeed speak of the sub-stantially medieval origin of modern science."[38]

Buridan's concept of impetus is a significant attempt to describe movement both on Earth and in the heavens by means of a single system of mechanics.[39] Since antiquity it had been taken for granted that the laws governing celestial motion were funda-mentally different from those governing terrestrial motion. Non-Western cultures that tended toward pantheism or that viewed the heavenly bodies as in some way divine likewise assumed that the motion of the divine bodies of the heavens must be accounted for differently from terrestrial motion. Isaac Newton finally demonstrated that a single set of laws could account for all the motion in the universe, both terrestrial and celestial. Buridan had already paved the way.

## THE CATHEDRAL SCHOOL OF CHARTRES

*The cathedral school of Chartres,* an institution of learning that came into its full maturity in the twelfth century, represents an important chapter in Western intellectual history and in the his-tory of Western science. The school made important strides toward excellence in the eleventh century under Fulbert, who had been a pupil of Gerbert of Aurillac, the bright light of the late tenth century who later became Pope Sylvester II. Practically everyone of the period who made any substantial contribution to the development of science was at one time or another associated with or influenced by Chartres.[40]

Fulbert conveyed a spirit of intellectual curiosity and versatil-ity by his own example. He was conversant with the most recent developments in logic, mathematics, and astronomy, and kept in touch with the influx of learning from Muslim Spain. In addition to being an accomplished physician, Fulbert also composed a variety of hymns. He was a fine example of the Catholic scholar; very far from his mind was any thought of despising the secular sciences or the works of the pagan ancients.

Something of the orientation of the School of Chartres can be gleaned from the cathedral's west façade. There each of the traditional seven liberal arts is personified in sculpture, with each discipline represented by an ancient teacher: Aristotle, Boethius, Cicero, Donatus (or, possibly, Priscian), Euclid, Ptolemy, and Pythagoras.[41] In the 1140s, Thierry of Chartres, the school's chancellor at the time, had supervised the construction of the west façade. Thierry was profoundly devoted to the study of the liberal arts and under his chancellorship Chartres became the most sought-after school of these venerable disciplines.

Thierry's religious convictions filled him with zeal for the liberal arts. For him, as well as for a great many other intellects of the Middle Ages, the disciplines of the *quadrivium*—arithmetic, geometry, music, and astronomy—invited students to contemplate the patterns with which God had ordered the world and to appreciate the beautiful art that was God's handiwork. The *trivium*—grammar, rhetoric, and logic—made it possible for people to express, persuasively and intelligibly, the insights that they gained from such investigation. Finally, in the words of a modern scholar, the liberal arts revealed to man "his place in the universe and [taught] him to appreciate the beauty of the created world."[42]

One of the characteristics of twelfth-century natural philosophy was a commitment to the idea of nature as something autonomous, operating according to fixed laws discernible by reason, and it was here that Chartres made perhaps its most significant contribution. Intellectuals interested in the workings of nature were anxious to develop explanations based on natural causation.[43] According to Adelard of Bath (c. 1080–1142), a student at Chartres, "It is through reason that we are men. For if we turned our backs on the amazing rational beauty of the universe we live in we should indeed deserve to be driven therefrom, like a guest unappreciative of the house into which he has been received."[44] He concluded, "I will detract nothing from God, for whatever is is from Him." But "we must listen to the very limits of human knowledge and only when this utterly breaks down should we refer things to God."[45]

William of Conches agreed. "I take nothing away from God," he said. "He is the author of all things, evil excepted. But the nature with which He endowed His creatures accomplishes a whole scheme of operations, and these too turn to His glory since it is He who created this very nature."[46] That is to say, the structure of nature that God created is usually capable of accounting for the phenomena we observe without recourse to supernatural explanations. William had only scorn and contempt for anyone who disparaged scientific investigation:

> Because they are themselves ignorant of nature's forces and wish to have all men as companions in their ignorance, they are unwilling for anybody to investigate them, but prefer that we believe like peasants and not inquire into the [natural] causes [of things]. However, we say that the cause of everything is to be sought.... But these people ... if they know of anybody so investigating, proclaim him a heretic.[47]

Naturally, such views as these raised suspicions: Could these Catholic philosophers maintain their commitment to investigating nature in terms of secondary causation and to nature as a rational entity without excluding the supernatural and miraculous altogether? But maintaining this balance is precisely what these thinkers did. They rejected the idea that rational investigation of natural causes could be an affront to God, or that it amounted to restricting His behavior to the confines of the natural laws that might be discovered. Such thinkers conceded, in accordance with the outlook described above, that God certainly could have created any kind of universe He wanted, but they contended that having created this one, God would allow it to operate according to its nature and would not typically interfere with its basic structure.[48]

In his discussion of the biblical creation account, Thierry of Chartres cast aside any suggestion that the celestial bodies might in some way be divine, that the universe itself was a large organism, or that the heavenly bodies were composed of imperishable matter not subject to earthly laws. To the contrary, Thierry explained that all things "have Him as their Creator, because they are all subject to change and can perish." Thierry described the stars and the firmament as being composed of water and air, rather than as semi-divine substances whose behavior must be explained according to principles fundamentally different from those seen to govern the things of earth.[49] That insight is positively crucial to the development of science.

Thomas Goldstein, a modern historian of science, describes the ultimate importance of the School of Chartres:

> Formulating the philosophical premises; defining the basic concept of the cosmos from which all later specialized sciences were to grow; systematically reconstructing the scientific knowledge of the past and thus placing the coming evolution of Western science on a solid traditional footing—each one of these steps seems so crucial that, taken together, they could

only mean one thing: that in a period of fifteen to twenty years, around the middle of the twelfth century, a handful of men were consciously striving to launch the evolution of Western science, and undertook every major step that was needed to achieve that end.[50]

Goldstein predicts that in the future, "Thierry will probably be recognized as one of the true founders of Western science."[51]

The century in which the school of Chartres most distinguished itself was a time of great intellectual excitement. As the Christians began to push back their Muslim conquerors in Spain and defeated them in Sicily in the late eleventh century, Catholic scholars came into possession of important Arab centers of learning. Muslims had come into contact with Greek science in the wake of their conquests of Alexandria and Syria and had studied and commented on the classical texts. Ancient Greek texts lost to Europeans for centuries, which Muslims had translated into Arabic, were now recovered and translated into Latin. In Italy, Latin translations could be made directly from the original Greek. Among these texts were Aristotle's key physics books, including *Physics*, *On the Heavens and World*, and *On Generation and Corruption*.

Many Catholic scholars had simply assumed that there could be no serious contradiction between the truths of the faith and the best of ancient philosophy. But contradictions there were, as these new texts made increasingly evident. Aristotle had posited an eternal universe, whereas the Church taught that God had created the world at a moment in time, out of nothing. Aristotle also denied the possibility of a vacuum. A modern reader could easily overlook the theological implications of this point, but a great many Catholics, particularly in the thirteenth century, did not. To deny the possibility of a vacuum was to deny God's creative power, for nothing was impossible to an omnipotent God. Still other problematic statements could be found within Aristotle's corpus of work and would have to be confronted.

One approach was taken by a group of people known as the Latin Averroists (after Averroës, one of the most famous and respected Muslim commentators on Aristotle). Their position has often been described, inaccurately, as the doctrine of the double truth: that what is false in theology could be true in philosophy and vice versa, and that contradictory statements could therefore both be true depending on whether they were considered from the point of view of religion or of philosophy.

What they actually taught was more subtle. They believed that Aristotle's views, such as the eternity of the earth, were the certain results of sound reasoning, and that no fault could be found in the logical process that led to them. Yet these views contradicted divine revelation. The Latin Averroists solved the problem by arguing that as philosophers they had to follow the dictates of reason wherever they led, but that since the conclusions they reached contradicted revelation, they could not be true in any absolute sense. After all, what was feeble human reason against the omnipotence of God, who transcended it? [52]

To conservative scholars, this solution seemed every bit as unstable and fraught with difficulty as it does to us, and it turned some Catholic thinkers away from philosophy altogether. Saint Thomas Aquinas, who deeply respected Aristotle, feared that a conservative reaction to the errors of the Averroists might lead to the abandonment of The Philosopher (as he referred to Aristotle) altogether. In his famous synthesis, Saint Thomas demonstrated that faith and reason were complementary and could not contradict each other. Any apparent contradictions that arose indicated errors in one's understanding either of religion or of philosophy.

In spite of Aquinas's brilliance, apprehension about the new texts and some scholars' responses to them still existed. It was in this context that shortly after Saint Thomas's death the bishop of Paris issued a series of 219 condemned propositions—known to history as the Condemnations of 1277—that professors at the University of Paris were forbidden to teach. These condemned propositions were statements of Aristotelian teaching—or in some cases merely the potential conclusion of an Aristotelian claim—that were irreconcilable with the Catholic understanding of God and the world. Although the condemnations applied only to Paris, there is good evidence that their influence was felt as far away as Oxford. The pope had not played any role in the condemnations; he had merely requested an investigation into the causes of all the intellectual turmoil that had beset the masters at Paris. (One scholar argues that there was "less than enthusiastic papal approval of the bishop of Paris' actions."[53])

Even the Condemnations of 1277, however, had a positive effect on the development of science. Pierre Duhem, one of the great twentieth-century historians of science, went so far as to argue that these condemnations represented the beginning of modern science. What Duhem and more recent scholars like A. C. Crombie and Edward Grant have suggested is that the condemnations forced thinkers to break out of the intellectual confinement that Aristotelian presuppositions had fastened upon them, and to think about the physical world in new ways. By condemning certain aspects of Aristotelian physical theory, they began to break Western scholars of the habit of relying so heavily on Aristotle, and gave them an opportunity to begin thinking in ways that departed from ancient assumptions.

Although scholars have disagreed over the relative influence of the condemnations, all agree that they forced thinkers to emancipate themselves from the restrictions of Aristotelian science and to consider possibilities that the great philosopher never envisioned.[54]

Let us consider one example. As we have noted, Aristotle denied the possibility of a vacuum, and thinkers in the High Middle Ages typically followed him in this view. After the condemnations were issued, scholars were now required to concede that the all-powerful God could indeed create a vacuum. This opened new and exciting scientific possibilities. To be sure, some scholars appear to have conceded the possibility of a vacuum in a merely formalistic way—that is, while they certainly admitted that God was all-powerful and therefore could create a vacuum, they were generally persuaded that in fact He would not do so. But some were intrigued by the possibilities the condemnations discussed and engaged in important scientific debate. Thus the condemnations, according to historian of science Richard Dales, "seem definitely to have promoted a freer and more imaginative way of doing science."[55]

This was clearly so in the case of another of the condemnations, namely the Aristotelian proposition that "the motions of the sky result from an intellective soul."[56] A condemnation of that statement was of great importance, since it denied that the heavenly bodies possessed souls and were in some way alive—a standard cosmological belief that had enjoyed currency since antiquity. Although we can find Church fathers who condemned this idea as incompatible with the faith, a great many Christian thinkers had adopted Aristotle's view and conceived of the planetary spheres as being propelled by intellectual substances of some kind.

This condemnation catalyzed new approaches to this central question of the behavior of the heavenly bodies. Jean Buridan, following in the footsteps of Robert Grosseteste, argued that the scriptural evidence for such intelligences was notably lacking, and Nicholas Oresme made still further strides against the idea.[57]

As early as the patristic period, Christian thought, albeit typically only by implication, began the de-animation of nature—that is, the removal from our conception of the universe any suggestion that the celestial bodies were themselves alive, or constituted intelligences in their own right, or were unable to operate in the absence of some kind of spiritual mover. Scattered throughout the writings of such saints as Augustine, Basil, Gregory of Nyssa, Jerome, and John Damascene are statements to this effect. But it was only later, when scholars began applying themselves more deliberately and consistently to the study of nature, that we begin to see thinkers who consciously conceived of the universe as an entity that was mechanistic and, by extension, intelligible to the inquiring human mind.[58] "During the twelfth century in Latin Europe," writes Dales, "those aspects of Judeo-Christian thought which emphasized the idea of creation out of nothing and the distance between God and the world, in certain contexts and with certain men, had the effect of eliminating all semi-divine entities from the realm of nature."[59] And according to Stanley Jaki, "nature had to be de-animized" in order for science to be born.[60]

Long after the condemnations themselves had been forgotten, the discussion that these anti-Aristotelian statements had provoked continued to influence European intellectual history through the seventeenth century and the onset of the Scientific Revolution.[61]

## THE SCIENTIST-PRIEST

*It is a relatively simple matter* to show that many great scientists, like Louis Pasteur, have been Catholic. Much more revealing, however, is the surprising number of Catholic *churchmen*, priests in particular, whose scientific work has been so extensive and significant. Here were men who in most cases had taken holy orders and had committed themselves to the highest and most significant spiritual commitment the Church affords. Their insatiable curiosity about the universe God created and their commitment to scientific research reveals, far more than could any merely theoretical discussion, that the relationship between Church and science is naturally one of friendship rather than of antagonism and suspicion.

Several important figures of the thirteenth century deserve mention. Roger Bacon, a Franciscan who taught at Oxford, was admired for his work in mathematics and optics, and is considered to be a forerunner of modern scientific method. Bacon wrote about the philosophy of science and emphasized the importance of experience and experiment. In his *Opus Maius*, Bacon observed: "Without experiment, nothing can be adequately known. An argument proves theoretically, but does not give the certitude necessary to remove all doubt; nor will the mind repose in the clear view of truth, unless it finds it by way of experiment." Likewise, in his *Opus Tertium*, he cautioned that "[t]he strongest arguments prove nothing, so long as the conclusions are not verified by experience."[62] He identified several obstacles to the transmission of truth, among them uninstructed popular opinion and long-standing but erroneous custom.[63]

Saint Albert the Great (c. 1200–1280), or Albertus Magnus, was educated at Padua and later joined the Dominican order. He taught in various priories in Germany before beginning his tenure at the University of Paris in 1241, where he would have a number of illustrious students, none more so than Saint Thomas Aquinas. Saint Albert also served in important positions of authority within the Church, including provincial of the German Dominicans for several years and bishop of Regensburg for two. "Proficient in all branches of science," writes the *Dictionary of Scientific Biography*, "he was one of the most famous precursors of modern science in the High Middle Ages." Canonized by Pope Pius XI in 1931, Saint Albert would be named the patron of all who cultivate the natural sciences ten years later by Pius XII.[64]

Saint Albert was a renowned naturalist and recorded an enormous amount about the world around him. His prodigious output spanned physics, logic, metaphysics, biology, psychology, and various earth sciences. Like Roger Bacon, Saint Albert was careful to note the importance of direct observation in the acquisition of knowledge about the physical world. In *De Mineralibus*, he explained that the aim of natural science was "not simply to accept the statements of others, that is, what is narrated by people, but to investigate the causes that are at work in nature for themselves."[65] His insistence on direct observation and—for all his admiration of Aristotle—his refusal to accept scientific authority on faith were essential contributions to the scientific frame of mind.

Robert Grosseteste, who served as chancellor of Oxford and as bishop of Lincoln, the largest diocese in England, shared the enormous range of scholarly interests and accomplishments that characterized Roger Bacon and Saint Albert the Great. Grosseteste had been influenced by the famous school at Chartres, particularly by Thierry.[66] Considered one of the most knowledgeable men of the Middle Ages, Grosseteste has been called the first man ever to write down a complete set of steps for performing a scientific experiment. In *Robert Grosseteste and the Origins of Experimental Science*, A. C. Crombie suggested that the thirteenth century possessed the rudiments of the scientific method, largely thanks to figures like Grosseteste. Thus, although the innovations of the seventeenth-century Scientific Revolution certainly deserve their due, a theoretical emphasis on observation and experiment is already evident in the High Middle Ages.

Standard textbooks very often do give Roger Bacon and Saint Albert the Great, and to a lesser extent Robert Grosseteste, their proper due. Other Catholic names in science, however, remain in undeserved obscurity. Father Nicolaus Steno (1638–1686), for example, a Lutheran convert who later became a Catholic priest, has been credited with "set[ting] down most of the principles of modern geology," and has sometimes been called the father of stratigraphy (the study of the strata, or layers, of the earth).[67] Born in Denmark, Father Steno lived and traveled throughout Europe over the course of his life, serving for a time as court physician to the grand duke of Tuscany. Yet despite his excellent reputation and creative work in medicine, he secured his scientific reputation in the study of fossils and the earth's strata.

His work began in an unlikely context: the dissection of the head of an enormous shark that a French fishing boat encountered in 1666. Weighing in at 2,800 pounds, the shark was the largest that most people had ever seen. Steno, who was known for his great skill as a dissector, was called upon to perform the dissection.

For our purposes, it suffices to concentrate on Steno's fascination with the shark's teeth. They bore a strange resemblance to so-called tongue stones, or glossopetrae, whose origins had been mysterious and obscure since ancient times. These stones, which the Maltese dug up from under the earth, were said to possess

THE CHURCH AND SCIENCE

curative powers. Countless theories were proposed to account for them. In the sixteenth century, Guillaume Rondelet had suggested that they might be shark teeth, but few were impressed with this idea. Now Steno had the chance to compare the objects side by side, and found the resemblance clear.

This was a significant moment in the history of science, since it pointed to a much larger and more significant issue than shark teeth and mysterious stones: the presence of shells and marine fossils embedded in rocks, far from the sea. The question of the glossopetrae, now almost certainly shark teeth, raised the broader question of the origin of fossils in general, and how they had come to exist in the state in which they were found. Why were these things being found inside rocks? Spontaneous generation was but one of the numerous explanations that had been proposed in the past.

Such explanations did not impress Steno, who found them scientifically dubious as well as offensive to his idea of God, who would not act in a manner so random and purposeless. He concluded for a number of reasons that existing theories of fossils could not be reconciled with the facts as they were known. He threw himself into study of the question, devoting the next two years to writing and compiling what would be his influential work, *De solido intra solidum naturaliter contento dissertationis prodromus* ("Preliminary Discourse to a Dissertation on a Solid Body Naturally Contained Within a Solid").

This was no easy task, for Steno was essentially striking out into uncharted territory. There was no existing science of geology to which he could refer for methodology or first principles. The speculations in which he engaged, dealing with events and processes that had occurred in the distant past, ruled out direct observation as a way of verifying some of his conclusions.

Nevertheless, he pressed ahead boldly. Rocks, fossils, and geological strata, Steno was certain, told a story about the history of the earth, and geological study could illuminate that history. This was a new and revolutionary idea. Previous writers had assumed, with Aristotle, that the earth's past was fundamentally unintelligible. "Steno," writes his most recent biographer, "was the first to assert that the world's history might be recoverable from the rocks and to take it upon himself to unravel that history."[68]

> Ultimately, Steno's achievement in *De solido* was not just that he proposed a new, and correct, theory of fossils. As he himself pointed out, writers more than a thousand years earlier had said essentially the same thing. Nor was it simply that he presented a new and correct interpretation of rock strata. It was that he drew up a blueprint for an entirely new scientific approach to nature, one that opened up the dimension of time. As Steno wrote, "from that which is perceived a definite conclusion may be drawn about what is imperceptible." From the present world one can deduce vanished worlds.[69]

Of the many insights found in Father Steno's text, three have generally been referred to as "Steno's principles." His is the first book of which we are aware that speaks of superposition, one of the key principles of stratigraphy.[70] The law of superposition is the first of Steno's principles. It states that sedimentary layers are formed in sequence, such that the lowest of the layers is the oldest, and that the layers decrease in age all the way through the most recent layer, on the very top.

But since most strata we find have been in some way disturbed, distorted, or tilted, this geological story is not always so easy to reconstruct. Which end is up, for instance, and thus in what direction does the age sequence go, in the case of strata that have been turned on their sides? Do we look from left to right or from right to left to learn the stratigraphic sequence? Thus Steno introduced his principle of original horizontality. Water, said Steno, is the source of sediments, whether in the form of a river, a storm, or similar phenomena. Water carries and then deposits the various layers of sediment. Once the sediments are in the basin, gravity and shallow water currents have a leveling effect on them, such that the layers of sediment, like water itself, match their surface shape on the bottom but become horizontal on the top. How to discover the sedimentary sequence in rocks that are no longer right side up? Since the largest and heaviest grains naturally settle first, with smaller and smaller ones following, we need simply to examine the layers and find where the largest particles were deposited. That is the bottom layer of the sequence.[71]

Finally, Steno's principle of lateral continuity posits that when both sides of a valley feature corresponding rock layers, the two sides were originally connected as continuous layers, with the valley itself a later geological event. Steno also noted that a stratum in which sea salt, or anything else that belongs in the sea—shark teeth, for example—is found reveals that the sea must have been there at some point.

As the years passed, Father Steno would be held up as a model of sanctity and scholarship. In 1722, his great-nephew, Jacob Winslow, wrote a biography of Steno that appeared in the section on prospective saints in a book called *Lives of the Saints for Each Day of the Year*. Winslow, a convert from Lutheranism to Catholicism, attributed his conversion to the intercession of Father Steno himself. In 1938, a group of Danish admirers looked to Pope Pius XI to have Father Steno declared a saint. Fifty years later, Pope John Paul II beatified Father Steno, praising his sanctity and his science.

# THE SCIENTIFIC ACHIEVEMENTS
## OF THE JESUITS

*It was in the Society of Jesus,* the priestly society founded in the sixteenth century by Ignatius Loyola, where the great bulk of Catholic priests interested in the sciences were found. A recent historian describes what the Jesuits accomplished by the eighteenth century:

> They had contributed to the development of pendulum clocks, pantographs, barometers, reflecting telescopes and microscopes, to scientific fields as various as magnetism, optics and electricity. They observed, in some cases before anyone else, the coloured bands on Jupiter's surface, the Andromeda nebula and Saturn's rings. They theorised about the circulation of the blood (independently of Harvey), the theoretical possibility of flight, the way the moon effected the tides, and the wave-like nature of light. Star maps of the southern hemisphere, symbolic logic, flood-control measures on the Po and Adige rivers, introducing plus and minus signs into Italian mathematics—all were typical Jesuit achievements, and scientists as influential as Fermat, Huygens, Leibniz and Newton were not alone in counting Jesuits among their most prized correspondents.[72]

Likewise, an important scholar of early electrical science has described the Society of Jesus as "the single most important contributor to experimental physics in the seventeenth century."[73] "Such an accolade," writes another scholar, "would only be strengthened by detailed studies of other sciences, such as optics, where virtually all the important treatises of the period were written by Jesuits."[74] Several of the great Jesuit scientists also performed the enormously valuable task of recording their data in massive encyclopedias, which played a crucial role in spreading scientific research throughout the scholarly community. "If scientific collaboration was one of the outgrowths of the scientific revolution," says historian William Ashworth, "the Jesuits deserve a large share of the credit."[75]

The Jesuits also boasted a great many extraordinary mathematicians who made a number of important contributions to their discipline. When Charles Bossut, one of the first historians of mathematics, compiled a list of the most eminent mathematicians from 900 B.C. through 1800 A.D., 16 of the 303 people he listed were Jesuits.[76] That figure—amounting to a full 5 percent of the greatest mathematicians over a span of 2,700 years— becomes still more impressive when we recall that the Jesuits existed for only two of those twenty-seven centuries![77] In addition, some thirty-five craters on the moon are named for Jesuit scientists and mathematicians.

The Jesuits were also the first to introduce Western science into such far-off places as China and India. In seventeenth-century China in particular, Jesuits introduced a substantial body of scientific knowledge and a vast array of mental tools for understanding the physical universe, including the Euclidean geometry that made planetary motion comprehensible. The Jesuits in China, according to one expert:

"[A]rrived at a time when science in general, and mathematics and astronomy in particular, were at a very low level there, contrasting with the birth of modern science in Europe. They made an enormous effort to translate western mathematical and astronomical works into Chinese and aroused the interest of Chinese scholars in these sciences. They made very extensive astronomical observation and carried out the first modern cartographic work in China. They also learned to appreciate the scientific achievements of this ancient culture and made them known in Europe. Through their correspondence European scientists first learned about the Chinese science and culture."[78]

Jesuits made important contributions to the scientific knowledge and infrastructure of other less developed nations not only in Asia but also in Africa and Central and South America. Beginning in the nineteenth century, these continents saw the opening of Jesuit observatories that studied astronomy, geomagnetism, meteorology, seismology, and solar physics. Such observatories provided these places with accurate timekeeping, weather forecasts (particularly important in the cases of hurricanes and typhoons), earthquake risk assessments, and cartography.[79] In Central and South America, the Jesuits worked primarily in meteorology and seismology, essentially laying the foundations of those disciplines there.[80] The scientific development of these countries, ranging from Ecuador to Lebanon to the Philippines, is indebted to Jesuit efforts.

A great many individual Jesuits have distinguished themselves in the sciences over the years. Father Giambattista Riccioli, for example, is known to us for a number of substantial achievements, among them the little-known fact that he was the first person to determine the rate of acceleration of a freely falling body. He was also an accomplished astronomer. Around 1640, Father Riccioli determined to produce for his order a massive encyclopedia of astronomy. Thanks to his persistence and the support of Father Athanasius Kircher, he got his project approved by the Society of Jesus. Issued in 1651, the *Almagestum novum* was "a deposit and memorial of energetic and devoted learning." It was a truly impressive achievement. "No serious astronomer could afford to ignore the *Almagestum novum*," writes a modern scholar.[81] John Flamsteed, for example, the Astronomer Royal of England, made considerable use of Father Riccioli's work in preparing his lectures on astronomy during the 1680s.[82]

The *Almagestum*, in addition to its sheer volume of information, also serves as a testament to the Jesuits' willingness to depart from Aristotelian astronomical ideas. They freely speak of the moon as made of the same material as earth, and honor astronomers (even Protestants) whose views had diverged from standard geocentrism.[83]

Scholars have noted the Jesuits' unusually keen appreciation of the importance of precision in the practice of experimental science, and Father Riccioli personifies that commitment. In order to develop an accurate one-second pendulum, he managed to persuade nine fellow Jesuits to count nearly 87,000 oscillations in a single day.[84] By means of this accurate pendulum, he was able to calculate the constant of gravity. A recent study describes the process:

> Riccioli and [Father Francesco Maria] Grimaldi chose a pendulum 3'4" long Roman measure, set it going, pushed it when it grew languid, and counted, for six hours by astronomical measure, as it swung, back and forth, 21,706 times. That came close to the number desired: $24 \times 60 \times 60/4 = 21,600$. But it did not satisfy Riccioli. He tried again, this time for an entire 24 hours, enlisting nine of his brethren including Grimaldi; the result, 87,998 swings against the desired 86,400. Riccioli lengthened the pendulum to 3'4.2" and repeated the count, with the same team: this time they got 86,999. That was close enough for them, but not for him. Going in the wrong direction, he shortened to 3'2.67" and, with only Grimaldi and one other staunch counter to keep the vigil with him, obtained, on three different

nights, 3,212 swings for the time between the meridianal cross-
ings of the stars Spica and Arcturus. He should have found
3,192. He estimated that the length required was 3'3.27",
which—such is the confidence of faith—he accepted without
trying. It was a good choice, only a little further out than his
initial one, as it implies a value of 955 cm/sec$^2$ for the constant
of gravity.[85]

Father Francesco Maria Grimaldi also went on to make a name
for himself in the history of science. Father Riccioli was con-
stantly impressed with his colleague's ability to fashion and then
use a variety of observational instruments, and insisted that
Father Grimaldi's assistance was absolutely essential to the
completion of his own *Almagestum novum*. "And so Divine Prov-
idence gave me," he later recalled, "although most unworthy, a
collaborator without whom I never could have completed my
[technical] works."[86] Father Grimaldi measured the height of
lunar mountains as well as the height of clouds. He and Father
Riccioli produced a notably accurate selenograph (a detailed dia-
gram depicting the features of the moon), which now adorns the
entrance to the National Air and Space Museum in Washington,
D.C.[87]

But Father Grimaldi's place in science was secured primarily
through his discovery of the diffraction of light, and indeed for
assigning the word "diffraction" to this phenomenon. (Isaac
Newton, who became interested in optics as a result of Father
Grimaldi's work, called it "inflection," but Father Grimaldi's
term became the norm.[88]) In a series of experiments, he demonstrated that the observed passage of light could not be reconciled
with the idea that it moved in a rectilinear (that is, straight-line)
path. In one experiment, for example, he allowed a beam of sunlight to pass through a small hole (one-sixtieth of an inch) into a

completely darkened room. The light that passed through the hole took on the shape of a cone. Into this cone of light, ten to twenty feet from the hole, Father Grimaldi inserted a rod to cast a shadow on the screen on the wall. He found that the shadow thus cast was far larger than purely rectilinear motion would allow, and therefore that light did not travel in an exclusively rectilinear path.[89] He also discovered what are known as diffraction bands, colored bands that appeared parallel to the edge of the shadow.

Father Grimaldi's discovery of diffraction led future scientists, eager to account for the phenomenon, to posit the wave nature of light. When the hole was larger than the wavelength of light, the light passed through it rectilinearly. But when the hole was smaller than the wavelength of light, diffraction was the result. Diffraction bands were also accounted for in terms of the wave nature of light; the interference of diffracted light waves produced the various colors observed in the bands.

One of the greatest Jesuit scientists was Father Roger Boscovich (1711–1787), whom Sir Harold Hartley, a twentieth-century fellow of the prestigious Royal Society, called "one of the great intellectual figures of all ages."[90] Father Boscovich was a genuine polymath accomplished in atomic theory, optics, mathematics, and astronomy and elected to learned societies and prestigious scientific academies across Europe. He also proved an accomplished poet, composing Latin verse under the auspices of Rome's prestigious Accademia degli Arcadi. It is little wonder that he has been called "the greatest genius Yugoslavia has ever produced."[91]

Father Boscovich's great genius became immediately apparent during his time at the Collegio Romano, the most prestigious and renowned of the Jesuit colleges. After completing his ordinary studies, he was appointed professor of mathematics at the Collegio.

Even in this early period of his career, prior to his ordination to the priesthood in 1744, he was notably prolific, publishing eight scientific dissertations before his appointment as professor and fourteen more afterward. They include *The Sunspots* (1736), *The Transit of Mercury* (1737), *The Aurora Borealis* (1738), *The Application of the Telescope in Astronomical Studies* (1739), *The Motions of the Heavenly Bodies in an Unresisting Medium* (1740), *The Different Effects of Gravity in Various Points of the Earth* (1741)—which pointed toward the important work he was to do in geodesy—and *The Aberration of the Fixed Stars* (1742).[92]

It was not long before a man of Father Boscovich's talents came to be known in Rome. Pope Benedict XIV, who ascended the papal throne in 1740, took special notice of Father Boscovich and his work. Benedict was one of the most learned of the popes of his day, an accomplished scholar in his own right and a man who encouraged learning, but it was his secretary of state, Cardinal Valenti Gonzaga, whose patronage of Father Boscovich would be especially important. Cardinal Gonzaga, who went out of his way to surround himself with scholars of high renown and whose own ancestors had come from the same Dalmatian town as had Father Boscovich, invited the accomplished priest to his Sunday gatherings.[93]

Benedict XIV turned to Father Boscovich for his technical expertise in 1742 after concerns had arisen that cracks in the dome of Saint Peter's Basilica portended possible collapse. He accepted the priest's recommendation that five iron rings be used to circle the cupola; Father Boscovich's report, which investigated the problem in theoretical terms, earned "the reputation of a minor classic in architectural statics."[94]

Father Boscovich developed the first geometric method for calculating a planet's orbit based on three observations of its position. His *Theory of Natural Philosophy*, originally published in

1758, attracted admirers in his day and ever since for its ambitious attempt to understand the structure of the universe with reference to a single idea.[95] According to a modern admirer, it "gave classical expression to one of the most powerful scientific ideas yet conceived and is unsurpassed for originality in fundamentals, clarity of expression, and precision in its view of structure—hence its immense influence."[96] And that influence was truly immense: top European scientists, particularly in England, repeatedly praised the *Theory* and devoted a great deal of attention to it throughout the nineteenth century. A revival of interest in Father Boscovich's work has begun to take place since the second half of the twentieth century.[97] A modern scholar says that this accomplished priest gave "the first coherent description of an atomic theory," well over a century before modern atomic theory emerged.[98] A recent historian of science calls Father Boscovich "the true creator of fundamental atomic physics as we understand it."[99]

Boscovich's original contributions "anticipated the aims, and many of the features, of twentieth-century atomic physics. Nor is this all that stands to the credit of the [*Theory*]. For it also qualitatively predicted several physical phenomena that have since been observed, such as the penetrability of matter by high-speed particles, and the possibility of states of matter of exceptionally high density."[100]

No wonder his work was the object of so much admiration and praise by some of the great scientists of the modern era. Thus Faraday wrote in 1844 that "the safest course appears to be to assume as little as possible, and that is why the atoms of Boscovich appear to me to have a great advantage over the more usual notion." Mendeleev said of Boscovich that "together with Copernicus [he] is the just pride of the Western Slavs," and that he "is regarded as the founder of modern atomism." Clerk Maxwell added in 1877 that "the best thing we can do is to get rid of the rigid nucleus and substitute an atom of Boscovich." In 1899, Kelvin spoke of "Hooke's exhibition of the forms of crystals by piles of globes, Navier's and Poisson's theory of the elasticity of solids, Maxwell's and Clausius' work in the kinetic theory of gases...all developments of Boscovich's theory pure and simple." Although Kelvin's own views were known to change frequently, he finally observed in 1905, "My present assumption is Boscovichianism pure and simple."[101] In 1958, an International Bicentenary Symposium was held in Belgrade to commemorate the two hundredth anniversary of the publication of the *Theory*. The presentations included papers by Niels Bohr and Werner Heisenberg.[102]

The life of Father Boscovich reveals to us a man who remained ever faithful to the Church he loved and the order of priests of which he was a member, and who also possessed an excitement about knowledge and learning. One anecdote must suffice: In 1745, this man of science spent his summer in Frascati, where a splendid summer residence was in the process of being built for the Jesuits. In the course of carrying out the project, builders managed to dig up the remains of a villa dating to the second century B.C. That was all it took: Father Boscovich was now an enthusiastic archaeologist, excavating and copying mosaic floors. He was convinced that the sundial he found was the one mentioned by the ancient Roman architect Vitruvius. He found time to write two studies: *On the Ancient Villa Discovered on the Ridge of Tusculum* and *On the ancient sundial and certain other treasures found among the ruins*. His discoveries were reported in the *Giornale de Letterati* the following year.[103]

Father Athanasius Kircher (1602–1680) resembled Father Boscovich in his enormous range of interests; he has been compared to Leonardo da Vinci and honored with the title "master of a hundred arts." His work in chemistry helped to debunk alchemy, which had been seriously entertained even by the likes of Isaac Newton and Robert Boyle, the father of modern chemistry.[104] A scholar writing in 2003 describes Kircher as "a giant among seventeenth-century scholars," and "one of the last thinkers who could rightfully claim all knowledge as his domain."[105]

Kircher's interests also included a fascination with ancient Egypt, where he distinguished himself in his scholarship. Thus, for example, he showed that the Coptic language was actually a vestige of early Egyptian. He has been called the real founder of Egyptology, no doubt because his work was carried out before the 1799 discovery of the Rosetta stone rendered Egyptian hieroglyphics comprehensible to scholars. Indeed it was "because of Kircher's work that scientists knew what to look for when interpreting the Rosetta stone."[106] Thus a modern scholar of ancient Egypt could conclude, "It is therefore Kircher's incontestable merit that he was the first to have discovered the phonetic value of an Egyptian hieroglyph. From a humanistic as well as an intellectual point of view Egyptology may very well be proud of having Kircher as its founder."[107]

The Jesuits' contributions to seismology (the study of earthquakes) have been so substantial that the field itself has sometimes been called "the Jesuit science." Jesuit involvement in seismology has been attributed both to the order's consistent presence in the universities in general and in the scientific community in particular, as well as to its priests' desire to minimize the devastating effects of earthquakes to whatever extent possible as a service to their fellow men.

In 1908, Father Frederick Louis Odenbach came up with the idea for what eventually became the Jesuit Seismological Service when he noted that the far-flung system of Jesuit colleges and universities throughout America held out the possibility of creating a network of seismographic stations. Having received the blessing of the presidents of Jesuit institutions of higher learning as well as that of American Jesuit provincials, Father Odenbach put his idea into practice the following year with the purchase of fifteen seismographs, each distributed to a Jesuit institution. Each of these seismographic stations would collect its data and send its findings to the central station in Cleveland. From there the data would be passed along to the International Seismological Center in Strasbourg. Thus was born the Jesuit Seismoloigcal Service, which has been described as "the first seismological network established of continental scale with uniform instrumentation."[108]

The best-known Jesuit seismologist, however, and indeed one of the most honored practitioners of the science of all time, was Father J. B. Macelwane. In 1925, Father Macelwane reorganized and reinvigorated the Jesuit Seismological Service (which was now known as the Jesuit Seismological Association), locating its central station this time at St. Louis University. A brilliant researcher, Father Macelwane published *Introduction to Theoretical Seismology*, the first textbook on seismology in America, in 1936. He served as president of the Seismological Society of America and of the American Geophysical Union. In 1962, the latter organization established a medal in his honor, still awarded to this day, to recognize the work of exceptional young geophysicists.[109]

In the field of astronomy, the public is left with the impression that churchmen, to the extent that they pursued the science at all, did so only in order to confirm their preconceived ideas rather than to follow the evidence wherever it led them. We have already seen how untrue that suggestion is, but a bit more additional evidence shall round out our discussion.

Johannes Kepler (1571–1630), the great astronomer whose laws of planetary motion constituted such an important scientific advance, carried on extensive correspondence with Jesuit astronomers over the course of his career. When at one point in his life Kepler found himself in financial difficulties as well as scientific ones, deprived even of a telescope, Father Paul Guldin urged his friend Father Nicolas Zucchi, the inventor of the reflecting telescope, to take one to Kepler. Kepler, in turn, both wrote a letter of appreciation to Father Guldin and, later, included a special note of gratitude at the end of his posthumously published *The Dream*. There we read:

> To the very reverend Father Paul Guldin, priest of the Society of Jesus, venerable and learned man, beloved patron. There is hardly anyone at this time with whom I would rather discuss matters of astronomy than with you.... Even more of a pleasure to me, therefore, was the greeting from your reverence which was delivered to me by members of your order who are here.... [I] think you should receive from me the first literary fruit of the joy that I have gained from trial of this gift [the telescope].[110]

Kepler's theory of elliptical planetary orbits had the advantage of simplicity over competing theories. The Ptolemaic (geocentric) and Copernican (heliocentric) models, both of which took circular planetary orbits for granted, had to introduce a complicated series of equants, epicycles, and deferents in order to account for apparently retrograde planetary motion. Tycho Brahe's system, which also posited circular orbits, featured these complications as well. But Kepler, by proposing elliptical planetary orbits, made these models look positively clumsy next to the elegant simplicity of his own system.

But was Kepler's system correct? The Italian astronomer Giovanni Cassini, a student of the Jesuits Riccioli and Grimaldi, used the observatory at the splendid Basilica of San Petronio in Bologna to lend support to Kepler's model.[111] Here we see an important way in which the Church contributed to astronomy that is all but unknown today: Cathedrals in Bologna, Florence, Paris, and Rome were designed in the seventeenth and eighteenth centuries to function as world-class solar observatories. Nowhere in the world were there more precise instruments for the study of the sun. Each such cathedral contained holes through which sunlight could enter and time lines (or meridian lines) on the floor. It was by observing the path traced out by the sunlight on these lines that researchers could obtain accurate measurements of time and predict equinoxes. (They could also make accurate calculations of the proper dates for Easter—the key initial function of these observatories.)[112]

Cassini would need equipment accurate enough that measurement errors of the sun's projected image would be no greater than 0.3 inches (the sun's image varied from five to thirty-three inches over the course of the year). The technology behind telescopes was not advanced enough in his day to provide such accuracy. It was the observatory at San Petronio that made Cassini's research possible. If the Earth's orbit were really elliptical, Cassini suggested, we should expect the sun's projected image on the floor of the cathedral to grow larger as the two bodies came closer together, at one focus of the ellipse, and smaller as they moved further apart, at the other one.[113]

Cassini was finally able to conduct his experiment during the mid-1650s, along with Jesuit colleagues, and accomplished what he set out to do: He confirmed Kepler's position on elliptical orbits.[114] As one scholar puts it, "Thus the Jesuits confirmed... the cornerstone of Kepler's version of the Copernican theory, and 'destroyed Aristotelian physics in the heavens,' by observations

made in the Church of San Petronio in the heart of the Papal
States."[115]

That was no small development. In fact, the use of *meridiana* in
Bologna's cathedral of San Petronio, in the words of the great
eighteenth-century French astronomer Jerome Lalande, "made
an epoch in the history of the renewal of the sciences." An earlier
eighteenth-century source averred that this achievement "would
be celebrated in ages to come for the immortal glory of the human
spirit, which could copy so precisely on the earth the eternal rule-
bound movements of the sun and the stars."[116] Who would have
guessed that Catholic cathedrals made such an important contribution to the advancement of science?

These cathedral observatories did substantially assist the
progress of scientific work. Between 1655 and 1736, astronomers
were able to make some 4,500 observations at San Petronio. As
the eighteenth century progressed, improvements in observational instruments rendered the cathedral observatories increasingly obsolete, but they continued to be used for timekeeping and
even for setting the time for railroads.

The fact remains, as J. L. Heilbron of the University of
California–Berkeley points out, that "[t]he Roman Catholic
Church gave more financial aid and social support to the study
of astronomy for over six centuries, from the recovery of ancient
learning during the late Middle Ages into the Enlightenment,
than any other, and, probably, all other, institutions."[117] And as
we have seen, the Church's contributions to science go well
beyond astronomy. Catholic theological ideas provided the
basis for scientific progress in the first place. Medieval thinkers
laid down some of the first principles of modern science. And
Catholic priests, loyal sons of the Church, have consistently displayed such interest and accomplishment in the sciences, from

mathematics to geometry, optics, biology, astronomy, geology, seismology, and a great many other fields.

How much of this is generally known, and how many Western civilization texts even mention it? To ask these questions is to answer them. Yet thanks to the excellent work by recent historians of science, who have been more and more willing to grant the Church her due, no serious scholar shall ever again be able to repeat the tired mythology about the alleged antagonism between religion and science. The appearance of modern science in the Catholic environment of Western Europe was no coincidence after all.

*Chapter Six*

# Art, Architecture, and the Church

T*he artistic inheritance* of the West is so strongly identi-fied with Catholic images that no one would wish to deny the Church's influence. Even here, though, the Catholic role has been significantly greater than simply providing the subject matter for Western art.

The very fact that we possess many of our artistic master-pieces at all is itself a reflection of Catholic ideas. The eighth and ninth centuries witnessed the growth of a destructive heresy called iconoclasm. Iconoclasm rejected the veneration of images, or icons, of religious figures. Indeed, iconoclasm went so far as to reject the depiction of Christ and the saints in art at all. Had that idea taken hold, the beautiful paintings, sculpture, mosaics, stained glass, illuminated manuscripts, and cathedral façades that have delighted and inspired Westerners and non-Westerners alike would never have come into exis-tence. But it could not take hold, since it ran directly counter to the Catholic understanding of and appreciation for the cre-ated world.

Iconoclasm originated in the Byzantine Empire rather than in the West, though it claimed to teach a doctrine that all believers in Christ must accept on pain of heresy. It was introduced by the Byzantine emperor Leo III (r. 717–741) for reasons that remain obscure. The Byzantine encounter with Islam likely played a role. From the first century of the existence of Islam, when Muslims had overrun the Middle Eastern portions of the Byzantine Empire, the emperor in Constantinople had had to organize and struggle against this persistent and powerful foe. In the course of that struggle he could not help but notice that Islamic art was not representational at all. No depictions of Muhammad, the founder of Islam, were to be found. Eventually, Leo III began to consider abolishing the use of icons among Eastern Christians, on the grounds that perhaps the reason for continuing Muslim victories and Byzantine defeats on the battlefield was that God was punishing the Byzantines for their use of icons.

As far as the West was concerned, iconoclasm was a flagrant heresy. Christian art had depicted Christ and the saints for centuries by the time the iconoclasm controversy developed. The depiction of Christ in art was a reflection of the Catholic doctrine of the Incarnation. With the Incarnation of God in Jesus Christ, the material world, while nevertheless fallen, had been elevated to a new level. It was not to be despised, for not only had God created it, but He had also dwelled in it.

These were some of the grounds on which Saint John of Damascus condemned iconoclasm. John spent much of his life as a monk near Jerusalem. Between the 720s and 740s he wrote his *Three Treatises on the Divine Images* in response to iconoclasm. Naturally, much of his argument was based on biblical and patristic citations, as well as the testimony of tradition as a whole, with regard to the specific question of whether God really opposed the veneration of images, as the iconoclasts claimed. But he also offered important theological defenses of religious art. John detected within the iconoclast position a tendency toward Manichaeism, a heresy that had divided the world into a realm of wickedness, that of matter, and one of goodness, that of the spirit. The idea that material things could communicate spiritual good was utter nonsense to the Manichee. (In the twelfth and thirteenth centuries, Catharism, a variant of Manichaeism, pursued the same line of thought to suggest that the Catholic sacramental system must be fraudulent, for how could wicked *matter*—in the form of water, consecrated oils, bread, and wine—communicate purely *spiritual* grace to the recipient?) "You abuse matter and call it worthless," John scolded the iconoclasts. "So do the Manichees, but the divine Scripture proclaims that it is good. For it says, 'And God saw everything that He had made, and behold it was exceedingly good.'"[1]

John was careful to point out that he did not "reverence [matter] as God—far from it; how can that which has come to be from nothing be God?"[2] But matter, which the Christian could not condemn as wicked in itself, could convey something of the divine:

I do not venerate matter, I venerate the fashioner of matter, who became matter [through the Incarnation] for my sake and accepted to dwell in matter and through matter worked my salvation, and I will not cease from reverencing matter, through which my salvation was worked.... Therefore I reverence the rest of matter and hold in respect that through which my salvation came, because it is filled with divine energy and grace. Is not the thrice-precious and thrice-blessed wood of the cross matter? Is not the holy and august mountain, the place of the skull, matter? Is not the life-giving and life-bearing rock, the holy tomb, the source of the resurrection, matter? Is not the ink and the all-holy book of the Gospels matter? Is not the life-bearing table, which offers to us the bread of life, matter? Is not the gold and silver matter, out of which crosses and tablets and bowls are fashioned? And, before all these things, is not the body and blood of my Lord matter? Either do away with reverence and veneration for all these or submit to the tradition of the Church and allow the veneration of images of God and friends of God, sanctified by name and therefore overshadowed by the grace of the divine Spirit.[3]

Thus theologians referred to Catholic theological principles in defense of art that depicted Christ, the saints, and the religious scenes that have defined so much of Western artistic life. In 843, the Byzantines themselves finally abandoned iconoclasm and returned to depicting Christ and the saints in art. The faithful greeted this reversal with joy; an annual celebration of the "Triumph of Orthodoxy"[4] commemorated the return to traditional practice in the veneration of icons.

It is difficult to overstate the significance of the Catholic Church's official opposition to iconoclasm (the Third Council of Nicaea in 787 condemned it). The ideas of Saint John of Damascus and his supporters later permitted us the luxury of the beautiful Madonnas of Raphael, the *Pietà* of Michelangelo, and countless other works of passion and genius, not to mention the great cathedral façades (which often depicted Christ, the apostles, and the saints) of the High Middle Ages. This favorable view of representational religious art cannot simply be taken for granted as something natural and inevitable; Islam, after all, has never abandoned its insistence on aniconic (non-image) art. Rehabilitating the iconoclast heresy in the sixteenth century, Protestants went on a rampage of smashing statues, altarpieces, stained-glass windows, and other great

treasures of Western art. John Calvin, arguably the most significant Protestant thinker of all, favored visually barren settings for his worship services, and even prohibited the use of
musical instruments. Nothing could have been further removed
from the Catholic Church's respect for the natural world,
inspired by the Incarnation, and its belief that human beings,
composed of body (matter) and soul, can be aided in their
ascent to God with the aid of material things.

Arguably the greatest Catholic contribution to art, and the one
that has undoubtedly and permanently influenced the European
landscape, is the medieval cathedral. One art historian recently
wrote, "The medieval cathedrals of Europe...are the greatest
accomplishments of humanity in the whole theatre of art."[5] Particularly stunning are Europe's Gothic cathedrals. Gothic architecture developed out of the Romanesque style in the twelfth
century and spread throughout Europe to varying degrees from
its origins in France and England. These buildings, monumental
in size and scope, are characterized by certain distinguishing features, including the flying buttress, the pointed arch, and the
ribbed vault. Their combined effect, including the much-admired
stained glass of the Gothic tradition, is an extraordinary testament to the supernatural faith of a civilization.

It is no accident that a closer study of these cathedrals reveals
an impressive geometric coherence. That coherence follows
directly from an important strain in Catholic thought. Saint
Augustine made repeated reference to Wisdom 11:21, an Old Testament verse that describes God as having "ordered all things by
measure, number, weight." This idea became common currency
among a great many Catholic thinkers, particularly those associated with the great cathedral school at Chartres in the twelfth
century. It played a central role in the construction of Gothic
cathedrals.[6]

At the time that Gothic architecture was evolving from its Romanesque predecessor, more and more Catholic thinkers were becoming persuaded of the link between mathematics—geometry in particular—and God. Ever since Pythagoras and Plato, an important strain of thought within Western civilization had identified mathematics with the divine. At Chartres, explains Robert Scott, scholars "believed that geometry was a means for linking human beings to God, that mathematics was a vehicle for revealing to humankind the innermost secrets of heaven. They thought the harmony of musical consonance was based on the same ratios as those forming cosmic order, that the cosmos was a work of architecture and God was its architect." These ideas led builders "to conceive of architecture as applied geometry, geometry as applied theology, and the designer of a Gothic cathedral as an imitator of the divine Master."[7] "Just as the great Geometer created the world in order and harmony," explains professor John Baldwin, "so the Gothic architect, in his small way, attempted to fashion God's earthly abode according to the supreme principles of proportion and beauty."[8]

The geometric proportionality that can be found in these cathedrals is quite striking. Consider England's Salisbury Cathedral. Measuring the cathedral's central crossing (where its principal transept intersects the east-west axis), we find it to be thirty-nine feet by thirty-nine feet. This primary dimension, in turn, is the basis for nearly all of the cathedral's remaining dimensions. For example, both the length and the width of each of the nave's ten bays is nineteen feet six inches—exactly half the length of the central crossing. The nave itself consists of twenty identical spaces measuring nineteen feet six inches square, and another ten spaces measuring nineteen feet six inches by thirty-nine feet. Other aspects of the structure offer still more examples of an overall geometric coherence permeating the cathedral.[9]

This attention to geometric proportion is evident throughout the Gothic tradition. Another striking example is the cathedral of Saint Remi in Rheims. Although Saint Remi, which still contains elements of the earlier Romanesque style, is not the purest example of a Gothic structure, it already exhibits the attention to geometry and mathematics that would constitute such an arresting quality of this tradition. The influence of St. Augustine and his belief in the symbolism of numbers, as well as his conviction (once again) that God had ordered "all things according to measure, number, weight," is immediately evident. The choir at Saint Remi is "among the most perfect Trinitarian symbols in Gothic architecture," explains Christopher Wilson, "for the play on the number three encompasses the triple windows lighting each of the three levels of the main apse and even the number obtained by multiplying the number of bays in the choir elevations—eleven—by the number of stories, that is thirty three."[10] Thirty-three, of course, is the age that Christ reached while on earth.

Again, this desire for geometric precision and numerical meaning, which contribute significantly to the pleasure that aesthetes derive from these great edifices, is no mere coincidence. It derives from specifically Catholic ideas traceable to the Church fathers. Saint Augustine, whose *De Musica* would become the most influential aesthetic treatise of the Middle Ages, considered architecture and music the noblest of the arts, since their mathematical proportions were those of the universe itself, and they therefore elevated our minds to the contemplation of the divine order.[11]

The windows of the Gothic cathedral and the emphasis on light as it flooded these enormous and majestic buildings are perhaps its most salient characteristic. It makes sense, then, that the architect would have appreciated the theological significance of light. Saint Augustine had conceived of human beings' acquisition of knowledge in terms of divine illumination: God *enlightens* the mind with knowledge. This idea of God pouring light into the minds of men proved a potent metaphor for architects in the Gothic tradition, in which physical light was meant to evoke thoughts of its divine source.[12]

We first see a great church in the Gothic style in the Abbey Church of St. Denis, seven miles north of Paris. Here the religious significance of the light pouring in through the windows in the choir and the nave cannot be missed. An inscription on the doors explained that the light elevated the mind upward from the material world and directed it toward the true light that was Christ.[13]

In designing his stupendous structure, the Gothic architect was thus profoundly influenced by Catholic thought. "As the worshippers' eyes rose toward heaven," writes a modern student of the subject, "God's grace, in the form of sunlight, was imagined to stream down in benediction, encouraging exaltation. Sinners could be led to repent and strive for perfection by envisioning the world of spiritual perfection where God resided—a world suggested by the geometric regularity of cathedrals."[14] Indeed, everything about the Gothic cathedral revealed its supernatural inspiration. "While the predominantly horizontal lines of Greco-Roman temples symbolized a nature-bound religious experience," writes one scholar, "Gothic spires symbolized the upward reach of a distinctly supernatural vision."[15] These great structures also convey to us something of the age in which they were conceived and built. No period of history that could have produced such magnificent works of architecture could have been utterly stagnant or dark, as the entirety of the Middle Ages has all too often been portrayed. The light that streamed into the Gothic cathedral symbolized the light of the thirteenth century, an age characterized as much by its universities, learning, and scholarship as by the religious fervor and heroism of Saint Francis of Assisi.

It is a rare soul who, in the twenty-first century, is not still overwhelmed by these cathedrals. One of the most recent studies of the Gothic cathedral, in fact, was written by a Stanford University sociologist with no professional training in architecture. He simply fell in love with Salisbury Cathedral in England and determined to read and write about this wondrous phenomenon in order to acquaint others with a treasure that so captivated him.[16] Even a hostile twentieth-century scholar could speak admiringly of the devotion and patient labors elicited by the construction of the great cathedrals:

> A splendid picture of the beautiful devotion of the people of a region in the erection of a magnificent cathedral is found in Chartres, France. That wonderful edifice was begun in 1194 and completed in 1240. To construct a building that would beautify their city and satisfy their religious aspirations the citizens contributed of their strength and property year after year for nearly half a century. Far from home they went to the distant quarries to dig out the rock. Encouraged by their priests they might be seen, men, women, and children, yoked to clumsy carts loaded with building materials. Day after day their weary journey to and from the quarries continued. When at night they stopped, worn out with the day's toil, their spare time was given up to confession and prayer. Others labored with more skill but with equal devotion on the great cathedral itself.... Its dedication and consecration marked an epoch in that part of France.[17]

The Scholastic frame of mind has sometimes been credited with giving rise to the Gothic cathedral. The Scholastics, of whom Saint Thomas Aquinas was the most illustrious example, were intellectual system builders. They sought not merely to answer this or that question, but to construct entire edifices of thought. Their *summae*, in which they sought to explore every significant question pertaining to their subject, were systematic, coherent wholes, in which each individual conclusion related harmoniously to every other—just as the various components of the Gothic cathedral worked together to create a structure of remarkable internal coherence.

Erwin Panofsky has provocatively suggested that this was no coincidence, and that both phenomena—Scholasticism and Gothic architecture—emerged as related products of a common intellectual and cultural milieu. He provides example after example of intriguing parallels between the Scholastic *summa* and the High Gothic cathedral. For instance, just as the Scholastic treatise, in its examination of disputed questions, reconciled the positions of conflicting sources of equal authority—two Church fathers seemingly at odds, for example—the Gothic cathedral synthesized the features of preceding architectural traditions rather than simply adopting one and suppressing the other.[18]

The greatest outburst of innovation and sheer accomplishment in the world of art since antiquity occurred during the Renaissance of the fifteenth and sixteenth centuries. The Renaissance is not easily pigeonholed. On the one hand, much of it appears to herald the coming of the modern world. Secularism is increasingly present, as is an increasing emphasis on worldly life rather than on the world to come. Tales of immorality are legion. Little wonder, then, that some Catholics are inclined to reject the Renaissance root and branch.

On the other hand, the Renaissance can with some justice be described as the fulfillment of the Middle Ages rather than as a radical break from them; medieval thinkers, like Renaissance figures, possessed a profound respect for classical antiquity (even if they did not accept the entire classical inheritance as uncritically as did some Renaissance humanists), and it was in the Late Middle Ages that we find the origins of important artistic techniques that would be perfected during the Renaissance. Moreover, so many of its masterpieces depict Catholic themes, and the popes themselves served as patrons of some of the greatest masters.

The truth of the matter appears to be as follows: 1) important artistic innovations were already occurring prior to the time frame traditionally associated with the Renaissance; 2) in areas other than art, the Renaissance period was one of stagnation or even retrogression; 3) a trend toward secularism was certainly evident during that time; but 4) the vast bulk of Renaissance art was religious in nature, and can be enjoyed by us today thanks to the patronage of the Renaissance popes.

Let us consider these points one at a time. A century before standard chronologies say the Renaissance had begun, the medieval Giotto di Bondone, known simply as Giotto, was already anticipating many of the technical innovations for which the Renaissance would be so celebrated. Giotto was born in 1267 near Florence. A possibly apocryphal story has it that at age ten, while tending sheep, the young Giotto was using chalk to draw a sheep on the rocks. Cimabue, an innovative artist in his own right, is said to have seen the lad drawing, and was so impressed that he felt compelled to ask the boy's father for permission to train Giotto as an artist.

Cimabue himself had been an artistic pioneer, transcending the formalism of Byzantine art in order to paint human beings with an eye to realism. Giotto would follow in his footsteps, carrying this emphasis on realism to new and important heights that would exert substantial influence on succeeding generations of painters. His techniques for depicting depth and rendering realistic art in three dimensions were of the greatest importance, as was his individualized depiction of human beings (as opposed to the more stylized approach that preceded him, in which the various individuals depicted were barely distinguishable from each other).

Thus in some sense it can be said that the Renaissance grew out of the Middle Ages. In areas unrelated to art, though, the Renaissance period actually constituted a time of retrogression. The study of English and continental literatures would hardly miss the removal of the fifteenth century. At the same time, the scientific life of Europe all but came to a standstill. With the exception of the Copernican theory of the universe, the history of Western science between 1350 and 1600 is one of relative stagnation. Western philosophy, which had flourished in the twelfth and thirteenth centuries, has comparatively little to show for itself during the same period.[19]

One could even say that the Renaissance was in many regards a time of irrationalism. It was during the Renaissance that alchemy reached its height, for example. Astrology grew ever more influential. Persecutions of witches, erroneously associated with the Middle Ages, became widespread only during the fifteenth and sixteenth centuries.

The spirit of secularism was certainly evident during the Renaissance. Although the doctrine of original sin was rarely denied in any explicit way, a much more favorable view of human nature and its potential now becomes evident. With the coming of the Renaissance we see a celebration of the natural man, apart from the regenerating effects of supernatural grace, and his dignity and potential. The contemplative virtues, so admired in the Middle Ages as manifested in the monastic tradition, began to give way to the active virtues as objects of admiration. In other words, a secular understanding of utility and practicality, which would later triumph during the Enlightenment, began to denigrate the life of the monk and to celebrate instead the life of worldly activity evident even in the ordinary townsman. Secularism extended even to political philosophy: In *The Prince* (1513), Machiavelli produced a purely secular treatment of politics and the state, an institution he described as morally autonomous and as exempt from the kind of standards against which we traditionally hold the behavior of individuals.

That secularism was also evident in art. For one thing, the subject matter of art began to change as the patronage of art extended to sources other than the Church. Self-portraits and landscape scenes, secular of their very nature, began to flourish. Whether secular or religious, though, the very desire to depict the natural world as accurately as possible, so evident in Renaissance art, suggests that the natural world, far from a mere way station between temporal existence and supernatural beatitude, was considered something good in and of itself and worthy of careful study and reproduction.

Yet the vast bulk of the artistic work during the Renaissance depicts religious themes, and much of it comes from men whose art was deeply inspired by a sincere and profound religious faith. According to Kenneth Clark, author of the widely acclaimed *Civilisation*:

> Guercino spent much of his mornings in prayer; Bernini frequently went on retreats and practiced the Spiritual Exercises of Saint Ignatius; Rubens went to Mass every day before beginning work. This conformity was not based on fear of the Inquisition, but on the perfectly simple belief that the faith which had inspired the great saints of the preceding generation was something by which a man should regulate his life. The mid-sixteenth century was a period of sanctity in the Roman Church...such people as Saint Ignatius Loyola, the visionary soldier turned psychologist. One does not need to be a

practicing Catholic to feel respect for a half-century that could produce these great spirits.[20]

The popes, particularly such figures as Julius II and Leo X, were great patrons of many of these artists. It was during the pontificate of Pope Julius II, and under his patronage, that such figures as Bramante, Michelangelo, and Raphael produced some of their most memorable works of art. The *Catholic Encyclopedia* points to the significance of this pope in contending that:

> [W]hen the question arose as to whether the Church would absorb or reject and condemn progress, whether or not it would associate itself with the humanistic spirit, Julius II deserves the credit for having taken sides with the Renaissance and prepared the stage for the moral triumph of the Church. The great creations of Julius II, Bramante's St. Peter's and Raphael's Vatican, are inseparable from the great ideas of humanity and culture represented by the Catholic Church. Here art surpasses itself, becoming the language of something higher, the symbol of one of the noblest harmonies ever realized by human nature. At the will of this extraordinary man Rome became at the end of the sixteenth century the meeting place and centre of all that was great in art and thought.[21]

Similar observations might be made of the pontificate of Leo X, even if we concede that he lacked the impeccable taste and judgment of Julius. "From all parts," wrote a cardinal in 1515, "men of letters are hurrying to the Eternal City, their common country, their support, their patroness." Raphael's work, if anything, grew still more impressive under Leo, who carried on his predecessor's patronage of this renowned painter. "Everything pertaining to art the pope turns over to Raphael," an ambassador observed in 1518.[22] Again we can profit from the judgment of Will Durant, who explains that Leo's court was:

> [T]he center of the intellect and wit of Rome, the place where scholars, educators, poets, artists, and musicians were welcomed or housed; the scene of solemn ecclesiastical functions, ceremonious diplomatic receptions, costly banquets, dramatic or musical performances, poetical recitations, and exhibitions of art. It was without question the most refined court in the world at that time. The labors of popes from Nicholas V to Leo himself in the improvement and adornment of the Vatican, in the assemblage of literary and artistic genius, and of the ablest ambassadors in Europe, made the court of Leo the zenith not of the art (for that had come under Julius) but of the literature and brilliance of the Renaissance. In mere quantity of culture history had never seen its equal, not even in Periclean Athens or Augustan Rome.[23]

This writer's own favorite Renaissance creation, the *Pietà* of Michelangelo, is a strikingly moving work that reveals a profoundly Catholic sensibility. The *pietà*, which depicted the Virgin Mary holding her divine Son after the crucifixion, had been an artistic genre in and of itself for hundreds of years by the time of Michelangelo. These earlier *pietàs* had often been horrific to see, as with the *Röttgen Pietà* (c. 1300–1325), in which a distorted and bloodied Christ figure lay in the lap of a mother overwhelmed with grief. The fourteenth century, a period of great disaster and human tragedy, would see a great deal more depictions of suffering in religious art.[24]

The depiction of suffering has played an important role in Western art, particularly because of the emphasis that Catholicism has placed on the crucifixion rather than (as in the Orthodox east as well as in Protestantism) on the resurrection as the central event in the drama of redemption. Yet the intensity of that suffering is significantly diminished in the first and by far more famous of Michelangelo's two *pietàs*. Michelangelo's work, which has been called the greatest marble sculpture ever created, preserves the tragedy of that terrible moment without any of the gruesome and disturbing images that characterized earlier such works. The face of Christ's mother is positively serene. Since the second century Mary had been called the "second Eve," for just as Eve's disobedience had led to mankind's perdition, Mary's conformity to God's will, in consenting to bear the God-Man in her womb, makes possible mankind's redemption. That is the woman we see in Michelangelo's sculpture: So confident is she in God's promises, and so perfectly resigned to God's will, that she can accept the terrible fate of her divine Son in a spirit of faithfulness and equanimity.

## ART AND SCIENCE

*In our discussion of the Church's* contributions to the development of modern science, we briefly explored how certain fundamental theological and philosophical ideas derived from Catholicism proved congenial to the enterprise of scientific inquiry. Oddly enough, our discussion of art can add still another explanation for the unique success of science in the West. It has to do with the development of linear perspective in art, perhaps the distinguishing feature of Renaissance painting.

It was in the West that perspective art, which involved the depiction of three dimensions in a two-dimensional artistic work, and chiaroscuro, the use of light and shadow, were developed. Both features had existed in the art of classical antiquity, and Western artists, beginning around 1300, revived them. It was only through Western influence that subsequent artists around the world applied these principles to their own traditional art.[25]

In *The Heritage of Giotto's Geometry*, Samuel Edgerton compares the perspective art developed in pre-Renaissance and Renaissance Europe with the art of other civilizations. He begins with a comparison of a Western and a Chinese rendering of a fly, and shows that the Westerner is much more attentive to the geometric structure of the fly. "In the West," he writes, "we take it for granted that if we are to understand the structure of an organic as well as an inorganic subject, we must first envisage it as nature mort (like a Chardin still life), with all constituent parts translated into impartial, static geometric relationships. In such pictures, as Arthur Waley wryly remarked, 'Pontius Pilate and a coffee-pot are both upright cylindrical masses.' To the traditional Chinese this approach is both scientifically and aesthetically absurd." The point of Edgerton's comparison is to emphasize that "the geometric perspective and chiaroscuro (light-and-shadow rendering) conventions of European Renaissance art, whether or not aesthetically styled, have proved extraordinarily useful to modern science."[26] This is why Edgerton suspects it is not a coincidence that Giotto, the forerunner and indeed the founder of Renaissance art, and Galileo, the brilliant physicist and astronomer who has sometimes been called the founder of modern science, both hailed from Tuscany, and that the Tuscan city of Florence was home to both artistic masterpieces *and* scientific advances.

The commitment of geometric perspective in art was itself a product of the distinct intellectual milieu of Catholic Europe. As we have seen, the idea of God as geometer, and of geometry as the basis upon which God ordered His creation, was one of long standing within the Catholic world. By the time of the Renaissance, explains Samuel Edgerton:

> [A] unique tradition rooted in medieval Christian doctrine was growing in the West: it was becoming socially de rigueur for the privileged gentry to know Euclidian geometry. Even before the twelfth century, the early church fathers suspected they might discover in Euclidian geometry God's very thinking process.
>
> Geometric linear perspective was quickly accepted in western Europe after the fifteenth century because Christians wanted to believe that when they beheld such an image in art, they were perceiving a replica of the same essential, underlying structure of reality that God had conceived at the moment of Creation. By the seventeenth century, as "natural philosophers" (such as Kepler, Galileo, Descartes, and Newton) came more and more to realize that linear perspective does in fact conform to the actual optical and physiological process of human vision, not only was perspective's Christian imprimatur upheld, but it now served to reinforce Western science's increasingly optimistic and democratic belief that God's conceptual process had at last been penetrated, and that knowledge (and control) of nature lay potentially within the grasp of any living human being.[27]

Thus did the Catholic Church's commitment to the study of Euclidean geometry, as a key to the mind of God and the basis upon which He ordered the universe, bear enormously important fruit both in the artistic and the scientific realms. This Catholic attraction to geometry led to a way of depicting the natural world that helped make the Scientific Revolution possible, and which would be copied by the rest of the world in the years to come.

*Chapter Seven*

# The Origins of
# International Law

W*hen the four hundredth* anniversary of Christopher Columbus's discovery of America was observed in 1892, the atmosphere was one of celebration. Columbus was a brave and skilled navigator who had brought two worlds together and changed history forever. The Knights of Columbus even put his name forward for canonization.

A century later, the prevailing mood was far more somber. Now Columbus was accused of all kinds of terrible crimes, ranging from environmental devastation to cruelties that culminated in genocide. Author Kirkpatrick Sale described the events of 1492 as the "conquest of paradise," as peaceful, environmentally friendly peoples were violently displaced by avaricious European conquerors. At the very least, the emphasis was now on European mistreatment of native populations, and particularly on the employment of natives as forced laborers.

The debate over the consequences of this meeting of cultures has remained contentious ever since. Those who would defend the Europeans in general and Columbus in particular have replied to the likes of Kirkpatrick Sale by suggesting that European crimes have been exaggerated, that the greatest toll on native lives came from disease (a non-volitional and therefore morally neutral source) rather than from exploitation or military force, that native populations were neither as peaceful nor as solicitous of environmental welfare as their modern-day admirers have suggested, and so on.

Here we shall consider the question from an angle that is frequently overlooked. Reports of Spanish mistreatment of the New World natives prompted a severe crisis of conscience among significant sectors of the Spanish population in the sixteenth century, not least among philosophers and theologians. This fact alone indicates that we are witnessing something historically unusual; nothing in the historical record suggests that Attila the Hun had any moral qualms about his conquests, and the large-scale human sacrifice that was so fundamental to Aztec civilization appears to have elicited no outpouring of self-criticism and philosophical reflection among Aztecs comparable to what European misbehavior provoked among Catholic theologians in sixteenth-century Spain.

It was in the course of that philosophical reflection that Spanish theologians achieved something rather substantial: the beginnings of modern international law. Thus the controversy surrounding the natives of America provided an opportunity for the elucidation of general principles that states were morally bound to observe in their interactions with each other.

Laws governing the interaction of states had remained vague throughout the years, and had never been articulated in any clear way. The circumstances arising from the discovery of the New World gave impetus to the study and delineation of those laws.[1] Students of international law have often looked to the sixteenth century, when theologians applied themselves to a serious reckoning with these issues, to find the origins of their discipline. Here again does the Catholic Church give birth to a distinctly Western idea.

The first major broadside by a churchman against Spanish colonial policy came in December 1511, on the island of Hispaniola (now Haiti and the Dominican Republic). In a dramatic sermon on the text "I am a voice crying in the wilderness," a Dominican friar named Antonio de Montesinos, speaking on behalf of the island's small Dominican community, proceeded to level a series of criticisms and condemnations at Spanish policy toward the Indians. According to historian Lewis Hanke, the sermon, delivered with important Spanish authorities in the audience, "was designed to shock and terrify its hearers." And indeed it must have:

> In order to make your sins against the Indians known to you I have come up on this pulpit, I who am a voice of Christ crying in the wilderness of this island, and therefore it behooves you to listen, not with careless attention, but with all your heart and senses, so that you may hear it; for this is going to be the strangest voice that ever you heard, the harshest and hardest and most awful and most dangerous that ever you expected to hear.... This voice says that you are in mortal sin, that you live and die in it, for the cruelty and tyranny you use in dealing with these innocent people. Tell me, by what right or justice do you keep these Indians in such a cruel and horrible servitude? On what authority have you waged a detestable war against these people, who dwelt quietly and peacefully on their own land?... Why do you keep them so oppressed and weary, not giving them enough to eat nor taking care of them in their illness? For with the excessive work you demand of them they fall ill and die, or rather you kill them with your desire to extract and acquire gold every day. And what care do you take

that they should be instructed in religion?... Are these not men? Have they not rational souls? Are you not bound to love them as you love yourselves?... Be certain that, in such a state as this, you can no more be saved than the Moors or Turks.[2]

Stunned by this withering rebuke, the leading men of the island, including Admiral Diego Columbus, engaged in lively and vocal protest, demanding that Father Montesinos retract his appalling statements. The Dominicans decided to send Father Montesinos to preach again on the following Sunday, at which time he would do his best to satisfy his antagonized hearers and to explain what he had said.

When it came time for what Diego Columbus and others hoped would be a retraction, Father Montesinos adopted as the basis for his retraction a verse from Job: "I will go back over my knowledge from the beginning and I will prove that my discourse is without falsehood." He proceeded to review the charges he had made the previous week and to demonstrate that none had been without foundation. He concluded by telling them that none of the friars would hear their confessions (since the Spanish colonial officials possessed neither contrition nor any plans to amend their behavior), and that they could write to Castile and tell that to anyone they liked.[3]

By the time the news of these two sermons reached King Ferdinand in Spain, the friar's remarks had been distorted to the point that they provoked the surprise both of the king and of the Dominicans' own provincial. Undaunted, Montesinos and his superior went to Spain to present their side of the story to the king. An attempt to interfere with Montesinos's determination to speak to Ferdinand backfired when a Franciscan, sent to the king's court to speak against the Dominicans in Hispaniola, was persuaded by Montesinos to adopt the Dominicans' position.

At this point, the king, faced with dramatic testimony regarding Spanish behavior in the New World, called together a group of theologians and jurists to develop laws that would govern Spanish officials in their interaction with the natives. In this way were born the Laws of Burgos (1512) and of Valladolid (1513), and similar arguments influenced the so-called New Laws of 1542. Much of this legislation on behalf of the natives proved disappointing in its application and enforcement, particularly since so much distance separated the Spanish Crown from the scene of activity in the New World. But this early criticism helped to set the stage for the more systematic and lasting work of some of the great sixteenth-century theological jurists.

Among the most illustrious of these thinkers was Father Francisco de Vitoria. In the course of his own critique of Spanish policy, Vitoria laid the groundwork for modern international law theory, and for that reason is sometimes called "the father of international law,"[4] a man who "propose[d] for the first time international law in modern terms."[5] With his fellow theological jurists, Vitoria "defended the doctrine that all men are equally free; on the basis of natural liberty, they proclaimed their right to life, to culture, and to property."[6] In support of his assertions, Vitoria drew from both Scripture and reason. In so doing he "furnished the world of his day with its first masterpiece on the law of nations in peace as well as in war."[7] It was a Catholic priest, therefore, who brought forth the first grand treatise on the law of nations—no small accomplishment.

Born around 1483, Vitoria had entered the Dominican order in 1504. He was skilled in languages and knowledgeable in the classics. He made his way to the University of Paris, where he completed his studies in the liberal arts and went on to study theology. He lectured at Paris until his departure in 1523, when he continued his theological lectures at Valladolid at the College of San Gregorio. Three years later he was elected to the Prime Chair of Theology at the University of Salamanca, where so much profound thought in so many areas would take place over the course of the sixteenth century. In 1532, he delivered a famous series of lectures that were later published as *Relección de los Indios*, usually rendered as *Readings on the Indians and on the Law of War*, which set forth important principles of international law in the context of a defense of the Indians' rights. When this great thinker was invited to attend the Council of Trent, he indicated that he would more likely go to the other world, which he did in 1546.

Father Vitoria was best known for his commentaries on Spanish colonialism in the New World, in which he and other Spanish theologians examined the morality of Spanish behavior. Did the Spanish possess just title to lands in the Americas that had been claimed on behalf of the Crown? What were their obligations to the natives? Such issues inevitably prompted more general and universal questions. What behavior were states obligated to observe in their interactions with one another? Under what circumstances may a state justly go to war? These questions are obviously fundamental to modern international law theory.

It was and is commonplace among Christian thinkers that man enjoys a unique position within God's creation. Having been created in God's image and endowed with a rational nature, he possesses a dignity that all other creatures lack.[8] It was on this basis that Vitoria continued the development of the idea that by virtue of his position, man was entitled to a degree of treatment from his fellow human beings that no other creature could claim.

## EQUALITY UNDER NATURAL LAW

*Vitoria borrowed two important* principles from Saint Thomas Aquinas: 1) the divine law, which proceeds from grace, does not annul human law, which proceeds from natural reason; and 2) those things that are natural to man are neither to be taken from nor given to him on account of sin.[9] Surely no Catholic would argue that it is a less serious crime to murder a non-baptized person than a baptized one. This is what Vitoria meant: The treatment to which all human beings were entitled—e.g., not to be killed, expropriated, etc.—derives from their status *as men* rather than as members of the faithful in the state of grace. Father Domingo de Soto, Vitoria's colleague at the University of Salamanca, stated the matter plainly: "Those who are in the grace of God are not a whit better off than the sinner or the pagan in what concerns natural rights."[10]

From these principles adopted from Saint Thomas, Vitoria argued that man was not deprived of civil dominion by mortal sin, and that the right to appropriate the things of nature for one's own use (i.e., the institution of private property) belonged to all men regardless of their paganism or whatever barbarian vices they might possess. The Indians of the New World, by virtue of being men, were therefore equal to the Spaniards in matters of natural rights. They owned their lands by the same principles that the Spaniards owned theirs.[11] As Vitoria wrote, "The upshot of all the preceding is, then, that the aborigines undoubtedly had true dominion in both public and private matters, just like Christians, and that neither their princes nor private persons could be despoiled of their property on the ground of their not being true owners."[12]

Vitoria also argued, as did fellow scholastics Domingo de Soto and Luis de Molina, that pagan princes ruled legitimately. He pointed out that the well-known scriptural admonitions to be subject to the secular powers had all been made in the context of pagan rule. If a pagan king has committed no other crime, says Vitoria, he may not be deposed simply because he is a pagan.[13] It was with this principle in mind that Christian Europe was to interact with the polities of the New World. "In the conception of the well-informed and well-balanced professor of Salamanca," writes a twentieth-century admirer, "states, irrespective of their size, their forms of government, their religion as well as that of their subjects, citizens, and inhabitants, their civilization, advanced or incipient, are equal in that system of law which he [Vitoria] professes."[14] Each state has the same rights as any other, and is under an obligation to respect the rights of others. In Vitoria's thinking, "the outlying principalities of America were regarded as States, and their subjects entitled to the same rights, and privileges, and subjected to the same duties as the Christian kingdoms of Spain, France, and of Europe generally."[15]

Vitoria did believe that the peoples of the New World had an obligation to permit Catholic missionaries to preach the Gospel in their lands. But he absolutely insisted that rejection of the Gospel did not constitute grounds for a just war. Himself a Thomist, Vitoria recalled the argument of Saint Thomas Aquinas whereby coercion was not to be applied in the conversion of pagans to the faith, since (in Saint Thomas's words) "to believe depends upon the will," and therefore must involve a free act.[16] Thus the Fourth Council of Toledo (633) had condemned the practice of compelling Jews to receive baptism.[17]

Vitoria and his allies believed that natural law existed not just among Christians but among all peoples. That is, they believed in the existence of "a natural system of ethics which neither depended on nor contradicted Christian revelation but could stand by itself."[18] This did not imply that societies would not pervert that law, or fail in their application of one of its precepts, or indeed simply be ignorant of its implications in a given area. Such difficulties aside, these Spanish theologians believed with Saint Paul that the natural law was written on the human heart, and they therefore possessed a basis on which to establish international rules of conduct that could morally bind even those who had never heard (or had actually rejected) the Gospel. Such peoples were still thought to possess the basic sense of right and wrong, summed up in the Ten Commandments and the Golden Rule—both of which some theologians all but identified with the natural law itself—from which international obligations could be derived.

Another conclusion followed from the natives' possession of the substance of the natural law. A number of theologians specifically described natural law as the unique inheritance of human beings rather than as a possession of man and brute alike. This point served as "the basis of a theory of the dignity of man and the gulf between him and the rest of the animal and created world."[19] One scholar concludes that this view of the natural law as something common to all human beings, and to human beings alone, led "to a firm belief that the Indians of the New World, as well as other pagans, had natural rights of their own, the infringement of which no superior civilization or even superior religion could justify."[20]

Some had argued that the natives of the New World lacked reason, or at the very least suffered from unsoundness of mind, and thereby could possess no dominion over things. Vitoria's reply to this argument was twofold. First, he said, a deficiency of reason among some population would not justify the subjugation or despoiling of that people, for their diminished intellectual capacities did not render nugatory their claims to private ownership. "It seems that they can still have dominion, because they can suffer wrong; therefore they have a right, but"—and here Vitoria hesitates—"whether they can have civil dominion is a question which I leave to the jurists."[21] Yet this was largely a hypothetical question in any event, Vitoria suggested, for the American Indians were not irrational in the first place. They were indeed endowed with reason, that characteristic possession of the human person. Developing Aristotle's principle that nature does nothing in vain, he wrote:

> According to the truth of the matter they are not irrational, but they have the use of reason in their own way. This is clear because they have a certain order in their affairs, ordered cities, separate marriages, magistrates, rulers, laws.... Also they do not err in things that are evident to others, which is evidence of the use of reason. Again, God and nature do not fail for a great part of a species in what is necessary. But the special quality in man is reason, and potency which is not actualized is in vain.

In his last two sentences, Vitoria meant that it was not possible to conceive of an entire portion of the human race deprived of reason, man's great distinguishing characteristic, for God would not fail to endow such a portion of mankind with that gift that gave man his special dignity among creatures.[22]

Although Vitoria's work was perhaps the most systematic of the sixteenth-century thinkers who explored these issues, perhaps the best-known native critic of Spanish policy was the priest and bishop Bartolomé de Las Casas, upon whom we rely for what information we possess about Antonio de Montesinos, the friar whose famous sermons had launched the entire controversy. Las Casas, whose doctrine appears to have been profoundly

influenced by the professors of Salamanca, shared Vitoria's position on the rationality of the natives: If a sizable portion of the
human race were without reason, we should be forced to speak of
a defect in the order of creation. If so considerable a portion of
mankind lacked the very faculty that distinguished man from the
brutes and by which he could call upon and love God, God's
intention to call all men to Himself would have failed. For the
Christian, such a conclusion was simply unthinkable. This was Las
Casas's reply to those who would argue that the natives constituted an example of what Aristotle had described as "slaves by
nature"—there were far too many of them, and in any case they did
not exhibit the level of debasement that Aristotle's conception
appeared to call for. Ultimately, though, Las Casas was prepared to
reject Aristotle on this point. He suggested that the natives "be
attracted gently, in accordance with Christ's doctrine," and proposed that Aristotle's views on natural slavery be abandoned,
since "we have in our favor Christ's mandate: love your neighbor
as yourself…although he [Aristotle] was a great philosopher,
study alone did not make him worthy of reaching God."[23]

In 1550, a momentous debate took place between Las Casas
and Juan Ginés de Sepúlveda, the philosopher and theologian
who famously contended for the use of force against the natives.
One scholar calls it "the clearest instance of an imperial power
openly questioning the legitimacy of its rights and the ethical
basis of its political actions."[24] Both men supported missionary
activity among the natives and wanted to win them for the
Church, but Las Casas insisted that the process occur peacefully.
Sepúlveda did not argue that the Spaniards had a right to con-
quer the native peoples simply because the latter were pagans; his
argument was that their low level of civilization and their barbaric practices were obstacles to their conversion, and that some
kind of Spanish tutelage was therefore necessary before the

evangelization process could proceed in earnest. He was well aware that circumstances or the difficulties that arise in the practical application of a sound theory—in this case, a theory that would morally justify war against the Indians—could affect the wisdom of putting it into practice at a given moment. What concerned him more was the fundamental question of whether war against the Indians could be shown theoretically to be just.

Las Casas was absolutely convinced that in practice such wars would be disastrous to the people involved and deleterious to the spread of the Gospel. In his view, the situation in America was "so dramatic and so all-inclusive that cold, academic speculation on the subject seems irresponsible, frivolous, and shocking."[25] Given the frailty of human nature, Las Casas considered these negative consequences to be inherent in the use of force against the natives, and argued accordingly that the use of coercion in any form was morally unacceptable. Las Casas forbade coercion both in compelling belief and also in the attempt to create a peaceful environment for missionaries to do their work, which Sepúlveda would have allowed.

Vitoria, on the other hand, allowed for the legitimate use of force against the natives on several limited grounds, including to protect them from subjection to the sometimes barbarian practices of their native cultures. For Las Casas, this argument was far too great a concession to the passions and imaginations of greedy and violent men, who would surely exploit such a potentially limitless concession for war. In his famous debate with Sepúlveda, after providing a lengthy list of arguments against his opponent's position, he noted that even in the hypothetical case that Sepúlveda was correct, his opponent should nevertheless keep his views to himself. Las Casas felt this way, two modern scholars explain, because of "the scandal he [Sepúlveda] was causing and the encouragement he was giving to men of violent tendencies."[26]

Las Casas believed that the myriad consequences of war, both intended and unintended, would more than offset any claim to be helping suffering natives—a point that critics of modern humanitarian military interventions continue to make to good effect to this day.[27]

"In order to put an end to all violence against the Indians," writes a modern study, "Las Casas needed to show that, for one reason or another, all war against them was unjust." For that reason, he made a strenuous effort to overturn any argument that, seeking to limit war, might nevertheless leave war open as a licit option.[28] Such "pacification" measures, Las Casas was convinced, would certainly harm the missionary effort, since the presence of armed men would dispose the wills and intellects of the natives against any member of the invading party, missionaries included.[29] Missionaries were to perform their good work "with gentle and divine words, and with examples and works of saintly life."[30] He was convinced that the natives could be made part of Christian civilization through persistent and sincere effort, and that enslavement or other coercion would be both unjust and counterproductive. Only peaceful interaction would ensure sincerity of heart among those who chose to convert.

Between writing, preaching, and political agitation, Las Casas devoted half a century to his labors on behalf of the natives, seeking reforms in their treatment and agitating against the *encomienda* system open to so much abuse. It was here that Las Casas identified an important source of injustice in the Spaniards' behavior in the New World. An *encomendero* was assigned a group of Indians; it was his job to protect them and to provide them with religious education. The natives on his *encomienda* were expected to pay tribute to the *encomendero* in return. The *encomienda* did not originally amount to a grant of political sovereignty over the natives, but in practice it often amounted to that, and the requisite tribute was exacted all too often by forced labor. Having once possessed an *encomienda* himself, Las Casas knew the injustices and abuses of the system firsthand and worked with limited success to put a stop to what he considered a grave evil.

In 1564, reflecting on his decades of labor as an advocate for the natives, Las Casas wrote in his will:

> In His goodness and mercy, God considered it right to choose me as his minister, though unworthy, to plead for all those peoples of the Indies, possessors of those kingdoms and lands, against wrongs and injuries never before heard of or seen, received from our Spaniards... and to restore them to the primitive liberty of which they were unjustly deprived....And I have labored in the court of the kings of Castile going and coming many times from the Indies to Castile and from Castile to the Indies, for about fifty years, since the year 1514, for God alone and from compassion at seeing perish such multitudes of rational men, domestic, humble, most mild and simple beings, well fitted to receive our Catholic faith...and to be endowed with all good customs.[31]

To this day, Las Casas is considered almost a saint throughout much of Latin America, and he continues to be admired both for his courage and for his painstaking labor. His Catholic faith, which taught him that a single code of morality bound all men, permitted him to render judgment on the behavior of his own society in a spirit of strict impartiality—no small thing. Las Casas's arguments, writes professor Lewis Hanke, "strengthened the hands of all those who in his time and the centuries to follow worked in the belief that all the peoples of the world are human beings with the potentialities and responsibilities of men."[32]

Thus far we have spoken of the early development of international law, a norm governing the behavior of states toward each other. The difficulty of enforcing international law is a separate matter. The resolution of this problem is left more or less open in the work of the Spanish theologians.[33] Vitoria's answer appears to have been connected to the idea of just war—that is, if a state had violated the norms of international law in its interaction with another state, the latter state could have grounds for waging a just war against it.[34]

We should not carelessly assume that the Spanish theologians would have supported an institution akin to the United Nations. Recall the original problem that a system of international law aims to solve. According to the seventeenth-century British philosopher Thomas Hobbes, human society, without a government capable of functioning as an umpire over all men, is condemned to a state of chaos and civil war. The creation of a sovereign office whose primary function is to keep order and enforce obedience to the law is, in Hobbes's view, the only mechanism by which we may escape the chronic insecurity and disorder of the so-called state of nature. In the same vein, it is sometimes said that in the absence of some kind of world government, the nations of the world are in the same situation vis-à-vis each other as are the individuals of a single nation before the creation of a government over them. Without the establishment of a sovereign to rule over the nations, Hobbesian analysis tells us that we can expect the same kind of conflict and disorder between nations as would exist, in the absence of civil government, between individual citizens.

The establishment of government does not solve the problem that Hobbes describes; it merely shifts that problem to another level. Government can enforce peace and prevent injustice among the people it rules. But the people are now in a state of nature vis-à-vis government itself, since there is no common umpire that stands above both government and people. If the government possesses the sovereign authority that Hobbes recommends, it must have the last word on the extent of its own powers, on right and wrong, and even on the adjudication of disputes between individual citizens and itself. Even if Hobbes believed in democracy, mere voting can hardly be expected to restrain such an institution. If a power above both government and people were established in order to ensure that government did not abuse its powers, it would only push the problem to yet another level, for there would now be no authority above this new power.

This is just one problem with the idea of an international institution with coercive powers to enforce international law. Proponents of this idea contend that such an authority would liberate the nations of the world from the Hobbesian state of nature in which they find themselves. But with the creation of such an authority, the problem of insecurity still exists: The nations of the world would then be in a state of nature vis-à-vis this new authority, whose behavior they would be unable to restrain.

The enforcement of international law, therefore, is no simple matter, and the establishment of a global institution for the purpose only shifts the Hobbesian problem rather than solving it. Yet other options remain. After all, advanced nations managed to observe the rules of so-called civilized warfare for two centuries following the Thirty Years' War (1618–1648). The threat of ostracism can have very real effects.

Whatever the practical difficulties of its enforcement, however, the *idea* of international law, which emerged in inchoate form as a result of the philosophical discussion prompted by the discovery of America, is supremely important. It suggests that each nation is not a moral universe unto itself, but is bound in its behavior by basic principles on which civilized peoples can agree. The state, in other words, is not morally autonomous.

In the early sixteenth century, Nicolo Machiavelli presaged the arrival of the modern state with his short book *The Prince* (1513). For Machiavelli, the state was indeed a morally autonomous institution, whose behavior on behalf of its own preservation could be judged against no external standard, whether the decrees of a pope or any code of moral principle. No wonder the Church condemned Machiavelli's political philosophy so severely: it was precisely this view that the great Catholic theologians of Spain so emphatically denied. The state, according to them, could indeed be judged according to principles external to itself, and could not act on the basis of mere expedience or narrow advantage if moral principles were trampled in the process.

In sum, Spanish theologians of the sixteenth century held the behavior of their own civilization up to critical scrutiny and found it wanting. They proposed that in matters of natural right the other peoples of the world were their equals, and that the commonwealths of pagan peoples were entitled to the same treatment that the nations of Christian Europe accorded to one another. That Catholic priests gave Western civilization the philosophical tools with which to approach non-Western peoples in a spirit of equality is quite an extraordinary thing. If we consider the Age of Discovery in the light of sound historical judgment, we must conclude that the Spaniards' ability to look objectively at these foreign peoples and recognize their common humanity was no small accomplishment, particularly when measured against the parochialism that has so often colored one people's conception of another.

Such impartiality could not have been expected to develop out of American Indian cultures. "The Indians of the same region or

language group did not even have a common name for themselves," explains Harvard historian Samuel Eliot Morison. "Each
tribe called itself something like 'We, the People,' and referred to
its neighbors by a word that meant 'the Barbarians,' 'Sons of She-
Dog,' or something equally insulting."[35] That a counterexample
like the Iroquois Confederation comes so readily to mind is an
indication of its exceptional character. The conception of an
international order of states large and small, of varying levels of
civilization and refinement, operating on a principle of equality,
could not have found fertile soil amid such narrow chauvinism.
The Catholic conception of the fundamental unity of the human
race, on the other hand, informed the deliberations of the great
sixteenth-century Spanish theologians who insisted on universal
principles that must govern the interaction of states. If we criti-
cize Spanish excesses in the New World, therefore, it is thanks to
the moral tools provided by the Catholic theologians of Spain
itself that we are able to do so.

Peruvian novelist Mario Vargas Llosa put European interaction with the natives of the New World into similar perspective:

> Father Las Casas was the most active, although not the only
> one, of those nonconformists who rebelled against abuses
> inflicted upon the Indians. They fought against their fellow
> men and against the policies of their own country in the name
> of the moral principle that to them was higher than any princi-
> ple of nation or state. This self-determination could not have
> been possible among the Incas or any of the other pre-Hispanic
> cultures. In these cultures, as in the other great civilizations of
> history foreign to the West, the individual could not morally
> question the social organism of which he was a part, because he
> existed only as an integral atom of that organism and because

for him the dictates of the state could not be separated from morality. The first culture to interrogate and question itself, the first to break up the masses into individual beings who with time gradually gained the right to think and act for themselves, was to become, thanks to that unknown exercise, freedom, the most powerful civilization of our world.[36]

That injustices were committed in the conquest of the New World no serious person will deny, and priests at the time chronicled and condemned them. But it is natural that we should wish to find some silver lining, some mitigating factor, amid the demographic tragedy that struck the peoples of the New World during the Age of Discovery. And that silver lining was that the encounters between these peoples provided an especially opportune moment for moralists to discuss and develop the fundamental principles that must govern their interaction. In this task they were aided enormously by the painstaking moral analysis of Catholic theologians teaching in Spanish universities.[37] As Hanke rightly concludes, "The ideals which some Spaniards sought to put into practice as they opened up the New World will never lose their shining brightness as long as men believe that other peoples have a right to live, that just methods may be found for the conduct of relations between peoples, and that essentially all the peoples of the world are men."[38] These are ideas with which the West has identified for centuries, and they come to us directly from the best of Catholic thought. Thus do we have another pillar of Western civilization constructed by the Catholic Church.

Chartres Cathedral, the site of the school that contributed so much to the development of Western science.

The Basilica of Saint Peter in Vatican City. Father Roger Boscovich is credited with saving the dome from collapse. In 1742, he advised Pope Benedict XIV to reinforce the cracking structure with five iron rings.

Spanish conquistadors fight—alongside their Indian allies—against the Aztecs. The foundations of international law are rooted in discussions among Spanish Catholic theologians about the inherent rights of peoples.

Michelangelo's famous *Pietà*.

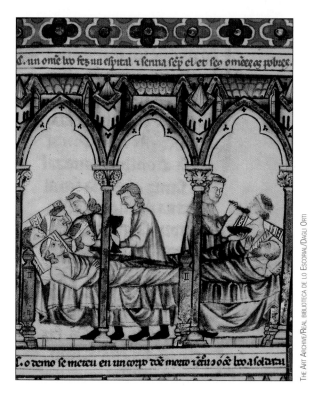

Monks tended the sick in the first hospitals in Europe.

Galileo Galilei and his drawings of the moon's phases as seen through his telescope. These are taken from Galileo's 1610 work *The Starry Messenger*.

This 1660 engraving shows the heliocentric universe posited by Copernicus. He appears at the lower right; his precursor Ptolemy is opposite him on the lower left.

Monks performed invaluable tasks for the continuity of Western civilization. In this thirteenth-century engraving, one monk is seen studying a globe while another painstakingly copies a manuscript.

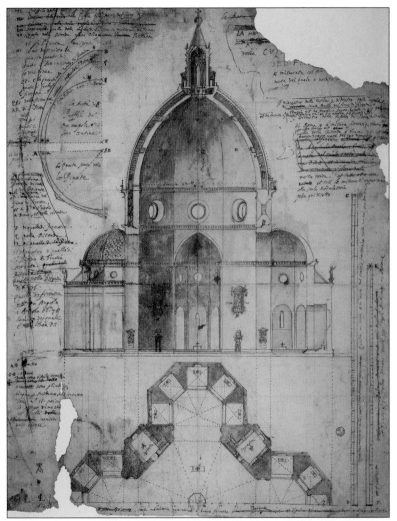

This cross-section of the dome of Santa Maria del Fiore in Florence, Italy, reveals the intricate mathematical proportions of medieval Catholic cathedrals. Architects honored God by using numbers and proportions with special significance, as seen in the three bays shown here. The number three represented the Holy Trinity.

England's Salisbury Cathedral, dedicated in 1258.

*Chapter Eight*

# The Church and Economics

T*he standard story of* the history of economic thought essentially begins with Adam Smith and other eighteenth-century thinkers. Catholics themselves, particularly those hostile to the market economy, have also tended to identify modern economic principles and insights more or less with thinkers of the Enlightenment. To the contrary, however, medieval and late Scholastic commentators understood and theorized about the free economy in ways that would prove profoundly fruitful for the development of sound economic thinking in the West. Modern economics, therefore, constitutes another important area in which Catholic influence has, until recently, all too often been obscured or overlooked. In fact, Catholics are now being called its founders.

Joseph Schumpeter, one of the great economists of the twentieth century, paid tribute to the overlooked contributions of the late Scholastics in *History of Economic Analysis* (1954). "[I]t is they," he wrote, "who come nearer than does any other group to having been the 'founders' of scientific economics."[1] In devoting scholarly attention to this unfortunately neglected chapter in the history of economic thought, Schumpeter would be joined by other accomplished scholars over the course of the twentieth century, including Raymond de Roover, Marjorie Grice-Hutchinson, and Alejandro Chafuen.[2]

Another great twentieth-century economist, Murray N. Rothbard, devoted a lengthy section of his critically acclaimed history of economic thought to the insights of the late Scholastics, whom he described as brilliant social thinkers and economic analysts. He made a compelling case that the insights of these men reached their culmination in the Austrian School of economics, an important school of economic thought that developed in the late nineteenth century and continues today. The Austrian School could itself boast a string of brilliant economists, from Carl Menger to Eugen von Böhm-Bawerk to Ludwig von Mises. F. A. Hayek, a distinguished member of the school, won the Nobel Prize in economics in 1974.

Before examining the Late Scholastics, however, we should consider the often overlooked economic contributions of still earlier Catholic scholars. Jean Buridan (1300–1358), for example, who served as rector of the University of Paris, made important contributions to the modern theory of money. Instead of viewing money as an artificial product of state intervention, Buridan showed how money emerged freely and spontaneously on the market, first as a useful commodity and then as a medium of exchange. In other words, money emerged not by government decree but out of the process of voluntary exchange, which people discover to be dramatically simplified by the adoption of a useful and widely desired commodity as a medium.[3]

This widely desired commodity, whatever it may be, must therefore first be valued for its role in satisfying non-monetary wants. It must also, if it is to be effective in its monetary role, possess certain important characteristics. It must be easily portable and divisible, it must be durable, and it must possess a high value per unit weight, such that small amounts of it are valuable enough to facilitate almost any transaction. "In that way," writes one expert, "Buridan began the classification of monetary qualities of commodities which was to constitute the first chapter of countless money and banking textbooks down to the end of the gold standard era in the 1930s."[4]

Nicolas Oresme (1325–1382), a pupil of Buridan, made his own significant contributions to monetary theory. Oresme, a polymath skilled in mathematics, astronomy, and physics, wrote *A Treatise on the Origin, Nature, Law and Alterations of Money*, which has been described as "a milestone in the science of money" that "set standards that would not be surpassed for many centuries, and which in certain respects have not been surpassed at all." He has even been called the "founding father of monetary economics."[5]

Oresme first stated the principle that would later become known as Gresham's Law. According to that law, if two currencies exist side by side in the same economy and the government fixes a ratio between them that diverges from the ratio that they can obtain on the free market, the currency that the government artificially overvalues will drive the one the government undervalues out of circulation. This is why Oresme argued that "if the fixed legal ratio of the coins differs from the market value of the metals, the coin which is underrated entirely disappears from circulation, and the coin which is overrated alone remains current."[6]

Thus suppose the two currencies are gold and silver, and that on the market sixteen ounces of silver and one ounce of gold are valued equally. Suppose further that the government establishes a legal ratio of 15:1, such that people are required to treat fifteen ounces of silver and one ounce of gold as if they were of equal value. This ratio overvalues silver, of course, since according to the two metals' market value it takes sixteen silver coins to equal one gold coin. But the government, with its 15:1 ratio, is telling the public that they can pay debts contracted in gold coins at a rate of only fifteen silver coins per gold coin instead of the sixteen silver coins per gold coin that market valuation would require. As a result, people begin to flee from gold and make all their payments in silver. In effect, it would be as if the government today declared that three quarters had to be treated as equivalent to one paper dollar. People would instantly cease using paper dollars and would wish to make all their payments in artificially overvalued quarters. Dollar bills would disappear from circulation. These are examples of overvalued money driving out undervalued money.

Oresme also understood the destructive effects of inflation. Government debasement of the monetary unit serves no good purpose, he explained. It interferes with commerce and increases the overall price level. It enriches the government at the expense of the people. Ideally, he suggested, government should not interfere in the monetary system at all.[7]

The late Scholastics shared Oresme's interest in monetary economics. They perceived clear relationships of cause and effect at work in the economy, particularly after observing the considerable price inflation that occurred in sixteenth-century Spain as a result of the influx of precious metals from the New World. From the observation that the greater supply of specie had led to a decline in the purchasing power of money, they came to the more general conclusion—an economic law, as it were—that an increase in the supply of any good will tend to bring about a decrease in its price. In what has been described by some scholars as the first formulation of the quantity theory of money, the Late Scholastic theologian Martín de Azpilcueta (1493–1586) wrote:

Other things being equal, in countries where there is a great scarcity of money, all other saleable goods and even the hands and labor of men, are given for less money than where it is abundant. Thus, we see by experience that in France, where money is scarcer than in Spain, bread, wine, cloth, and labor are worth much less. And even in Spain, in times when money is scarcer, saleable goods and labor were given for very much less than after the discovery of the Indies, which flooded the country with gold and silver. The reason for this is that money is worth more where and when it is scarce than where and when it is abundant. What some men say, that a scarcity of money brings down other things, arises from the fact that its excessive rise [in value] makes other things seem lower, just as a short man standing beside a very tall one looks shorter than when he is beside a man of his own height.[8]

Other important work in economic theory was done by Thomas de Vio, Cardinal Cajetan (1468–1534). Cardinal Cajetan was an extraordinarily influential and important churchman, who, among other things, had engaged in debate with Martin Luther, the founder of Protestantism, tripping him up in a discussion of papal authority. Luther rejected the notion that Matthew 16:18, which spoke of Christ giving the keys to the kingdom of heaven to the apostle Peter, had meant to imply that the successors of Peter were intended to wield teaching and disciplinary authority throughout the Christian world. But Cajetan showed that a parallel verse from the Old Testament, Isaiah 22:22, also used the symbolism of the key, and that there the key was indeed a sign of authority that would be handed down to successors.[9]

In his 1499 treatise *De Cambiis*, which sought to vindicate the foreign exchange market from a moral point of view, Cajetan also

pointed out that the value of money *in the present* could be
affected by expectations of the likely state of the market *in the
future*. Thus the current value of money can be affected by people's expectations of disruptive and damaging events ranging
from poor harvests to war, as well as by expectations of changes
in the money supply. In that way, writes Murray Rothbard, "Cardinal Cajetan, a sixteenth-century prince of the Church, can be
considered the founder of expectations theory in economics."[10]

Among the most momentous and important economic principles that developed and matured with the help of the Late
Scholastics, as well as under their immediate predecessors, was
the subjective theory of value. Inspired partly by their own analysis and partly by St. Augustine's comments on value in his *City of
God*, these Catholic thinkers contended that value derived not
from objective factors like cost of production or the amount of
labor employed but from the subjective valuation of individuals.
Any theory that attributed value to objective factors such as
labor or other costs of production was therefore faulty.

Franciscan friar Pierre de Jean Olivi (1248–1298) first proposed a value theory based on subjective utility. He argued that,
in economic terms, the value of a good derived from individuals'
subjective assessments of its usefulness and desirability to them.
The "just price" could therefore not be calculated on the basis of
objective factors, such as the labor and other production costs
that went into producing it. Rather, the just price emerged out of
the interaction of buyers and sellers on the market, where individuals' subjective appraisals of goods manifested themselves in
their buying or abstention from buying at given prices.[11] A century and a half later, San Bernardino of Siena, one of the greatest
economic thinkers of the Middle Ages, adopted Olivi's subjective
value theory practically word for word.[12] Who would have

guessed that the correct value theory in economics originated with a thirteenth-century Franciscan friar?

The late Scholastics adopted this position as well. As Luis Saravía de la Calle put it in the sixteenth century:

> Those who measure the just price by the labor, costs, and risk incurred by the person who deals in the merchandise or produces it, or by the cost of transport or the expense of traveling...or by what he has to pay the factors for their industry, risk, and labor, are greatly in error, and still more so are those who allow a certain profit of a fifth or a tenth. For the just price arises from the abundance or scarcity of goods, merchants, and money...and not from costs, labor, and risk. If we had to consider labor and risk in order to assess the just price, no merchant would ever suffer loss, nor would abundance or scarcity of goods and money enter into the question. Prices are not commonly fixed on the basis of costs. Why should a bale of linen brought overland from Brittany at great expense be worth more than one which is transported cheaply by sea?... Why should a book written out by hand be worth more than one which is printed, when the latter is better though it costs less to produce?...The just price is found not by counting the cost but by the common estimation.[13]

The Jesuit Cardinal Juan de Lugo (1583–1660) concurred, offering his own argument in favor of subjective value:

> Price fluctuates not because of the intrinsic and substantial perfection of the articles—since mice are more perfect than corn, yet are worth less—but on account of their utility in respect of human need, and then only on account of estimation;

for jewels are much less useful than corn in the house and yet their price is much higher. And we must take into account not only the estimation of prudent men but also of the imprudent, if they are sufficiently numerous in a place. This is why our glass trinkets are in Ethiopia justly exchanged for gold, because they are commonly more esteemed there. And among the Japanese, old objects made of iron and pottery, which are worth nothing to us, fetch a high price because of their antiquity. Communal estimation, even when foolish, raises the natural price of goods, since price is derived from estimation. The natural price is raised by abundance of buyers and money, and lowered by the contrary factors.[14]

Luis de Molina, another Jesuit, likewise declared:

[T]he just price of goods is not fixed according to the utility given to them by man, as if, *caeteris paribus*, the nature and the need of the use given to them determined the quantity of price.... [I]t depends on the relative appreciation which each man has for the use of the good. This explains why the just price of a pearl, which can be used only to decorate, is higher than the just price of a great quantity of grain, wine, meat, bread, or horses, even if the utility of these things (which are also nobler in nature) is more convenient and superior to the use of a pearl. That is why we can conclude that the just price for a pearl depends on the fact that some men wanted to grant it value as an object of decoration.[15]

Carl Menger, whose *Principles of Economics* (1871) had such a profound influence on the development of modern economics (and which has been identified with the Thomistic-Aristotelian tradition[16]), explained the implications of subjective value in a helpful way. Suppose tobacco should suddenly cease to perform any useful function for human beings—no one wanted or needed it any longer for any purpose at all. Imagine, furthermore, a machine that had been designed exclusively for the processing of tobacco and could serve no other purpose. As a result of the shift in people's tastes entirely away from tobacco—tobacco's loss of *use-value*, as Menger would say—the value of this machine would likewise fall to zero. Thus the value of the tobacco is not derived from its cost of production. According to subjective value theory, the exact opposite is closer to the truth. The factors of production that are employed in tobacco processing derive *their own value* from the subjective value that consumers impute to tobacco, the final product toward whose production these factors are employed.[17]

Subjective value theory, an essential economic insight, has nothing to do with anthropocentrism or moral relativism. Economics deals with the fact and implications of human choice. In order to understand and explain people's choices, one must make use of the values they actually hold. (Needless to say, that does not imply endorsement of those values.) In the case described by Menger, it simply boils down to the common-sense conclusion that if people do not value object A, they will likewise impute no value to factors specifically designed for the production of A.

Subjective value theory also amounts to a direct rebuttal to the labor theory of value, associated most closely with Karl Marx, the father of communism. Marx did not believe in objective morality, but he did believe that objective values could be assigned to economic goods. That objective economic value was based on the number of labor hours that went into the production of a particular good. Now Marx's labor theory did not contend that the mere expenditure of labor automatically rendered the resulting product valuable. Thus he did not say that if I spent the day gluing empty beer cans together, the fruits of my labor would be ipso facto valuable. Things were considered valuable, admitted Marx, only if individuals attributed use-value to them. But *once individuals imputed use-value to a good*, the value of that good would be determined by the number of labor hours expended in its production. (We shall leave aside some of the immediate difficulties of such a theory, including its inability to account for the rise in value of an artist's works following his death; certainly no additional labor is applied to them between the moment of their completion and the moment of his death, so the labor theory appears to be at a loss in explaining this commonly observed phenomenon.)

Marx derived from his labor theory of value the idea that laborers in a free economy were "exploited" because although their labor effort was the source of all value, the wages they received did not fully reflect this effort. Profits retained by the employer were entirely unearned, according to Marx, and amounted to an unjust deduction from what rightfully belonged to the workers.

A systematic refutation of Marx is beyond our purposes here. But with the help of late Scholastic insights, we can understand at least the primary error in his labor theory of value. (Supplementary arguments, included in the notes, can then establish why Marx's ideas about the exploitation of labor were fundamentally wrongheaded.[18]) Marx was not incorrect to perceive a relationship between the value of a good and the value of the labor exerted in the production of that good; these two phenomena are indeed often related. His error was that he had the causal relationship exactly backwards. A good does not derive its value from the labor expended upon it. The labor expended upon it derives *its* value from the degree to which consumers value the final product.

Thus when San Bernardino of Siena and the sixteenth-century Scholastics argued in favor of subjective value theory, they were setting forth a crucial economic concept that implicitly anticipated and refuted one of the great economic errors of the modern period. Even Adam Smith, known to history as the great champion of free markets and economic liberty, was ambiguous enough in his exposition of value theory to leave the impression that goods derived their value from the labor expended to make them. Rothbard has gone so far as to suggest that Smith's eighteenth-century labor theory of value fed into Marx's theory in the following century, and that the economics profession—to say nothing of the world as a whole—would have been far better off if economic thought had remained faithful to the value theory expounded by the important Catholic thinkers we have discussed here. French and Italian economists, influenced by the Scholastics, by and large maintained the correct position; it was British economists who diverged so tragically into lines of thought that culminated in Marx.

A discussion of the influence of Catholic thought on the development of economics cannot overlook the contributions of Emil Kauder. Kauder authored a substantial body of work in which he sought to discover, among other things, why the (correct) subjective value theory should have developed and flourished in Catholic countries, while the (incorrect) labor theory of value should have been so influential in Protestant ones. More specifically, he was intrigued to find that British thinkers were so inclined toward the labor theory while French and Italian thinkers came down so consistently on the side of subjective value.

In *A History of Marginal Utility Theory* (1965), Kauder suggested that the answer to this puzzle could be found in the
importance that Protestant luminary John Calvin ascribed to
work. For Calvin, work—of essentially any kind—enjoyed divine
sanction, and was a crucial arena within which man could glorify
God. This emphasis on work led thinkers in Protestant countries
to emphasize labor as the central determinant of value. "Any
social philosopher or economist exposed to Calvinism," Kauder
explained, "will be tempted to give labor an exalted position in
his social or economic treatise, and no better way of extolling
labor can be found than by combining work with value theory,
traditionally the very basis of an economic system. Thus value
becomes labor value."[19]

According to Kauder, this was true even in the cases of such
thinkers as John Locke and Adam Smith, both of whom placed
great emphasis on labor in their writing and whose own views
were largely deistic rather than Protestant.[20] Such men
absorbed the Calvinist ideas that dominated their cultural
milieu. Smith, for example, was always sympathetic to Presby-
terianism (organized Calvinism, in effect) in spite of his own
departures from orthodoxy, and this sympathy for Calvinism
may well account for Smith's emphasis on labor as a determinant of value.[21]

Catholic countries, on the other hand, more deeply influenced
by an Aristotelian and Thomist line of thought, felt no such
attraction to a labor theory of value. Aristotle and Saint Thomas
envisioned the purpose of economic activity to be the derivation
of pleasure and happiness. Thus the goals of economics were profoundly *subjective*, insofar as pleasure and happiness were non-
quantifiable states of being whose intensity could not be
articulated with precision or in a manner that could be compared
from one person to another. Subjective value theory follows from

this premise as night follows day. "If pleasure in a moderate form is the purpose of economics," wrote Kauder, "then following the Aristotelian concept of the final cause, *all principles of economics including valuation must be derived from this goal.* In this pattern of Aristotelian and Thomistic thinking, valuation has the function of showing how much pleasure can be derived from economic goods."[22]

In other words, then, the Calvinist emphasis on the importance of labor led thinkers in Protestant countries to make it the determining factor in their theory of what made goods valuable—how much labor had been expended on them? The Aristotelian and Thomist view that dominated Catholic countries, on the other hand, which held happiness to be the purpose of economic activity, was naturally far more inclined to look for the source of value in individuals' subjective valuations of goods, as they assess the amount of pleasure that the good in question will afford them.

It is impossible to prove such a theory, of course, though Kauder assembles suggestive evidence that Protestant and Catholic thinkers at the time possessed an inchoate sense of the theological source of their disagreement over economic value. The fact remains, however, that Catholic thinkers, informed by their own distinct intellectual tradition, reached the correct conclusion with regard to the nature of value while Protestant ones by and large did not.

It would be interesting enough if Catholic thinkers had happened fortuitously upon these important economic principles, only to have them languish in obscurity without influencing any subsequent thinker. In fact, however, the economic ideas of the late Scholastics were profoundly influential, and the existing evidence permits us the happy luxury of tracing that influence through the centuries.

Into the seventeenth century, the Dutch Protestant Hugo Grotius, known for his contributions to international law theory, expressly cited the late Scholastics in his own work, and adopted much of their economic outlook. Scholastic influence in the seventeenth century also persists in the work of such influential Jesuits as Father Leonardus Lessius and Father Juan de Lugo.[23] In eighteenth-century Italy, there is strong evidence of Scholastic influence on Abbé Ferdinando Galiani, who is sometimes cited as the originator of the ideas of utility and scarcity as determinants of price.[24] (Likewise for Antonio Genovesi, a contemporary of Galiani who was also indebted to Scholastic thought.) "From Galiani," writes Rothbard, "the central role of utility, scarcity, and the common estimation of the market spread to France, to the late eighteenth-century French abbé Étienne Bonnot de Condillac (1714–80), as well as to that other great abbé Robert Jacques Turgot (1727–81).... François Quesnay (1694–1774) and the eighteenth-century French physiocrats—often considered to be the founders of economic science—were also heavily influenced by the Scholastics."[25]

Alejandro Chafuen, in his important book *Faith and Liberty: The Economic Thought of the Late Scholastics* (2003), shows that on one issue after another these sixteenth- and seventeenth-century thinkers not only understood and developed crucial economic principles, but also defended the principles of economic liberty and a free-market economy. From prices and wages to money and value theory, the late Scholastics anticipated the very best economic thought of later centuries. Specialists in the history of economic thought have become more and more aware of the late Scholastics' contribution to economics, but this is yet another example of a Catholic innovation well known to specialized scholars that has, for the most part, not made its way to the general public.[26] This is why it is so silly to claim, as some controversialists have, that the idea of the free market was developed in the eighteenth century by anti-Catholic zealots. These ideas had been current for hundreds of years by the time of the publication of the virulently anti-Catholic French *Encyclopedie,* which repeated the Scholastic analysis of price determination.[27]

*Chapter Nine*

# How Catholic Charity Changed the World

*In the early fourth century,* famine and disease struck the army of the Roman emperor Constantine. Pachomius, a pagan soldier in that army, watched in amazement as many of his fellow Romans brought food to the afflicted men and, without discrimination, bestowed help on those in need. Curious, Pachomius inquired about these people and found out that they were Christians. What kind of religion was it, he wondered, that could inspire such acts of generosity and humanity? He began to learn about the faith—and before he knew it, he was on the road to conversion.[1]

This kind of amazement has attended Catholic charitable work throughout the ages. Even Voltaire, perhaps the most prolific anti-Catholic propagandist of the eighteenth century, was awed by the heroic spirit of self-sacrifice that animated so many of the Church's sons and daughters. "Perhaps there is nothing greater on earth," he said, "than the sacrifice of youth and beauty, often of high birth, made by the gentle sex in order to work in hospitals for the relief of human misery, the sight of which is so revolting to our delicacy. Peoples separated from the Roman religion have imitated but imperfectly so generous a charity."[2]

It would take many large volumes to record the complete history of Catholic charitable work carried on by individuals, parishes, dioceses, monasteries, missionaries, friars, nuns, and lay organizations. Suffice it to say that Catholic charity has had no peer in the amount and variety of good work it has done and the human suffering and misery it has alleviated. Let us go still further: *The Catholic Church invented charity as we know it in the West.*

Just as important as the sheer volume of Catholic charity was the qualitative difference that separated the Church's charity from what had preceded it. It would be foolish to deny that some noble sentiments were voiced by the great ancient philosophers when it came to philanthropy, or that men of wealth made impressive and substantial voluntary contributions to their communities. The wealthy were expected to finance baths, public buildings, and all manner of public entertainment. Pliny the Younger, for example, was far from alone in endowing his hometown with a school and a library.

Yet for all the benefactions thus offered, the spirit of giving in the ancient world was in a certain sense deficient when set against that of the Church. Most ancient giving was self-interested rather than purely gratuitous. The buildings financed by the wealthy prominently displayed their names. Donors gave what they did either to put the recipients in their debt or to call attention to themselves and their great liberality. That those in need were to be served with a cheerful heart and provided for without thought of reward or reciprocity was certainly not the governing principle.

Stoicism, an ancient school of thought dating back to around 300 B.C. and still alive and well in the early centuries of the

Christian era, is sometimes cited as a pre-Christian line of thought that recommended doing good to one's fellow man without expecting anything in return. To be sure, the Stoics did teach that the good man was a citizen of the world who enjoyed a spirit of fraternity with all men, and for that reason they may appear to have been messengers of charity, but they also taught the suppression of feeling and emotion as things unbecoming of a man. Man should be utterly unperturbed by outside events, even of the most tragic kind. He must possess a self-mastery so strong as to be able to face the worst catastrophe in a spirit of absolute indifference. That was also the spirit in which the wise man should assist the less fortunate: not one of sharing the grief and sorrow of those he helps or of making an emotional connection with them, but in the disinterested and emotionless spirit of one who is simply discharging his duty. Rodney Stark describes classical philosophy as having "regarded mercy and pity as pathological emotions—defects of character to be avoided by all rational men. Since mercy involves providing unearned help or relief, it was contrary to justice."[3] Thus the Roman philosopher Seneca could write:

> The sage will console those who weep, but without weeping with them; he will succor the shipwrecked, give hospitality to the proscribed, and alms to the poor...restore the son to the mother's tears, save the captive from the arena, and even bury the criminal; but in all his mind and his countenance will be alike untroubled. He will feel no pity. He will succor, he will do good, for he is born to assist his fellows, to labor for the welfare of mankind, and to offer each one his part.... His countenance and his soul will betray no emotion as he looks upon the withered legs, the tattered rags, the bent and emaciated frame of the

beggar. But he will help those who are worthy, and, like the gods, his leaning will be towards the wretched.... It is only diseased eyes that grow moist in beholding tears in other eyes.[4]

It is true that, simultaneously with the development of Christianity, some of the harshness of earlier Stoicism began to dissolve. One can hardly read the *Meditations* of Marcus Aurelius, the second-century Roman emperor and Stoic philosopher, without being struck by the degree to which the thought of this noble pagan resembled that of Christianity, and it was for this reason that Saint Justin Martyr could praise later Stoicism. But the ruthless suppression of emotion and feeling that had characterized so much of this school had already taken its toll. It was certainly alien to human nature in its refusal to acknowledge such an important dimension of what it truly means to be human. We recoil from such examples of Stoicism as Anaxagoras, a man who, upon learning of his son's death, merely remarked, "I never supposed that I had begotten an immortal." Likewise, one can only marvel at the moral emptiness of Stilpo, who when faced with the ruin of his country, the capture of his native city, and the loss of his daughters to slavery or concubinage, proclaimed that after all he had really lost nothing, since the wise man transcended and rose above his circumstances.[5] It was only natural that men so insulated from the reality of evil would be slow to alleviate its effects on their fellow men. "Men who refused to recognize pain and sickness as evils," notes one observer, "were scarcely likely to be very eager to relieve them in others."[6]

The spirit of Catholic charity did not arise in a vacuum but took its inspiration from the teaching of Christ. "A new commandment I give unto you: that you love one another, as I have loved you, that you also love one another. By this shall all men know that you are my disciples, if you have love one for another"

(John 13:34-35; cf. James 4:11). Saint Paul explains that those who do not belong to the community of the faithful should also be accorded the care and charity of Christians, even if they should be enemies of the faithful (cf. Roman 12: 14-20; Galatians 6:10). Here was a new teaching for the ancient world.

According to W. E. H. Lecky, frequently a harsh critic of the Church, there can be "no question that neither in practice nor in theory, neither in the institutions that were founded nor in the place that was assigned to it in the scale of duties, did charity in antiquity occupy a position at all comparable to that which it has obtained by Christianity. Nearly all relief was a State measure, dictated much more by policy than by benevolence, and the habit of selling young children, the innumerable expositions, the readiness of the poor to enroll themselves as gladiators, and the frequent famines, show how large was the measure of unrelieved distress."[7]

The practice of offering oblations for the poor developed early in Church history. The faithful's offerings were placed on the altar within the context of the Mass. Other forms of giving included the *collecta*, in effect on certain fast days, in which the faithful donated some portion of the fruits of the earth just prior to the reading of the epistle. Financial contributions to the church treasury were also made, and extraordinary collections were solicited from richer members of the faithful. Early Christians would often fast, consecrating the money they would have spent on food as a sacrificial offering. Saint Justin Martyr reports that many people who had loved riches and material things prior to their conversion now sacrificed for the poor in a spirit of joy.[8]

One could go on at great length citing the good works of the early Church, carried out by both the lowly and the rich. Even the Church fathers, who bequeathed to Western civilization an enormous corpus of literary and scholarly work, found time to devote themselves to the service of their fellow men. Saint Augustine established a hospice for pilgrims, ransomed slaves, and gave away clothing to the poor. (He warned people not to give him expensive garments, since he would only sell them and give the proceeds to the poor.[9]) Saint John Chrysostom founded a series of hospitals in Constantinople.[10] Saint Cyprian and Saint Ephrem organized relief efforts during times of plague and famine.

The early Church also institutionalized the care of widows and orphans and saw after the needs of the sick, especially during epidemics. During the pestilences that struck Carthage and Alexandria, the Christians earned respect and admiration for the bravery with which they consoled the dying and buried the dead, at a time when the pagans abandoned even their friends to their terrible fate.[11] In the North African city of Carthage, the third-century bishop and Church father Saint Cyprian rebuked the pagan population for not helping victims of the plague, preferring instead to plunder them: "No compassion is shown by you to the sick, only covetousness and plunder open their jaws over the dead; they who are too fearful for the work of mercy, are bold for guilty profits. They who shun to bury the dead, are greedy for what they have left behind them." Saint Cyprian summoned followers of Christ to action, calling on them to nurse the sick and bury the dead. Recall that this was still the age of intermittent persecution of Christians, so the great bishop was asking his followers to help the very people who had at times persecuted them. But, he said, "If we only do good to those who do good to us, what do we more than the heathens and publicans? If we are the children of God, who makes His sun to shine upon good and bad, and sends rain on the just and the unjust, let us prove it by our acts, by blessing those who curse us, and doing good to those who persecute us."[12]

In the case of Alexandria, which also fell prey to the plague in the third century, the Christian bishop Dionysius recorded that the pagans "thrust aside anyone who began to be sick, and kept aloof even from their dearest friends, and cast the sufferers out upon the public roads half dead, and left them unburied, and treated them with utter contempt when they died." He was able to report, however, that very many Christians "did not spare themselves, but kept by each other, and visited the sick without thought of their own peril, and ministered to them assiduously... drawing upon themselves their neighbors' diseases, and willingly taking over to their own persons the burden of the sufferings of those around them."[13] (Martin Luther, who famously broke with the Catholic Church in the early sixteenth century, nevertheless maintained this spirit of self-sacrifice in his famous essay on whether a Christian minister was morally entitled to flee from a plague. No, Luther said, his place was by the side of his flock, tending to their spiritual needs even to the moment of their deaths.)

Saint Ephrem, a hermit in Edessa, was remembered for his heroism when famine and pestilence struck that unfortunate city. Not only did he coordinate the collection and distribution of alms, but he also established hospitals, cared for the sick, and tended to the dead.[14] When a famine struck Armenia during the reign of Maximius, Christians lent assistance to the poor regardless of religious affiliation. Eusebius, the great fourth-century ecclesiastical historian, tells us that as a result of the Christians' good example many pagans "made inquiries about a religion whose disciples are capable of such disinterested devotion."[15] Julian the Apostate, who detested Christianity, complained of Christian kindness toward the pagan poor: "These impious Galileans not only feed their own poor, but ours also; welcoming them to their *agapae*, they attract them, as children are attracted, with cakes."[16]

## EARLY HOSPITALS AND THE KNIGHTS OF SAINT JOHN

*It is open to debate whether* institutions resembling hospitals in the modern sense can be said to have existed in ancient Greece and Rome. Many historians have doubted it, while others have pointed out an unusual exception here and there. Yet even these exceptions involved the care of sick or wounded soldiers rather than of the general population. With regard to the establishment of institutions staffed by physicians who made diagnoses and prescribed remedies, and where nursing provisions were also available, the Church appears to have pioneered.[17]

By the fourth century, the Church began to sponsor the establishment of hospitals on a large scale, such that nearly every major city ultimately had one. These hospitals originally provided hospitality to strangers but eventually cared for the sick, widows, orphans, and the poor in general.[18] As Guenter Risse puts it, Christians set aside "the reciprocal hospitality that had prevailed in ancient Greece and the family-oriented obligations of the Romans" in order to cater to "particular social groups marginalized by poverty, sickness, and age."[19] Likewise, medical historian Fielding Garrison observes that before the birth of Christ "the spirit toward sickness and misfortune was not one of compassion, and the credit of ministering to human suffering on an extended scale belongs to Christianity."[20]

A woman named Fabiola, in an act of Christian penance, established the first large public hospital in Rome; she would scour the streets for poor and infirm men and women in need of its care.[21] Saint Basil the Great, known to contemporaries as the Apostle of Almsgiving, established a hospital in fourth-century Caesarea. He was known to embrace the miserable lepers who sought care there, displaying a tender mercy toward these outcasts for which Saint Francis of Assisi would later become famous. Not surprisingly, the monasteries also played an important role in the care of the sick.[22] According to the most thorough study of the history of hospitals:

> [F]ollowing the fall of the Roman Empire, monasteries gradually became the providers of organized medical care not available elsewhere in Europe for several centuries. Given their organization and location, these institutions were virtual oases of order, piety, and stability in which healing could flourish. To provide these caregiving practices, monasteries also became sites of medical learning between the fifth and tenth centuries, the classic period of so-called monastic medicine. During the Carolingian revival of the 800s, monasteries also emerged as the principal centers for the study and transmission of ancient medical texts.[23]

Although the importance of caring for sick monks is duly emphasized in the Rule of Saint Benedict, there is no evidence that the father of Western monasticism imagined the monastery undertaking the task of providing medical care to the laity. Yet, as with so much else in the monastic enterprise, the force of circumstances significantly influenced the role and expectations of the monastery.

The military orders, established during the Crusades, administered hospitals all over Europe. One such order, the Knights of

Saint John (also known as the Hospitallers), an early instantiation of what later became the Knights of Malta, left an especially significant imprint on the history of European hospitals, most notably with their unusually extensive facility in Jerusalem. Established around 1080, this hospice sought to provide for the poor and to render safe and secure lodging for pilgrims, of whom there were many in Jerusalem (particularly after the Christian victory in the First Crusade at the end of the century). The scope of the hospital's operations increased significantly after Godfrey of Bouillon, who had led the Crusaders into Jerusalem, endowed the institution with a string of properties. With Jerusalem in Christian hands and routes to the city open, still more donations began to arrive from other sources.

John of Würzburg, a German priest, was overwhelmed by what he saw during his visit to the hospital. In addition to the care it dispensed, it also served as a substantial source of charitable relief. According to John, "The house feeds so many individuals outside and within, and it gives so huge an amount of alms to poor people, either those who come to the door, or those who remain outside, that certainly the total expenses can in no way be counted, even by the managers and dispensers of this house." Theoderic of Würzburg, another German pilgrim, marveled that "going through the palace we could in no way judge the number of people who lay there, but we saw a thousand beds. No king nor tyrant would be powerful enough to maintain daily the great number fed in this house."[24]

In 1120, the Hospitallers elected Raymond du Puy as administrator of the hospital, replacing the deceased Brother Gerard. The new administrator placed dramatic emphasis on service to the sick who had been entrusted to the hospital's care, and expected the staff to make heroic sacrifices on their behalf. We read in "How Our Lords the Sick Should be Received and Served"—article sixteen of du Puy's code regarding the administration of the hospital—that "in that obedience in which the master and the chapter of the hospital shall permit an hospital to exist when the sick man shall come there, let him be received thus: let him partake of the Holy Sacrament, first having confessed his sins to the priest, and afterwards let him be carried to bed, and there as if he were a Lord." "As a model for both charitable service and unconditional devotion to the sick," explains a modern history of hospitals, "du Puy's decree became a milestone in the development of the hospital."[25] As described by Guenter Risse:

> Not surprisingly, the new stream of pilgrims to the Latin King-
> dom of Jerusalem and their testimonials concerning the charity
> of the Hospitallers of Saint John spread rapidly throughout
> Europe, including England. The existence of a religious order
> that strongly expressed its fealty to the sick inspired the cre-
> ation of a network of similar institutions, especially at ports of
> embarkation in Italy and southern France where pilgrims
> assembled. At the same time, grateful ex-inmates, charitable
> nobles, and royals from one end of Europe to the other pro-
> vided substantial land donations. In 1131, King Alfonso of
> Aragon bequeathed one-third of his realm to the Hospitallers.[26]

Over the course of the twelfth century, the hospital began to look more and more like a modern hospital and less like a hospice for pilgrims. The hospital's mission became more specifically defined as the care of the sick, as opposed to providing shelter to needy travelers. At first an institution solely for Christians, the Hospital of Saint John began to admit Muslims and Jews as well.

Saint John's was also impressive for its professionalism, organization, and strict regimen. Modest surgeries were carried out. The sick received twice-daily visits from physicians, baths, and two main meals per day. The hospital workers were not permitted to eat until the patients had been fed. A female staff was on hand to perform other chores and ensured that the sick had clean clothes and bed linens.[27]

The sophisticated organization of Saint John's, coupled with its intense spirit of service to the sick, served as a model for Europe, where institutions inspired by the great hospital of Jerusalem began to pop up everywhere, in modest villages and major cities alike. The Hospitallers themselves, by the thirteenth century, were administering perhaps twenty hospices and leper houses.[28]

So impressive has Catholic charitable work been that even the Church's own enemies have grudgingly acknowledged it. The pagan writer Lucian (130–200) observed in astonishment, "The earnestness with which the people of this religion help one another in their needs is incredible. They spare themselves nothing for this end. Their first lawgiver put it into their heads that they were all brethren!"[29] Julian the Apostate, the Roman emperor who made a futile, if energetic, attempt in the 360s to return the empire to its earlier paganism, conceded that the Christians outshone the pagans in their devotion to charitable work. "Whilst the pagan priests neglect the poor," he wrote, "the hated Galileans [that is, the Christians] devote themselves to works of charity, and by a display of false compassion have established and given effect to their pernicious errors. See their love-feasts, and their tables spread for the indigent. Such practice is common among them, and causes a contempt for our gods."[30] Martin Luther, as inveterate an enemy of the Catholic Church as ever lived, was forced to admit: "Under the papacy the people were at least charitable, and force was not required to obtain alms. Today, under the reign of the Gospel [by which he meant Protestantism], in place of giving they rob each other, and it might be said that no one thinks he has any-thing till he gets possession of the property of his neighbor."[31]

Speaking about the Church, Simon Patten, a twentieth-century economic thinker, observed: "It provided food and shel-ter for the workers, charity for the unfortunate, and relief from disease, plague, and famine, which were but too common in the Middle Ages. When we note the number of the hospitals and infirmaries, the bounties of the monks, and the self-sacrifice of the nuns, we cannot doubt that the unfortunate of that time were at least as well provided for as they are at the present."[32] Frederick Hurter, a nineteenth-century biographer of Pope Innocent III, went so far as to declare: "All the institutions of beneficence which the human race this day possesses for the solace of the unfortunate, all that has been done for the protection of the indi-gent and afflicted in all the vicissitudes of their lives, and under all kinds of suffering, have come directly or indirectly from the Church of Rome. That Church set the example, carried on the movement, and often supplied the means of giving it effect."[33]

The extent of the Church's charitable activity sometimes became clearest when it was taken away. In sixteenth-century England, for example, King Henry VIII suppressed the monas-teries and confiscated their property, distributing it at rock-bottom prices to men of influence within his realm. The pretext for the suppression was that the monasteries had become sources of scandal and immorality, though there can be little doubt that such contrived accusations merely concealed royal avarice. The social consequences of the dissolution of the monasteries must have been substantial. The Northern Risings of 1536, a popular rebellion also known as the Pilgrimage of Grace, had much to do with popular anger at the disappearance of monastic charity, and a petitioner to the king observed two years later:

[T]he experience which we have had by those houses that already be suppressed shows plainly unto us that a great hurt & decay is thereby come & hereafter shall come to this your realm & great impoverishing of many your poor obedient subjects, for lack of hospitality & good householding that was wont in them to be kept to the great relief of the poor people of all the [areas] adjoining the said monasteries.[34]

The monasteries were known to be generous and easy landlords, making land available at low rents and for leases of long duration. "The monastery was a proprietor that never died; its tenantry had to do with a deathless landlord; its lands and houses never changed owners; its tenants were liable to none of the many... uncertainties that other tenants were."[35] Thus the dissolution of the monasteries and the redistribution of their lands could only mean "ruin to scores of thousands of the poorest of the peasantry, the breakup of the small communities which were their world, and a future that was truly beggary."[36]

The favorable terms on which people had once worked these lands by and large disappeared in the wake of the monasteries' dissolution. According to one historian, "The new owners [of these lands], shopkeepers, bankers or needy noblemen, had no attachment to the rural past, and they exploited their lands in a spirit that was solely business-like. Rents were increased, arable land converted to pasture and large areas enclosed. Thousands of unemployed farm hands were thrown on to the streets. Social distinctions became accentuated and pauperism increased in an alarming fashion."[37]

The effects of the dissolution were also felt in charitable provision and the care of the truly needy. Until relatively recently, the historical consensus regarding Catholic charitable activity in England took for granted a frequently heard Protestant criticism—that monastic poor relief had been neither as quantitatively substantial nor as qualitatively beneficial as its Catholic defenders had claimed. To the contrary, went this argument, monastic charitable provision had been relatively scant, and what meager amounts of charity the monasteries did dispense were distributed recklessly and without sufficient care to distinguish the genuinely needy from the chronically improvident and the merely lazy. In effect, then, they rewarded (and thereby tended to increase the instances of) the very condition they claimed to alleviate.

Modern scholars have at last begun to overturn this gross distortion of the historical record, a distortion that can be traced as far back as the late seventeenth and early eighteenth centuries with the Protestant bias of Gilbert Burnet and his *History of the Reformation of the Church of England.*[38] According to Paul Slack, a modern researcher, "The dissolution of the monasteries, chantries, religious gilds and fraternities in the 1530s and 1540s radically reduced existing sources of charity. The real aid which they had provided for the poor was no doubt concentrated geographically, but it was more substantial than has often been supposed, and its destruction left a real vacuum."[39]

Likewise, Neil Rushton gives substantial evidence that the monasteries were indeed careful to direct their aid to the truly needy. And when they did not, explains Barbara Harvey in her revisionist study *Living and Dying in England, 1100–1540,* the culprit was not the conservatism or soft-heartedness of the monks but rather the constraints that donors placed on how the monasteries were to disburse their funds. Some donors endowed a distribution of alms in their wills. In other words, they gave a monastery a sum of money that was to be distributed to the needy as alms. But while part of the purpose of such endowments was to alleviate the suffering of the poor, they were also intended to reach a great many people, in order to win the prayers of as many people as possible for the repose of the soul of the benefactor. Such endowments therefore tended to encourage indiscriminate almsgiving. But over time the monasteries did tend to be more cautious and discriminating with their ordinary revenues.[40]

During the several centuries following the death of Charlemagne in 814, much of the care of the poor, until then mostly the province of the local parish church, began to migrate to the monasteries. In the words of France's King Louis IX, the monasteries were the *patrimonio pauperum*—the patrimony of the poor; indeed it had been customary ever since the fourth century to speak of all of the Church's possessions as the *patrimonio pauperum*. But the monasteries distinguished themselves in particular. "In every district," according to one scholar, "alike on towering mountain and in lowly valley, arose monasteries which formed the centers of the organized religious life of the neighborhood, maintained schools, provided models for agriculture, industry, pisciculture, and forestry, sheltered the traveler, relieved the poor, reared the orphans, cared for the sick, and were havens of refuge for all who were weighed down by spiritual or corporal misery. For centuries they were the centers of all religious, charitable, and cultural activity."[41] Monasteries distributed alms daily to those in need. W. E. H. Lecky wrote of monastic charity: "As time rolled on, charity assumed many forms, and every monastery became a center from which it radiated. By the monks the nobles were overawed, the poor protected, the sick tended, travelers sheltered, prisoners ransomed, the remotest spheres of suffering explored. During the darkest period of the Middle Ages, the monks found a refuge for pilgrims amid the horrors of the Alpine snows."[42] The Benedictines, Cistercians, and Premonstratensians, as well as the mendicant orders, the Franciscans and Dominicans later on, distinguished themselves in their attention to charitable work.

Poor travelers could rely on monastic hospitality, and the records indicate that even well-to-do travelers were often made welcome as well, in conformity with Saint Benedict's instruction in his Rule that the visitor was to be received as the monks would receive Christ. But the monks did not merely wait for the poor to come their way in the course of their travels. They sought out the poor who lived in the surrounding area. Lanfranc, for example, gave the almoner (the distributor of alms) the responsibility of discovering the sick and the poor near the monastery and providing them with monastic alms. In some cases, we read of the poor being given lodging, at times even indefinitely, in the monastic almonry.[43]

In addition to more institutionalized giving, the monks also provided food for the poor from their own leftovers. Gilbert of Sempringham, whose own leftovers were rather substantial, placed them on a plate he called "Lord Jesus' dish," in clear view of his fellow monks and with the obvious intent of urging them to emulate his generosity. It was also traditional for food and drink to be set out in commemoration of deceased monks, and distributed to the poor at the conclusion of the meal. This practice would be observed for as few as thirty days or as much as a full year following a monk's death—and in the case of an abbot, sometimes even in perpetuity.[44]

Just as the sixteenth-century attack on the monasteries by the Crown debilitated the network of charity that those institutions had supported, the French Revolution's eighteenth-century attack on the Church likewise struck at the source of so much good work. In November 1789, the revolutionary French government nationalized (that is, confiscated) Church property. The archbishop of Aix en Provence warned that such an act of theft threatened educational and welfare provisions for the French people. He was right, of course. In 1847, France had 47 percent fewer hospitals than in the year of the confiscation, and in 1799 the 50,000 students enrolled in universities ten years earlier had dwindled to a mere 12,000.[45]

Although you'd never know it from reading the standard Western civilization text, the Catholic Church revolutionized the practice of charitable giving, in both its spirit and its application. The results speak for themselves: previously unheard-of amounts of charitable giving and systematic, institutionalized care of widows, orphans, the poor, and the sick.

*Chapter Ten*

# The Church and Western Law

I n most Western countries, if a person is convicted of murder and sentenced to death, but goes insane between the moment of sentencing and the moment of execution, he is kept alive until he regains his sanity and only then is he executed. The reason for this unusual proviso is entirely theological: Only if the man is sane can he make a good confession, receive forgiveness for his sins, and hope to save his soul. Cases like this have led legal scholar Harold Berman to observe that modern Western legal systems "are a secular residue of religious attitudes and assumptions which historically found expression first in the liturgy and rituals and doctrine of the church and thereafter in the institutions and concepts and values of the law. When these historical roots are not understood, many parts of the law appear to lack any underlying source of validity."[1]

Professor Berman's scholarly work, particularly his magisterial *Law and Revolution: The Formation of the Western Legal Tradition*, has documented the influence of the Church on the development of Western law. "Western concepts of law," he argues, "are in their origins, and therefore in their nature, intimately bound up with distinctively Western theological and liturgical concepts of the atonement and of the sacraments."[2]

Our story begins in the early centuries of the Church. The first millennium, following the emperor Constantine's Edict of Milan (which extended toleration to Christianity in 313), saw a frequent conflation of the roles of Church and state, often to the detriment of the former. To be sure, Saint Ambrose, the great fourth-century bishop of Milan, once proclaimed, "Palaces belong to the emperor, churches to the priesthood," and Pope Gelasius famously formulated what became known as the "two swords" doctrine, according to which the world was ordered by two powers, one temporal and the other secular. In practice, though, this line was often blurred, and secular authority came to exercise more and more authority over sacred matters.

In 325, Constantine was already issuing a call for what became the Council of Nicaea, the first ecumenical council in Church history, to deal with the divisive issue of Arianism, a heresy that denied the divinity of Christ. Succeeding centuries saw far more involvement in Church affairs by secular rulers. The kings (and later emperors) of the Franks appointed Church personnel and even instructed them in matters of sacred doctrine. The same would later be true of French and English monarchs, as well as of other rulers of northern and eastern Europe. Charlemagne himself convened and presided over an important Church council at Frankfurt in 794. By the eleventh century the king-emperors of the German lands were appointing not only bishops but also popes.

In the ninth and tenth centuries, the problem of lay control of Church institutions grew particularly intense. The collapse of central authority in Western Europe during those centuries, as monarchs found themselves unable to cope with the waves of

Viking, Magyar, and Muslim invasions, created opportunities for powerful landholders to extend their authority over churches, monasteries, and even bishoprics. Thus abbots of monasteries, parish priests, and even bishops were being appointed by laymen instead of by the Church.

Hildebrand, as Pope Saint Gregory VII was known before his elevation to the papacy, belonged to the party of radical reformers who sought not merely to persuade secular rulers to appoint good men but, more fundamentally, to exclude laymen from the selection of Church personnel altogether. The Gregorian Reform, which began several decades before the pontificate of the man after whom it is named, originated as an effort to improve the moral level of the clergy by insisting upon the observance of clerical celibacy and to abolish the practice of simony (the buying and selling of Church offices). Problems arising from efforts to reform these aspects of Church life brought the Gregorian party face to face with the real problem: lay domination of the Church. Pope Gregory had little chance of reversing the decadence within the Church if he lacked the power to name the Church's bishops—a power that in the eleventh century was being exercised by the various European monarchs instead. Likewise, as long as laymen could name parish priests and abbots of monasteries, the multiplication of spiritually unfit candidates for these offices would only continue.

## THE SEPARATION OF CHURCH AND STATE

*Pope Gregory took a dramatic step* when he described the king as simply and solely a layman, with no more of a religious function than any other layman. In the past, even Church reformers had taken for granted that while the appointment of Church officials by lesser secular rulers was indeed wrong, the king was an exception. The king was said to be a sacred figure with religious rights and responsibilities; some had even gone so far as to propose that the consecration of a king was a sacrament (a ritual that, like baptism and Holy Communion, imparted God's sanctifying grace to the soul of the recipient). For Gregory, though, the king was just another layman, a non-ordained figure who had no right to intervene in the affairs of the Church. By extension, the state that the king ruled likewise possessed no powers over the Church.

The Gregorian Reform clarified the boundaries that must separate Church and state if the Church is to enjoy the liberty she needs to carry out her mission. Shortly thereafter, we find legal codes being drawn up in both Church and state, in which the powers and responsibilities of each in post-Hildebrand Europe are set down and made explicit. As the first systematic body of law in medieval Europe, canon law (that is, Church law) became the model for the various secular legal systems that would now begin to emerge.

Prior to the development of canon law in the twelfth and thirteenth centuries, nothing resembling a modern legal system existed anywhere in Western Europe. Since the advent of the barbarian kingdoms in the western Roman Empire, law had been intimately bound up with custom and kinship, and was not thought of as a distinct branch of learning and analysis independent of these things and capable of discerning general rules by which human beings could be bound. Canon law, too, had been in just such a state as late as the eleventh century. It had never been systematically codified, and consisted instead of scattered remarks from ecumenical councils, penitentials (books that assigned penances for sins), popes, individual bishops, the Bible, the Church fathers, and the like. Much of Church law was regional in nature, moreover, and was not universally applicable throughout Christendom as a whole.

The twelfth century began to change all that. The key treatise of canon law was the work of the monk Gratian, called *A Concordance of Discordant Canons* (also known as the *Decretum Gratiani*, or simply the *Decretum*), written around 1140. It is an enormous work, both in size and scope. It also constituted a historic milestone. According to Berman, it was "the first comprehensive and systematic legal treatise in the history of the West, and perhaps in the history of mankind—if by 'comprehensive' is meant the attempt to embrace virtually the entire law of a given polity, and if by 'systematic' is meant the express effort to present that law as a single body, in which all the parts are viewed as interacting to form a whole."[3] In a world in which custom rather than statutory law ruled so much of both the ecclesiastical and secular domains, Gratian and other canonists developed criteria, based on reason and conscience, for determining the validity of given customs, and held up the idea of a pre-political natural law to which any legitimate custom had to conform. Scholars of Church law showed the barbarized West how to take a patchwork of custom, statutory law, and countless other sources, and produce from them a coherent legal order whose structure was internally consistent and in which previously existing contradictions were synthesized or otherwise resolved. Such ideas would bear important fruit not only in Church law, as in the work of Gratian himself, but also in the secular legal systems that would be codified in its wake. Catholic legal thinkers "took a variety of texts—the Old Testament, the Gospel, 'The Philosopher'—Aristotle, 'The Jurist'—Justinian, the Church fathers, Saint Augustine, the Church councils; and by the use of the scholastic method and of a natural-law theory they were able to create out of these various sources, as well as out of the existing customs of their contemporary ecclesiastical and secular society, a coherent and rational legal science."[4]

Twelfth-century European jurists, in the process of assembling modern legal systems for the emerging states of Western Europe, were thus indebted to canon law as a model. Equally important was the *content* of canon law, whose scope was so sweeping that it contributed to the development of Western law in such areas as marriage, property, and inheritance. Berman cites "the introduction of rational trial procedures to replace magical mechanical modes of proof by ordeals of fire and water, by battles of champions, and by ritual oaths [all of which had played a central role in Germanic folklaw]; the insistence upon consent as the foundation of marriage and upon wrongful intent as the basis of crime; the development of equity to protect the poor and helpless against the rich and powerful."[5]

At the time that canon lawyers and Catholic jurists in the medieval universities sought to establish legal systems for Church and state, they were faced with an unfortunate fact: As late as the eleventh century, the peoples of Europe still lived under a barbaric mode of law. These scholars faced a situation in which "the prevailing law remained the law of blood feud, of trial by battle and by ordeals of fire and water and by compurgation."[6] We have already seen what trial by ordeal amounted to in practice: holding up people accused of crimes to tests devoid of anything like modern or rational rules of evidence. The rational procedures called for by canon law thus hastened the end of these primitive methods. Law is one of the important areas of Western civilization in which we are deeply indebted to the ancient Romans. But where the Church did not innovate she restored—a contribution often equally important—and her own canon law, with its rules of evidence and rational procedures, recalled the best of the Roman legal order in a milieu in which innocence and guilt were determined all too often by means of superstition.

The canon law of marriage held that a valid marriage required the free consent of both the man and the woman, and that a marriage could be held invalid if it took place under duress or if one of the parties entered into the marriage on the basis of a mistake regarding either the identity or some important quality of the other person. "Here," writes Berman, "were the foundations not only of the modern law of marriage but also of certain basic elements of modern contract law, namely, the concept of free will and related concepts of mistake, duress, and fraud."[7] And by implementing these crucial principles in law, Catholic jurists were at last able to overcome the common practice of infant marriage that owed its origins to barbarian custom.[8] Barbarian practice thus gave way to Catholic principle. Through the codification and promulgation of a systematic body of law, the salutary principles of Catholic belief were able to make their way into the daily practices of European peoples who had adopted Catholicism but who had all too often failed to draw out all its implications. These principles remain central to the modern legal orders under which Westerners, and more and more non-Westerners, continue to live.

When we examine the rules by which canon law sought to determine the criminality of a particular act, we discover legal principles that have since become standard in all modern Western legal systems. Canon lawyers were concerned with the intent of an act, with various kinds of intent, and with the moral implications of various kinds of causal connections. With regard to the last point, canonists considered examples such as this: Someone throws a stone to frighten his companion, but in the course of avoiding it the companion runs into a rock and causes himself great injury. He seeks medical assistance, but a doctor's negligence causes him to die. To what extent was the throwing of the stone a cause of the man's death? This was the kind of sophisticated legal question for which canon lawyers sought an answer.[9]

The same canonists introduced the equally modern principle that extenuating factors could exempt someone from legal liability. Thus, if one were insane, asleep, mistaken, or intoxicated, his apparently criminal actions might not be actionable. But these mitigating factors could excuse someone from legal liability only if as a result of them the accused could not have known that he was doing something wrong, and only if he had not wrongfully brought one or more of these conditions upon himself, as in the case of someone who purposely makes himself drunk.[10]

To be sure, ancient Roman law had distinguished between deliberate and accidental actions, and so had helped to introduce the idea of intent into the law. The eleventh- and twelfth-century canonists, as with the contemporaneous architects of the emerging legal systems of the secular states of Western Europe, drew upon the newly rediscovered law code that had been drawn up during the reign of the sixth-century emperor Justinian. But they made important contributions and refinements of their own and introduced them into European societies that had known nothing of these distinctions during the numerous centuries under barbarian influence.

The secular legal systems we have been describing here would also bear the distinct imprint of Catholic theology. For this part of our story we must examine the work of Saint Anselm of Canterbury (1033–1109).

Saint Anselm belongs to the early history of Scholasticism, that enormously significant and influential chapter of Western intellectual history that reached its height in the work of Saint

Thomas Aquinas (1225–1274) but which persisted through the sixteenth and seventeenth centuries. We have already seen something of Saint Anselm's devotion to reason in the brief overview of his ontological proof for the existence of God. That proof, an a priori argument for God's existence, drew nothing from divine revelation and rested instead on the power of reason alone.

But it is to Saint Anselm's work *Cur Deus Homo* that we turn in our discussion of the Western legal tradition, since that tradition was deeply influenced by this classic discussion of the purpose of the Incarnation and crucifixion of Christ. In that book, Saint Anselm was concerned with demonstrating on the basis of human reason why it was fitting that God should have become man in the person of Jesus Christ, and why Christ's crucifixion— as opposed to some other method of redemption—was an indispensable ingredient in the redemption of mankind after the Fall and the expulsion of Adam and Eve from paradise. In particular, the author wished to address the natural objection: Why could God not simply have forgiven the human race for this original transgression? Why could he not have reopened the gates of Heaven to the descendants of Adam by means of a simple declaration of forgiveness, a gratuitous act of grace? Why, in other words, was the crucifixion necessary?[11]

Anselm's answer went as follows.[12] God originally created man in order that he might enjoy eternal blessedness. Man in a certain sense frustrated God's intention by rebelling against Him and introducing sin into the world. In order for the demands of justice to be satisfied, man must be punished for his sin against God. Yet his offense against the all-good God is so great that no punishment he might suffer could offer Him adequate recompense. Whatever punishment he did suffer, moreover, would have to be so severe that at the very least he would have to forfeit eternal blessedness, but since eternal blessedness was God's plan for man in the first place, such a punishment would undermine God's purposes yet again.

The reason that God cannot simply forgive man's sin in the absence of some form of punishment is that when man rebelled against God he disturbed the moral order of the universe. That moral order must be repaired. God's honor must be restored, and that restoration cannot occur so long as the rupture of the moral order that occurred as a result of man's rebellion remains in existence.

Since man owes restitution to God but is incapable of making it, while God could vindicate His own honor through a gratuitous act (but should not), the only way that atonement for original sin can take place is through the mediation of a God-Man. Thus does Anselm provide a rational account for the need for the atoning death of Jesus Christ.

The law of crimes as it emerged in Western civilization did so amid a religious milieu deeply influenced by Saint Anselm's exposition of the doctrine of the atonement. That exposition rested fundamentally on the idea that a violation of the law was an offense against justice and against the moral order itself, that such a violation required a punishment if the moral order were to be repaired, and that the punishment should befit the nature and extent of the violation.

The atonement, according to Anselm, had to be carried out the way it was because by violating God's law man had disturbed justice itself, and justice required the infliction of some punishment in order to vindicate the moral order. With the passage of time, it became common to think not just about Adam and Eve and original sin but also about the perpetrator of crime in the temporal realm: Having violated justice in the abstract, he had to be subject to some punishment if the order of justice were to be restored. Crime became in large measure depersonalized, as criminal actions came to be viewed less as actions directed at particular persons (victims) and more as violations of the abstract principle of justice, and whose disturbance of the moral order could be rectified through the application of punishment.[13]

> Contracts, it was said, must be kept, and if they were not, a price must be paid for their breach. Torts must be remedied by damages equivalent to the injury. Property rights must be restored by those who had violated them. These and similar principles became so deeply embedded in the consciousness—indeed, in the sacred values—of Western society that it became hard to imagine a legal order founded on different kinds of principles and values. Yet contemporary non-Western cultures do have legal orders founded on different kinds of principles and values, and so did European culture prior to the eleventh and twelfth centuries. In some legal orders, ideas of fate and honor prevail, of vengeance and reconciliation. In others, ideas of covenant and community dominate; in still others, ideas of deterrence and rehabilitation.[14]

## THE ORIGINS OF NATURAL RIGHTS

*The Church's influence on the legal* systems and legal thought of the West extends also to the development of the idea of natural rights. For a long time, scholars took for granted that the idea of natural rights, universal moral claims possessed by all individuals, emerged more or less spontaneously in the seventeenth century. Thanks to the work of Brian Tierney, one of the world's great authorities on medieval thought, that thesis can no longer be sustained. When seventeenth-century philosophers set forth theories of natural rights, they were building upon an already existing tradition dating as far back as the Catholic scholars of the twelfth century.[15] The idea of rights is one of the most distinctive aspects of Western civilization, and scholars are increasingly coming to acknowledge that it, too, comes to us from the Church. Prior to Tierney's work, few people, scholars included, would have supposed that the origins of the idea of natural rights dated to twelfth-century commentators on the *Decretum*, Gratian's famous compendium of the canon law of the Catholic Church. But it is with these scholars, known as the decretists, that the tradition in fact began.

The twelfth century exhibited great interest in and concern for the rights of certain institutions and certain categories of people. Beginning with the investiture controversy of the eleventh century, kings and popes engaged in lively exchanges over their rights vis-à-vis one another, a debate that was still alive and well over two centuries later in the pamphlet war that broke out between supporters of Pope Boniface VIII and King Philip the Fair of France in their seminal Church-state struggle. The lords and vassals of feudal Europe existed within a relationship of rights and obligations. The towns and cities that began to dot the European landscape with the renewal of urban life in the eleventh century insisted on their rights against other political authorities.[16]

To be sure, these were not assertions of what we would call *natural* rights, since in each case they involved rights of particular groups rather than rights that inhered in all human beings by nature. But it was in the context of a culture that frequently asserted the concept of rights that the canonists and other legal thinkers of the twelfth century began to derive the vocabulary and the conceptual apparatus that we associate with modern natural rights theories.

It happened this way. The various sources that were cited in the early chapters of Gratian's *Decretum*—which appealed to everything from the Bible to the Church fathers, Church councils of varying import, papal statements, and the like—made frequent reference to the term *ius naturale*, or natural law. These sources, however, defined the term variously, and in ways that at times seemed to contradict each other. Commentators thus sought to sort out the various meanings that the term could hold. According to Tierney:

> The important point for us is that, in explaining the various possible senses of *ius naturale*, the jurists found a new meaning that was not really present in their ancient texts. Reading the old texts with minds formed in their new, more personalist, rights-based culture, they added a new definition. Sometimes they defined natural right in a subjective sense as a power, force, ability, or faculty inhering in human persons.... [O]nce the old concept of natural right was defined in this subjective way the argument could easily lead to the rightful rules of conduct prescribed by natural law or to *the licit claims and powers inhering in individuals that we call natural rights.*[17]

The canonists, argues Tierney, "were coming to see that an adequate concept of natural justice had to include a concept of individual rights."[18]

Specific examples of natural rights soon began to be identified. One was the right to appear and defend oneself against charges in a court of law. Medieval jurists denied that this right was merely *granted* to individuals by government statute, insisting instead that it was a *natural right* of individuals that derived from the universal moral law. More and more, the idea gained currency that individuals possessed certain subjective powers, or natural rights, by virtue of being human. No ruler could abridge them. As historian Kenneth Pennington explains, by 1300, European jurists "had developed a sturdy language of rights derived from natural law. During the period from 1150 to 1300, they defined the rights of property, self-defense, non-Christians, marriage, and procedure as being rooted in natural, not positive, law. By placing these rights squarely within the framework of natural law, the jurists could and did argue that these rights could not be taken away by the human prince. The prince had no jurisdiction over rights based on natural law; consequently these rights were inalienable."[19] These all sound like fairly modern principles. But they come to us from medieval Catholic thinkers, who yet again established the crucial foundations of Western civilization as we know it.

Pope Innocent IV considered the question of whether fundamental rights of property and of establishing lawful governments belonged only to Christians, or whether these things rightly belonged to all men. At the time, an exaggerated pro-papalist opinion could be found in some circles, according to which the pope, as God's representative on earth, was lord of the whole world, and therefore that legitimate authority and ownership could be exercised only by those who recognized papal authority. Innocent rejected this position, and instead held that "ownership, possession and jurisdiction can belong to infidels licitly...for these things were made not only for the faithful but for every rational creature."[20] This text would be cited to great effect by later Catholic rights theorists.

Rights language and the philosophy of rights continued to develop with the passage of time. Particularly significant was the debate that ensued in the early fourteenth century over the

Franciscans, an order of mendicant friars founded in the early thirteenth century that shunned worldly goods and embraced lives of
poverty. With the death of Saint Francis in 1226 and the continuing expansion of the order he founded, some were in favor of mod-
erating the traditional Franciscan insistence on absolute poverty,
often considered unreasonable for such a large, far-flung order. An
extreme wing of the Franciscans, known as the "Spirituals,"
refused all compromise, insisting that their lives of absolute
poverty were a faithful replication of the lives of Christ and the
apostles and therefore amounted to the highest and most perfect
form of the Christian life. What began as a controversy over
whether Christ and the apostles had in fact really shunned all
property then developed into a profoundly fruitful and important
debate over the nature of property that raised some of the central
questions that would dominate the treatises of seventeenth-
century rights theorists.[21]

What really solidified the natural-rights tradition within the
West was the European discovery of America and the questions
that Spanish Scholastic theologians raised with regard to the
rights of the inhabitants of these new lands, a story we previously
explored. (These theologians frequently quoted the statement of
Innocent IV, above.) In developing the idea that the American
natives possessed natural rights that Europeans had to respect,
sixteenth-century theologians were building upon a much older
tradition of discourse whose origins lay in the work of twelfth-
century canon lawyers.

Thus it was in the Church's canon law that the West saw the
first example of a modern legal system, and it was in light of that
model that the modern Western legal tradition took shape. Likewise, the Western law of crimes was deeply influenced not only
by legal principles enshrined in canon law but also by Catholic

theological ideas, particularly the doctrine of the atonement as developed by Saint Anselm. Finally, the very idea of natural rights, for a long time assumed to have emerged fully formed from liberal thinkers of the seventeenth and eighteenth centuries, in fact derives from Catholic canonists, popes, university professors, and philosophers. The more scholars investigate Western law, the greater the imprint of the Catholic Church on our civilization turns out to be, and the more persuasive her claim as its architect.

*Chapter Eleven*

# The Church and Western Morality

*Not surprisingly,* Western standards of morality have been decisively shaped by the Catholic Church. Many of the most important principles of the Western moral tradition derive from the distinctly Catholic idea of the sacredness of human life. The insistence on the uniqueness and value of each person, by virtue of the immortal soul, was nowhere to be found in the ancient world. Indeed, the poor, weak, or sickly were typically treated with contempt by non-Catholics and sometimes even abandoned altogether. That, as we have seen, is what made Catholic charity so significant, and something new in the Western world.

Catholics spoke out against, and eventually abolished, the practice of infanticide, which had been considered morally acceptable even in ancient Greece and Rome. Plato, for example, had said that a poor man whose sickness made him unable to work any longer should be left to die. Seneca wrote: "We drown children who at birth are weakly and abnormal."[1] Deformed male children and many healthy female children (inconvenient in patriarchal societies) were simply abandoned. As a result, the male population of the ancient Roman world outnumbered the female population by some 30 percent.[2] The Church could never accept such behavior.

We see the Church's commitment to the sacred nature of human life in the Western condemnation of suicide, a practice that had its defenders in the ancient world. Aristotle had criticized the practice of suicide, but others among the ancients, particularly the Stoics, favored suicide as an acceptable method of escaping physical pain or emotional frustration. A number of well-known Stoics themselves committed suicide. What better proof of one's detachment from the world than control of the moment of departure?

In *The City of God*, Saint Augustine dismissed the elements of pagan antiquity that portrayed suicide as somehow noble:

> [G]reatness of spirit is not the right term to apply to one who has killed himself because he has lacked strength to endure hardships, or another's wrongdoing. In fact we detect weakness in a mind which cannot bear physical oppression, or the stupid opinion of the mob; we rightly ascribe greatness to a spirit that has the strength to endure a life of misery instead of running away from it, and to despise the judgment of men . . . in comparison with the pure light of a good conscience.[3]

The example of Christ, Augustine continued, likewise forbade such behavior. Christ could have urged suicide upon his followers in order to escape the punishments of their persecutors, but He did not. "If He did not advise this way of quitting this life," Augustine reasoned, "although He promised to prepare eternal dwellings for them after their departure, it is clear that this course is not allowed to those who worship the one true God."[4]

Saint Thomas Aquinas likewise took up the question of suicide, in the treatise on justice in his *Summa Theologiae*. Two of
his three principal arguments against suicide rest are based in reason, defensible apart from divine revelation, but he concludes
with a rationale that finds suicide to be absolutely forbidden on
specifically Catholic grounds:

> [L]ife is a gift divinely given to man and subject to the power
> that gives life and takes it away. Therefore, one who takes his
> own life sins against God, much as one who kills another's ser-
> vant sins against the master whose servant it was, or as one sins
> who usurps judgment in a matter not in his jurisdiction. To
> God alone pertains the judgment of death and of life, according
> to Deuteronomy 32:39: "I will kill and I will make live."[5]

Although perhaps not a simple thing to measure, one might
well argue that the Church had particular success in instilling an
aversion to suicide among the Catholic faithful. Early in the
twentieth century, one scholar pointed to the sharp difference in
suicide rates between the Catholic and Protestant cantons of
Switzerland, as well as to the very low rate in heavily Catholic
Ireland, a land of so much tragedy and misfortune.[6]

Likewise, it was the Church and the teachings of Christ that
helped to abolish the gladiatorial contests, in which men fought
each other to the death as a form of entertainment. Such trivial-
ization of human life could not have been more at odds with the
Catholic emphasis on the dignity and worth of each individual.
In his *Daily Life in Ancient Rome*, Jerome Carcopino states flatly
that "the butcheries of the arena were stopped at the command
of Christian emperors." Indeed, they had been suppressed in
the western half of the empire by the late fourth century, and
in the eastern half by the early fifth. W. E. H. Lecky put this

development into perspective: "There is scarcely any single reform so important in the moral history of mankind as the suppression of the gladiatorial shows, a feat that must be almost exclusively ascribed to the Christian church."[7]

The Church was equally critical of what eventually became the widespread practice of dueling. Those who sanctioned the practice alleged that it actually discouraged violence by institutionalizing it, developing codes of honor surrounding its proper use, and providing for witnesses. This was better than, say, ceaseless blood feuds carried out in the dead of night or with reckless disregard for human life. Since only utopians believed violence could ever be fully eradicated, it was thought better to channel it in the least socially disruptive ways. Such was the rationale for dueling.

Yet there was still something off-putting about men using swords and pistols to vindicate their honor. Not surprisingly, the Church applied sanctions against those who engaged in the practice. The Council of Trent (1545–1563), which dealt primarily with matters of Church reform and the clarification of Catholic doctrine in the wake of the Protestant Reformation, in effect expelled duelers from the Church, cutting them off from the sacraments and forbidding them Church burials. Pope Benedict XIV reaffirmed these penalties in the mid–eighteenth century, and Pope Pius IX made clear that not only the duelers themselves but also any witnesses and accomplices incurred the penalties.

Pope Leo XIII continued the Church's opposition to the practice at a time when secular laws against dueling were being disregarded. He summed up the religious principles that had informed Catholic condemnation of dueling for centuries:

Clearly, divine law, both that which is known by the light of reason and that which is revealed in Sacred Scripture, strictly forbids anyone, outside of public cause, to kill or wound a man unless compelled to do so in self-defense. Those, moreover, who provoke a private combat or accept one when challenged, deliberately and unnecessarily intend to take a life or at least wound an adversary. Furthermore, divine law prohibits anyone from risking his life rashly, exposing himself to grave and evident danger when not constrained by duty or generous charity. In the very nature of the duel, there is plainly blind temerity and contempt for life. There can be, therefore, no obscurity or doubt in anyone's mind that those who engage in battle privately and singly take upon themselves a double guilt, that of another's destruction and the deliberate risk of their own lives.

The reasons given by duelers for their contests were, said the pope, ludicrously inadequate. At root they were based on a simple desire for vengeance. "It is, to be sure, the desire of revenge that impels passionate and arrogant men to seek satisfaction," Leo wrote. "God commands all men to love each other in brotherly love and forbids them to ever violate anyone; he condemns revenge as a deadly sin and reserves to himself the right of expiation. If people could restrain their passion and submit to God, they would easily abandon the monstrous custom of dueling."[8]

Another important way in which the Catholic Church has shaped Western conceptions of morality involves the tradition of just war. To be sure, the world of classical antiquity took up this issue to one degree or another, and Cicero discussed the rights and wrongs of war. But although the ancient philosophers did refer to particular wars as just or unjust, they did not erect a full-fledged theory of the just war. "Neither in Plato nor in Aristotle," attests Ernest Fortin, "do we find anything that quite compares with, say, the famous question 'On War' in Thomas Aquinas' *Summa Theologiae*." Thus the development of a distinct intellectual tradition in the West whereby the moral rectitude of wars is held up to scrutiny according to certain fixed principles has been the work of the Catholic Church. It is true that Cicero advanced something like a theory of the just war in his evaluation of the history of Rome's own conflicts. Yet the Church fathers who inherited the idea from him expanded it into a tool of moral reckoning far more ambitious in scope. Fortin adds that "one has to admit that the problem of warfare has always been fraught with greater urgency for the Christian theologian than it was for any of the philosophers of classical antiquity," particularly given "the force of the biblical teaching concerning the sacredness of life."[9]

The most significant early Catholic treatment of the issue of war and the moral criteria necessary for a war to be considered just appears in the writings of Saint Augustine. In his view, a just war was "justified only by the injustice of an aggressor, and that injustice ought to be a source of grief to any good man, because it is human injustice." Although Augustine did not expressly include the immunity of noncombatants in his conception of the just war, as did later contributors to the theory, he appears to have taken for granted that civilians should be spared the violence of a belligerent army. Thus when Augustine warned against being motivated by revenge and insisted that a just war could not be waged on the basis of mere human passion, he was insisting on a certain internal disposition in the soldier that would militate against the indiscriminate use of force.[10]

Saint Thomas Aquinas memorably addressed the issue as well, citing three conditions that had to be met in order for a war to claim the mantle of justice:

> In order for a war to be just, three things are necessary. First, the authority of the sovereign by whose command the war is to be waged. For it is not the business of a private individual to declare war.

Secondly, a just cause is required, namely that those who are attacked, should be attacked because they deserve it on account of some fault. Wherefore Augustine says, "A just war is wont to be described as one that avenges wrongs, when a nation or state has to be punished, for refusing to make amends for the wrongs inflicted by its subjects, or to restore what it has seized unjustly."

Thirdly, it is necessary that the belligerents should have a rightful intention, so that they intend the advancement of good, or the avoidance of evil....For it may happen that the war is declared by the legitimate authority, and for a just cause, and yet be rendered unlawful through a wicked intention. Hence Augustine says, "The passion for inflicting harm, the cruel thirst for vengeance, an unpacific and relentless spirit, the fever of revolt, the lust of power, and such like things, all these are rightly condemned in war."[11]

This tradition continued to evolve into the later Middle Ages and into the modern period, particularly with the work of the sixteenth-century Spanish Scholastics. Father Francisco de Vitoria, who played a major role in establishing the rudiments of international law, also devoted himself to the question of the just war. In *De Jure Belli*, he identified three major rules of war, as explained by Catholic historians Thomas A. Massaro and Thomas A. Shannon:

First Canon: Assuming that a prince has authority to make war, he should first of all not go seeking occasions and causes of war, but should, if possible, live in peace with all men as St. Paul enjoins on us.

Second Canon: When war for a just cause has broken out it must not be waged so as to ruin the people to whom it is directed, but only so as to obtain one's rights and the defense of one's country and in order that from that war peace and security may in time result.

Third Canon: When victory has been won, victory should be utilized with moderation and Christian humility, and the victor ought to deem that he is sitting as judge between two states, the one which has been wronged and the one which has done the wrong, so that it will be as judge and not as accuser that he will deliver the judgment whereby the injured state can obtain satisfaction, and this, so far as possible, should involve the offending state in the least degree of calamity and misfortune, the offending individuals being chastised within lawful limits.[12]

Father Francisco Suárez likewise summarized the conditions for a just war:

In order that war may be justly waged, certain conditions are to be observed and these may be brought under three heads. First, it must be waged by a legitimate power. Second, its cause must be just and right. Third, just methods should be used, that is, equity in the beginning of the war and the prosecution of it and in victory.... The reason of the general conclusion is that although war, in itself, is not an evil, yet on account of the many ills which it brings in its train, it is to be numbered among those undertakings which are often wrongly done. And thus it needs many circumstances to make it honest.[13]

Nicolo Machiavelli's book *The Prince* was a purely secular examination of politics.[14] His view of the relationship between morality and the state, which still exerts influence over Western political thought, helps us to appreciate the significance and importance of just-war theory. In the Machiavellian scheme of things, the state could be judged by nothing and no one, and was accountable to no higher authority. No pope or moral code was permitted to stand in judgment of the state's behavior. This was one reason that Machiavelli so disliked Catholicism; it believed that states, not just individuals, were subject to moral correction. Politics for Machiavelli became, as one writer put it, "a game, like chess, and the removal of a political pawn, though it comprised fifty thousand men, was no more disquieting than the removal from the board of an ivory piece."[15]

It was precisely in order to counter that kind of thinking that the just-war tradition, and particularly the contributions of the sixteenth-century Scholastics, developed in the first place. According to the Catholic Church, no one, not even the state, was exempt from the demands of morality. In subsequent centuries just-war theory has proven an indispensable tool for proper moral reflection, and philosophers working in this tradition in our own day have drawn from these traditional principles to meet the specific challenges of the twenty-first century.

---

Our ancient sources inform us that sexual morality had reached a particularly degraded point at the time of the Church's appearance in history. Widespread promiscuity, wrote the satirist Juvenal, had caused the Romans to lose the goddess Chastity. Ovid observed that sexual practices in his day had grown especially perverse, even sadistic. Similar testimonies to the state of marital fidelity and sexual immorality around the time of Christ can be found in Catullus, Martial, and Suetonius. Caesar Augustus attempted to curb this kind of immorality through the law, though law can rarely reform a people who have already succumbed to the allures of immediate gratification. By the early second century, Tacitus contended that a chaste wife was a rare phenomenon.[16]

The Church taught that intimate relations were to be confined to husband and wife. Even Edward Gibbon, who blamed Christianity for the fall of the Roman Empire in the West, was compelled to admit: "The dignity of marriage was restored by the Christians." The second-century Greek physician Galen, so struck by the rectitude of Christian sexual behavior, described them as "so far advanced in self-discipline and...intense desire to attain moral excellence that they are in no way inferior to true philosophers."[17]

Adultery, according to the Church, was not confined to a wife's infidelity to her husband, as the ancient world so often had it, but also extended to a husband's unfaithfulness to his wife. The Church's influence in this area was of great historical significance, which is why Edward Westermarck, an accomplished historian of the institution of marriage, credited Christian influence with the equalization of the sin of adultery.[18]

These principles account in part for why women formed so much of the Christian population of the early centuries of the Church. So numerous were female Christians that the Romans used to dismiss Christianity as a religion for women. Part of the attraction that the faith held for women was that the Church sanctified marriage, elevating it to the level of a sacrament, and prohibited divorce (which really meant that men could not leave their wives with nothing to go marry another woman). Women also attained substantially more autonomy thanks to Catholicism. "Women found protection in the teachings of the Church," writes philosopher Robert Phillips, "and were permitted to form communities of religious who would be self-governing—

something unheard of in any culture of the ancient world.... Look at the catalogue of saints filled up with women. Where in the world were women able to run their own schools, convents, colleges, hospitals and orphanages, outside of Catholicism?"[19]

One aspect of ancient Greek philosophy that constituted a bridge to Catholic thought is the suggestion that there is a certain kind of life that befits a chimpanzee, and one that befits a human being. Possessed of reason, the human being is not condemned to act on mere instinct. He is capable of moral reflection, an ability that must always elude even the cleverest specimens of the animal kingdom. Should he fail to exercise this faculty, then he never lives up to his own nature. If he will not engage in intellectual activity or serious moral reckoning when it comes to his own behavior, then what is the point of his being human in the first place? If one's guiding principle is to do whatever brings immediate pleasure, one is in a sense no different from a beast.

The Church teaches that a life truly befitting humanity requires the assistance of divine grace. Even pagan Romans perceived something of the degraded condition of man: "What a contemptible thing is man," wrote Seneca, "if he fail to rise above the human condition!" The grace of God could help him do so. Here the Church has held out the examples of the saints, who demonstrate that lives of heroic virtue are possible when human beings let themselves decrease so that Christ may increase.

The Church teaches that a good life is not simply one in which our external actions are beyond reproach. Christ insists that it is not enough merely to refrain from murder or adultery; not only must the body not yield to such crimes, but the soul must also keep from leaning toward them. Not only should we not steal from our neighbor, but we should also not allow ourselves to indulge in envious thoughts about his possessions. Although we are certainly permitted to hate what is evil—sin, for example, or Satan himself—we are to divorce ourselves from the kind of anger and hatred that only corrode the soul. We are not only not to commit adultery, but we are also not to entertain impure thoughts, for to do so turns one of our fellow human beings into a thing, a mere object. Someone wishing to lead a good life should not want to make a fellow human being into a thing.

It has been said that to do anything well is difficult, and that living as a human being rather than as a beast is no exception. It requires moral seriousness and self-discipline. Socrates had famously said that knowledge was virtue, that to know the good was to do the good. Aristotle and St. Paul knew better, for we can all recall moments in our lives at which we knew perfectly well what the good was but did not do it, and likewise knew what was wrong but did do that. This is why Catholic spiritual directors instruct those under their charge to eat a carrot the next time we want a cupcake; not because cupcakes are evil, but because if we can get into the habit of disciplining our wills in cases in which no moral principle is at stake, then we shall be better prepared in the moment of temptation, when we are indeed faced with a choice between good and evil. And just as the more habituated we become to sin the easier further sin becomes, it is also true, as Aristotle observed, that virtuous living becomes ever easier the more we engage in it and the more it becomes a matter of habit.

These are some of the distinctive ideas that the Church has introduced into Western civilization. Today, all too many younger people have heard the Church's teaching on human intimacy only in caricature, and given the culture within which they live, cannot begin to understand why the Church proposes it. Faithful to the mission she has fulfilled for two millennia, however, the Church still holds out a moral alternative to young people immersed in a culture that relentlessly teaches them to pursue immediate gratification. The Church recalls the great men of Christendom—like Charlemagne, Saint Thomas Aquinas, Saint Francis of Assisi, and Saint Francis Xavier, to name a few—and holds them up as models for how true men live. Its message? Essentially this: You can aspire to be one of these men—a builder of civilization, a great genius, a servant of God and men, or a heroic missionary—or you can be a self-absorbed nobody fixated on gratifying your appetites. Our society does everything in its power to ensure that you wind up on the latter path. Be your own person. Rise above the herd, declare your independence from a culture that thinks so little of you, and proclaim that you intend to live not as a beast but as a man.

*Conclusion*

# A World Without God

R *eligion is a central* aspect of any civilization. For two thousand years, the way Western man typically thinks about God has been overwhelmingly indebted to the Catholic Church.

Four characteristics in particular differentiate the Church's view of God from the views ancient Near Eastern civilizations held of the divine.[1] First, God is one. Polytheistic systems, in which less-than-omnipotent deities are charged with custodianship of particular natural phenomena or physical locations, seem alien to the Western mind, which is accustomed to viewing God as a single being supremely powerful over all aspects of His creation.

Second, God is absolutely sovereign, in that He derives His own existence from no prior realm and is subject to no other force. Neither illness, nor hunger and thirst, nor the power of fate—one or more of which applied to the various Near Eastern gods—has any power over Him.

Third, God is transcendent, utterly beyond and other than His creation. He is not reposed in any physical location; neither does He animate any created thing, as with the nature gods of animism. This attribute makes possible the emergence of science and the growth of the idea of regular laws of nature, since it deprives material nature of divine attributes. Since the various objects of the created world therefore do not possess wills of their own, it becomes possible to conceive of them as conforming to regular patterns of behavior.

Finally, God is good. Unlike the gods of ancient Sumer, who appeared at best indifferent to human welfare, or the gods of ancient Greece, who were at times petty and vindictive in their dealings with mankind, the God of Catholicism loves mankind and wills man's good. Moreover, although like pagan gods He is pleased by ritual sacrifice—namely, the Holy Sacrifice of the Mass—unlike many of them He is also pleased by the good behavior of human beings.

All of these characteristics are also evident in the God of Old Testament Judaism. The Catholic conception of God is distinct from that tradition as well, however, as a result of the Incarnation of Jesus Christ. With the birth of Christ and His sojourn in this world, we learn that God seeks not only man's worship but also his friendship. The great twentieth-century Catholic writer Robert Hugh Benson could thus write a book called *The Friendship of Christ* (1912). In his *Philosophical Fragments*, Søren Kierkegaard once compared God to a king who wished to win the love of a common woman. If he approached her in his capacity as king, she would be too awed by him to be able to offer him the kind of love spontaneously exchanged between equals. She could also be attracted only to his wealth and power, or could simply fear to refuse the king's desire.

For these reasons, the king approached the common woman in the guise of a commoner. Only then would he be able to elicit her sincere love, and only then would he be able to know that her love for him was truly genuine. This, says Kierkegaard, is what God does when He is born into the world as Jesus Christ, the Second Person of the Blessed Trinity. He seeks out our love not by over-whelming us with the majesty and awe of the beatific vision (which is not available to us in this world, only in the world to come) but by condescending to interact with us on our level, adopting a human nature and taking human flesh.[2] This is an extraordinary idea in the history of religion, yet so embedded has it become within Western culture that Westerners even today scarcely give the matter a second thought.

So ingrained are the concepts that Catholicism introduced into the world that very often even movements opposing it are nevertheless imbued with Christian ideas. Murray Rothbard pointed out the extent to which Marxism, a relentlessly secular ideology, borrowed from the religious ideas of sixteenth-century Christian heresies.[3] The intellectuals of the American progressive era of the early twentieth century congratulated themselves for having abandoned their (largely Protestant) faith, yet a dis-tinctly Christian idiom nevertheless continued to dominate their speech.[4]

These points only underscore what we have already seen: The Catholic Church did not merely contribute to Western civilization—the Church *built* that civilization. The Church borrowed from the ancient world, to be sure, but she typically did so in a way that transformed the classical tradition for the better. There was hardly a human enterprise of the Early Mid-dle Ages to which the monasteries did not contribute. The Sci-entific Revolution took root in a Western Europe whose theological and philosophical foundations, Catholic at their very core, proved fertile soil for the development of the scientific enterprise. The mature idea of international law emerged from the Late Scholastics, as did concepts central to the emergence of economics as a distinct discipline.

These latter two contributions emerged from the European universities, a creation of the High Middle Ages that occurred under the auspices of the Church. Unlike the academies of ancient Greece, each of which tended to be dominated by a single school of thought, the universities of medieval Europe were places of intense intellectual debate and exchange. David Lindberg explains:

> [I]t must be emphatically stated that within this educational system the medieval master had a great deal of freedom. The stereotype of the Middle Ages pictures the professor as spineless and subservient, a slavish follower of Aristotle and the church fathers (exactly how one could be a slavish follower of both, the stereotype does not explain), fearful of departing one iota from the demands of authority. There were broad theological limits, of course, but within those limits the medieval master had remarkable freedom of thought and expression; there was almost no doctrine, philosophical or theological, that was not submitted to minute scrutiny and criticism by scholars in the medieval university.[5]

The Catholic Scholastics' eagerness to search for the truth, to study and employ a great diversity of sources, and treat objections to their positions with precision and care, endowed the medieval intellectual tradition—and by extension the universities in which that tradition developed and matured—with a vitality of which the West may rightly boast.

All of these areas: economic thought, international law, science, university life, charity, religious ideas, art, morality—these are the very foundations of a civilization, and in the West every single one of them emerged from the heart of the Catholic Church.

Paradoxically, the importance of the Church to Western civilization has sometimes become clearer as its influence has waned. During the eighteenth-century Enlightenment, the Church's privileged position and the respect it was traditionally accorded were both called into serious question, to an extent without precedent in the history of Catholicism. The nineteenth century saw more attacks on Catholicism, particularly with the German *Kulturkampf* and the anticlericalism of the Italian nationalists. France secularized its school system in 1905. Although the Church flourished in the United States during the late nineteenth and early twentieth centuries, attacks on the Church's liberty elsewhere in the West did untold damage.[6]

The world of art provides perhaps the most dramatic and visible evidence of the consequences of the Church's partial eclipse in the modern world. Jude Dougherty, dean emeritus of the School of Philosophy at Catholic University, has spoken of a connection "between the impoverished anti-metaphysical philosophy of our day and its debilitating effect on the arts." According to Dougherty, there is a link between a civilization's art and its belief in and consciousness of the transcendent. "Without a metaphysical recognition of the transcendent, without the recognition of a divine intellect at once the source of nature's order and the fulfillment of human aspiration, reality is construed in purely materialistic terms. Man himself becomes the measure, unaccountable to an objective order. Life itself is empty and without purpose. That aridity finds its expression in the perverseness and sterility of modern art, from Bauhaus to Cubism to post-modernism."

Professor Dougherty's claim is more than plausible; it is positively compelling. When people believe that life has no purpose and is the result of random chance, guided by no greater force or principle, who can be surprised when that sense of meaninglessness is reflected in their art?

A sense of meaninglessness and disorder had been growing since the nineteenth century. In *Joyful Wisdom*, Friedrich Nietzsche wrote: "At last the horizon lies free before us, even granted that it is not bright; at least the sea, *our* sea, lies open before us. Perhaps there has never been so open a sea." That is to say, there is no order or meaning to the universe apart from what man himself, in the most supreme and unfettered act of will of all, chooses to bestow upon it. Frederick Copleston, the great historian of philosophy, summed up the Nietzschean point of view: "The rejection of the idea that the world has been created by God for a purpose or that it is the self-manifestation of the absolute Idea or Spirit sets man free to give to life the meaning which he wills to give it. And it has no other meaning."[7]

Meanwhile, modernism in literature was busy challenging the pillars of order within the written word—such aspects as giving stories and novels a beginning, middle, and end. They featured bizarre plots in which the main character was forced to contend with a chaotic and irrational universe he was unable to comprehend. Thus Franz Kafka's *The Metamorphosis* begins: "As Gregor Samsa awoke one morning from uneasy dreams he found himself transformed in his bed into a giant insect."

In music, the spirit of the age was especially apparent in the atonality of Arnold Schoenberg and the chaotic rhythms of Igor Stravinsky, particularly in his notorious *Rite of Spring* but also in some of his later works, like his 1945 Symphony in Three Movements. We need hardly point out the degeneration of architecture, which is evident today even among buildings purporting to be Catholic churches.[8]

The point is not necessarily to contend that these works are utterly without merit, but rather to suggest that they reflect an intellectual and cultural milieu at variance with the Catholic belief in an orderly universe that was endowed with ultimate meaning. By the mid-twentieth century, the time had come to take the final, fateful step: to declare, as did Jean-Paul Sartre (1905–1980) and his school of existentialist thought, that the universe was utterly absurd and life itself completely meaningless. How, then, ought one to live life? By courageously facing the void, frankly acknowledging that all is without meaning and that there are no such things as absolute values. And, of course, by constructing one's own values and living by them (shades of Nietzsche, to be sure).

The visual arts were certain to be affected by such a philosophical milieu. The medieval artist, aware that his role was to communicate something greater than himself, did not typically sign his work. He wished to call attention not to himself but to the subject of his work. A newer conception of the artist, which began to emerge during the Renaissance, reached its full maturity in nineteenth-century Romanticism. A reaction against the cold scientism of the Enlightenment, Romanticism emphasized feeling, emotion, and spontaneity. Thus the artist's own feelings, struggles, emotions, and idiosyncracies were to be given expression in his art; art itself became a form of self-expression. The focus of the artist's work began to shift toward depicting his interior disposition. The invention of photography in the late nineteenth century gave added impetus to this trend, since by making the precise reproduction of the natural world an easy task it freed the artist to engage in self-expression.

With the passage of time, this Romantic self-preoccupation degenerated into the simple narcissism and nihilism of modern art. In 1917, French artist Marcel Duchamp shocked the art world when he signed a urinal and placed it on display as a work of art. That a poll of five hundred art experts in 2004 yielded Duchamp's *Fountain* as the single most influential work of modern art speaks for itself.[9]

Duchamp was a formative influence on London-based artist Tracey Emin. Emin's *My Bed*, which was nominated for the prestigious Turner Prize, consisted of an unmade bed complete with bottles of vodka, used prophylactics, and bloodied undergarments. While on display at the Tate Gallery in 1999, the bed was vandalized by two nude men who proceeded to jump on it and drink the vodka. The world of modern art being what it is, everyone at the gallery applauded, assuming that the vandalism was part of the show. Emin is now employed as a professor at the European Graduate School.

These examples symbolize the departure from the Church that many Westerners have undertaken in recent years. The Church, which calls on her children to be generous in the transmission of life, finds even this most fundamental message falling on deaf ears in Western Europe, which is not having enough children even to reproduce itself. So far has Europe abandoned the faith that built her that the European Union could not bring itself even to acknowledge the continent's Christian heritage in its constitution. Many of the great cathedrals that once testified to the religious convictions of a people have in our own day become like museum pieces, interesting curiosities to an unbelieving world.

The self-imposed historical amnesia of the West today cannot undo the past or the Church's central role in building Western civilization. "I am not a Catholic," wrote French philosopher Simone Weil, "but I consider the Christian idea, which has its roots in Greek thought and in the course of the centuries has nourished all of our European civilization, as something that one cannot renounce without becoming degraded." That is a lesson that Western civilization, cut off more and more from its Catholic foundations, is in the process of learning the hard way.

# ACKNOWLEDGMENTS

Over the course of writing this book I received helpful suggestions from Dr. Michael Foley, Dr. Diane Moczar, Dr. John Rao, and Professor Carol Long. I also wish to thank Dr. Anthony Rizzi, director of the Institute for Advanced Physics and author of the important book *The Science Before Science: A Guide to Thinking in the 21st Century*, for vetting Chapter Five. Any errors of fact or interpretation are, of course, solely my own.

I must make special mention of Doreen Munna and Marilyn Ventiere of my college's interlibrary loan department for cheerfully fulfilling my requests for old, hard-to-find, and long-forgotten titles.

Once again, working with Regnery has been a pleasure. The book certainly benefited from the comments and suggestions of executive editor Harry Crocker, and managing editor Paula Decker reviewed the manuscript with her usual attention to detail.

I started writing this book before I was approached with the idea for *The Politically Incorrect Guide to American History*, my third book. To meet the deadline for that project I put this one aside for a little while and eventually returned to it last year. I completed the manuscript two days before our second child, Veronica Lynn, was born. My dear wife, Heather, was her usual supportive self throughout what was often a difficult nine months for her, and I am deeply grateful.

The book is dedicated to Veronica and Regina (born 2003), our two daughters. I hope it will reinforce what we intend to teach them: that in their Catholic faith they possess the pearl of great price with which they would not want to part for anything in the world. For as Saint Thomas More once said, no one on his deathbed ever regretted having been a Catholic.

THOMAS E. WOODS, JR.
*Coram, New York*
*March 2005*

# BIBLIOGRAPHY

Bainton, Roland H. *Christian Attitudes Toward War and Peace.* New York: Abingdon Press, 1960.

Baldwin, John W. *The Scholastic Culture of the Middle Ages, 1000–1300.* Lexington, Mass.: D.C. Heath, 1971.

Baluffi, Cajetan. *The Charity of the Church.* Translated by Denis Gargan. Dublin: M. H. Gill and Son, 1885.

Bangert, William V., S.J. *A History of the Society of Jesus.* St. Louis: Institute of Jesuit Sources, 1972.

Barzun, Jacques. *From Dawn to Decadence.* New York: Harper Collins, 2001.

Benestad, J. Brian, ed. *Ernest Fortin: Collected Essays.* Vol. 3: *Human Rights, Virtue, and the Common Good: Untimely Meditations on Religion and Politics.* Lanham, Md.: Rowman & Littlefield, 1996.

Berman, Harold J. *Faith and Order: The Reconciliation of Law and Religion.* Atlanta: Scholars Press, 1993.

——. "The Influence of Christianity Upon the Development of Law," *Oklahoma Law Review* 12 (February 1959): 86–101.

———. *The Interaction of Law and Religion.* Nashville, Tenn.: Abingdon Press,1974.

———. *Law and Revolution: The Formation of the Western Legal Tradition.* Cambridge: Harvard University Press, 1983.

Broad, William J. "How the Church Aided 'Heretical' Astronomy," *New York Times,* October 19, 1999.

Brodrick, James. *The Life and Work of Blessed Robert Francis Cardinal Bellarmine, S.J., 1542–1621.* Vol. 2. London: Burns, Oates and Washbourne, 1928.

Butterfield, Herbert. *The Origins of Modern Science, 1300–1800,* rev. ed. New York: Free Press, 1957.

Cahill, Thomas. *How the Irish Saved Civilization.* New York: Doubleday, 1995.

Carroll, Vincent and David Shiflett. *Christianity on Trial.* San Francisco: Encounter Books, 2001.

Chafuen, Alejandro A. *Faith and Liberty: The Economic Thought of the Late Scholastics.* Lanham, Md.: Lexington, 2003.

Clark, Kenneth. *Civilisation: A Personal View.* New York: HarperPerennial, 1969.

Cobban, A. B. *The Medieval Universities: Their Development and Organization.* London: Methuen & Co., 1975.

Cobbett, William. *A History of the Protestant Reformation in England and Ireland.* Rockford, Ill.: TAN, 1988 [1896].

Collins, Randall. *Weberian Sociological Theory.* Cambridge: Cambridge University Press, 1986.

Copleston, Frederick, S.J. *A History of Philosophy.* Vol. 7: *Modern Philosophy from the Post-Kantian Idealists to Marx, Kierkegaard, and Nietzsche.* New York: Doubleday, 1994 [1963].

Crocker, H. W., III. *Triumph.* Roseville, Calif.: Prima, 2001.

Crombie, A. C. *Medieval and Early Modern Science.* 2 vols. Garden City, N.Y.: Doubleday, 1959.

Cutler, Alan. *The Seashell on the Mountaintop.* New York: Dutton, 2003.

Dales, Richard C. "The De-Animation of the Heavens in the Middle Ages," *Journal of the History of Ideas* 41 (1980): 531–50.

——. *The Intellectual Life of Western Europe in the Middle Ages.* Washington, D.C.: University Press of America, 1980.

——. "A Twelfth Century Concept of the Natural Order," *Viator* 9 (1978): 179–92.

Daly, Lowrie J. *The Medieval University, 1200–1400.* New York: Sheed and Ward, 1961.

Daniel-Rops, Henri. *Cathedral and Crusade.* Translated by John Warrington. London: J. M. Dent & Sons, 1957.

——. *The Church in the Dark Ages.* Translated by Audrey Butler. London: J. M. Dent & Sons, 1959.

——. *The Protestant Reformation.* Translated by Audrey Butler. London: J. M. Dent & Sons, 1961.

Davies, Michael. *For Altar and Throne: The Rising in the Vendée.* St. Paul, Minn.: Remnant Press, 1997.

Dawson, Christopher. *Religion and the Rise of Western Culture.* New York: Image Books, 1991 [1950].

De Roover, Raymond. *Business, Banking, and Economic Thought in Late Medieval and Early Modern Europe: Selected Studies of Raymond de Roover.* Edited by Julius Kirshner. Chicago: University of Chicago Press, 1974.

——. "The Concept of the Just Price: Theory and Economic Policy," *Journal of Economic History* 18 (1958): 418–34.

Derbyshire, David. "Henry 'Stamped Out Industrial Revolution,'" *Telegraph* [U.K.], June 21, 2002.

Dijksterhuis, E. J. *The Mechanization of the World Picture.*
Translated by C. Dikshoorn. London: Oxford University
Press, 1961.

Durant, Will. *The Age of Faith.* New York: MJF Books, 1950.

——. *Caesar and Christ.* New York: MJF Books, 1950.

——. *The Renaissance.* New York: MJF Books, 1953.

Edgerton, Samuel Y., Jr. *The Heritage of Giotto's Geometry:
Art and Science on the Eve of the Scientific Revolution.*
Ithaca: Cornell University Press, 1991.

Fernandez-Santamaria, J. A. *The State, War and Peace:
Spanish Political Thought in the Renaissance, 1516–1559.*
Cambridge: Cambridge University Press, 1977.

Flick, Alexander Clarence. *The Rise of the Mediaeval Church.*
New York: Burt Franklin, 1909.

Franklin, James. "The Renaissance Myth," *Quadrant* 26
(November 1982): 51–60.

Friede, Juan and Benjamin Keen, eds. *Bartolome de Las Casas
in History: Toward an Understanding of the Man and His
Work.* DeKalb, Ill.: Northern Illinois University Press, 1971.

Gillispie, Charles C., ed. *Dictionary of Scientific Biography.*
New York: Charles Scribner's Sons, 1970.

Gilson, Etienne. *Reason and Revelation in the Middle Ages.*
New York: Charles Scribner's Sons, 1938.

Gimpel, Jean. *The Medieval Machine: The Industrial Revolution of the Middle Ages.* New York: Holt, Rinehart, and
Winston, 1976.

Goldstein, Thomas. *Dawn of Modern Science: From the Ancient
Greeks to the Renaissance.* New York: Da Capo Press, 1995
[1980].

Goodell, Henry H. "The Influence of the Monks in Agriculture."
Address delivered before the Massachusetts State Board of

Agriculture, August 23, 1901. Copy in the Goodell Papers at the University of Massachusetts.

Grant, Edward. "The Condemnation of 1277, God's Absolute Power, and Physical Thought in the Late Middle Ages," *iator* 10 (1979): 211–44.

——. *The Foundations of Modern Science in the Middle Ages: Their Religious, Institutional, and Intellectual Contexts.* Cambridge: Cambridge University Press, 1996.

——. *God and Reason in the Middle Ages.* Cambridge: Cambridge University Press, 2001.

Grégoire, Réginald, Léo Moulin, and Raymond Oursel. *The Monastic Realm.* New York: Rizzoli, 1985.

Grice-Hutchinson, Marjorie. *Early Economic Thought in Spain, 1177–1740.* London: George Allen & Unwin, 1978.

——. *The School of Salamanca: Readings in Spanish Monetary Theory, 1544–1605.* Oxford: Clarendon Press, 1952.

Haffner, Paul. *Creation and Scientific Creativity.* Front Royal, Va.: Christendom Press, 1991.

Hamilton, Bernice. *Political Thought in Sixteenth-Century Spain.* London: Oxford University Press, 1963.

Hanke, Lewis. *Bartolomé de Las Casas: An Interpretation of His Life and Writings.* The Hague: Martinus Nijhoff, 1951.

——. *The Spanish Struggle for Justice in the Conquest of America.* Boston: Little, Brown and Co., 1965 [1949].

Harvey, Barbara. *Living and Dying in England, 1100–1540: The Monastic Experience.* Oxford: Clarendon Press, 1993.

Haskins, Charles Homer. *The Renaissance of the Twelfth Century.* Cleveland: Meridian, 1957 [1927].

——. *The Rise of Universities.* Ithaca: Cornell University Press, 1957 [1923].

Heilbron, J. L. *Electricity in the 17th and 18th Centuries: A Study of Early Modern Physics*. Berkeley: University of California Press, 1979.

———. *The Sun in the Church: Cathedrals as Solar Observatories*. Cambridge: Harvard University Press, 1999.

Hillgarth, J. N., ed., *Christianity and Paganism, 350–750: The Conversion of Western Europe*. Philadelphia: University of Pennsylvania Press, 1986.

Howell, Benjamin F., Jr. *An Introduction to Seismological Research: History and Development*. Cambridge: Cambridge University Press, 1990.

Hughes, Philip. *A History of the Church*. Vol. 1, rev. ed. London: Sheed and Ward, 1948.

———. *A Popular History of the Reformation*. Garden City, N.Y.: Hanover House,1957.

Hülsmann, Jörg Guido. "Nicholas Oresme and the First Monetary Treatise." May 8, 2004. http://www.mises.org/fullstory.aspx?control=1516.

Jaki, Stanley L. *Patterns or Principles and Other Essays*. Bryn Mawr, Pa.: Intercollegiate Studies Institute, 1995.

———. *The Savior of Science*. Grand Rapids, Mich.: Eerdmans, 2000.

———. *Science and Creation: From Eternal Cycles to an Oscillating Universe*. Edinburgh: Scottish Academic Press, 1986.

John of Damascus. *Three Treatises on the Divine Images*. Translated by Andrew Louth. Crestwood, N.Y.: St. Vladimir's Seminary Press, 2003.

Johnson, Paul. *Art: A New History*. New York: HarperCollins, 2003.

Kauder, Emil. *A History of Marginal Utility Theory*. Princeton: Princeton University Press, 1965.

Klibansky, Raymond. "The School of Chartres." In *Twelfth Century Europe and the Foundations of Modern Society*, Marshall Clagett, Gaines Post, and Robert Reynolds. eds. Madison: University of Wisconsin Press, 1961.

Knowles, David. *The Evolution of Medieval Thought*, 2nd ed. London: Longman, 1988.

Langan, John, S.J. "The Elements of St. Augustine's Just War Theory," *Journal of Religious Ethics* 12 (spring 1984): 19–38.

Langford, Jerome J., O.P. *Galileo, Science and the Church*. New York: Desclee, 1966.

Lecky, William Edward Hartpole. *History of European Morals from Augustus to Charlemagne*. 2 vols. New York: D. Appleton and Company, 1870.

Leff, Gordon. *Paris and Oxford Universities in the Thirteenth and Fourteenth Centuries: An Institutional and Intellectual History*. New York: John Wiley and Sons, 1968.

Lindberg, David C. "On the Applicability of Mathematics to Nature: Roger Bacon and His Predecessors," *British Journal for the History of Science* 15 (1982): 3–25.

——. *The Beginnings of Western Science*. Chicago: University of Chicago Press, 1992.

—— and Ronald L. Numbers, eds. *God and Nature: Historical Essays on the Encounter Between Christianity and Science*. Berkeley: University of California Press, 1986.

Lynch, Joseph H. *The Medieval Church: A Brief History*. London: Longman, 1992.

MacDonnell, Joseph E. *Companions of Jesuits: A Tradition of Collaboration*. Fairfield, Conn.: Humanities Institute, 1995.

——. *Jesuit Geometers*. St. Louis: Institute of Jesuit Sources, 1989.

Massaro, Thomas A., S.J., and Thomas A. Shannon. *Catholic Perspectives on Peace and War*. Lanham, Md.: Rowman & Littlefield, 2003.

Menger, Carl. *Principles of Economics*. Translated by James Dingwall and Bert F. Hoselitz. Grove City, Penn.: Libertarian Press, 1994.

Montalembert, Charles. *The Monks of the West: From St. Benedict to St. Bernard*. 5 vols. London: Nimmo, 1896.

Morison, Samuel Eliot. *The Oxford History of the American People*. Vol. 1: *Prehistory to 1789*. New York: Meridian, 1994 [1965].

Newman, John Henry. *Essays and Sketches*. Vol. 3. Charles Frederick Harrold, ed. New York: Longmans, Green and Co., 1948.

O'Connor, John B. *Monasticism and Civilization*. New York: P. J. Kennedy & Sons, 1921.

Oldroyd, David R. *Thinking About the Earth: A History of Ideas in Geology*. Cambridge: Harvard University Press, 1996.

Panofsky, Erwin. *Gothic Architecture and Scholasticism*. New York: Meridian Books, 1985 [1951].

Partington, J. R. *A History of Chemistry*. Vol. 2. London: Macmillan, 1961.

Pennington, Kenneth. "The History of Rights in Western Thought," *Emory Law Journal* 47 (1998): 237–52.

Phillips, Robert. *Last Things First*. Fort Collins, Colo: Roman Catholic Books, 2004.

Reid, Charles J., Jr. "The Canonistic Contribution to the Western Rights Tradition: An Historical Inquiry," *Boston College Law Review* 33 (1991): 37–92.

Reynolds, L. D. and N. G. Wilson. *Scribes and Scholars: A Guide to the Transmission of Greek and Latin Literature*, 3rd ed. Oxford: Clarendon Press, 1991.

Risse, Guenter B. *Mending Bodies, Saving Souls: A History of Hospitals*. New York: Oxford University Press, 1999.

Rothbard, Murray N. *An Austrian Perspective on the History of Economic Thought*. Vol. 1: *Economic Thought Before Adam Smith*. Hants, England: Edward Elgar, 1995.

———. "New Light on the Prehistory of the Austrian School." In *The Foundations of Modern Austrian Economics*. Edwin G. Dolan, ed. Kansas City: Sheed & Ward, 1976.

Royal, Robert C. *Columbus On Trial: 1492 v. 1992*, 2nd ed. Herndon, Va.: Young America's Foundation, 1993.

Rushton, Neil S. "Monastic Charitable Provision in Tudor England: Quantifying and Qualifying Poor Relief in the Early Sixteenth Century," *Continuity and Change* 16 (2001): 9–44.

Russell, Frederick H. *The Just War in the Middle Ages*. Cambridge: Cambridge University Press, 1975.

Sadowsky, James A., S.J. "Can There Be an Endless Regress of Causes?" In *Philosophy of Religion: A Guide and Anthology*. Brian Davies, ed. New York: Oxford University Press, 2000.

Schmidt, Alvin J. *Under the Influence: How Christianity Transformed Civilization*. Grand Rapids, Mich.: Zondervan, 2001.

Schmidt, C[harles Guillaume Adolphe]. *The Social Results of Early Christianity*. London: Sir Isaac Pitman & Sons, 1907.

Schnürer, Gustav. *Church and Culture in the Middle Ages*. Translated by George J. Undreiner. Paterson, NJ: St. Anthony Guild Press, 1956.

Schumpeter, Joseph A. *History of Economic Analysis*. New York: Oxford University Press, 1954.

Scott, James Brown. *The Spanish Origin of International Law.* Washington, D.C.: School of Foreign Service, Georgetown University, 1928.

Scott, Robert A. *The Gothic Enterprise.* Berkeley: University of California Press, 2003.

Stark, Rodney. *For the Glory of God.* Princeton: Princeton University Press, 2003.

Stuewer, Roger H. "A Critical Analysis of Newton's Work on Diffraction," *Isis* 61 (1970): 188–205.

Tierney, Brian. *The Idea of Natural Rights: Studies on Natural Rights, Natural Law, and Church Law, 1150–1625.* Grand Rapids, Mich.: William B. Eerdmans, 2001 [1997].

——. "The Idea of Natural Rights: Origins and Persistence," *Northwestern University Journal of International Human Rights* 2 (April 2004): 2–12.

Udías, Agustín. *Searching the Heavens and the Earth: The History of Jesuit Observatories.* Dordrecht, Netherlands: Kluwer Academic Publishers, 2003.

—— and William Stauder. "Jesuits in Seismology," *Jesuits in Science Newsletter* 13 (1997).

Uhlhorn, Gerhard. *Christian Charity in the Ancient Church.* New York: Charles Scribner's Sons, 1883.

Walsh, James J. *The Popes and Science.* New York: Fordham University Press, 1911.

Watner, Carl. "'All Mankind Is One': The Libertarian Tradition in Sixteenth Century Spain," *Journal of Libertarian Studies* 8 (summer 1987): 293–309.

West, Andrew Fleming. *Alcuin and the Rise of the Christian Schools.* New York: Charles Scribner's Sons, 1892.

White, Kevin, ed. *Hispanic Philosophy in the Age of Discovery.* Washington, D.C.: Catholic University of America Press, 1997.

White, Lynn, Jr. "Eilmer of Malmesbury, an Eleventh-Century Aviator: A Case Study of Technological Innovation, Its Context and Tradition," *Technology and Culture* 2 (1961): 97–111.

Whyte, Lancelot Law, ed. *Roger Joseph Boscovich, S.J., F.R.S., 1711–1787.* New York: Fordham University Press, 1961.

Wilson, Christopher. *The Gothic Cathedral: The Architecture of the Great Church, 1130–1530.* London: Thames and Hudson, 1990.

Wolf, A. *A History of Science, Technology, and Philosophy in the 16th and 17th Centuries.* London: George Allen & Unwin, 1938.

Wolff, Philippe. *The Awakening of Europe.* New York: Penguin Books, 1968.

Woods, Thomas E., Jr. *The Church and the Market: A Catholic Defense of the Free Economy.* Lanham, Md.: Lexington Books, 2005.

Wright, Jonathan. *The Jesuits: Missions, Myths and Histories.* London: HarperCollins, 2004.

# NOTES

### Chapter One
## THE INDISPENSABLE CHURCH

1. See, for example, Henry Kamen, *The Spanish Inquisition: A Histori-cal Revision* (New Haven: Yale University Press, 1999); Edward M. Peters, *Inquisition* (Berkeley: University of California Press, 1989).
2. Christopher Knight and Robert Lomas, *Second Messiah* (Glouces-ter, Mass.: Fair Winds Press, 2001), 70.
3. Ibid., 71.
4. J. L. Heilbron, *The Sun in the Church: Cathedrals as Solar Obser-vatories* (Cambridge: Harvard University Press, 1999), 3.
5. Réginald Grégoire, Léo Moulin, and Raymond Oursel, *The Monas-tic Realm* (New York: Rizzoli, 1985), 277.
6. Harold J. Berman, *The Interaction of Law and Religion* (Nashville, Tenn.: Abingdon Press, 1974), 59.

### Chapter Two
## A LIGHT IN THE DARKNESS

1. Will Durant, *Caesar and Christ* (New York: MJF Books, 1950), 79.
2. Henri Daniel-Rops, *The Church in the Dark Ages*, trans. Audrey Butler (London: J. M. Dent & Sons, 1959), 59.

3.  J. N. Hillgarth, ed., *Christianity and Paganism, 350–750: The Conversion of Western Europe* (Philadelphia: University of Pennsylvania Press, 1986), 69.

4.  Ibid., 70.

5.  Gustav Schnürer, *Church and Culture in the Middle Ages*, vol. 1, trans. George J. Undreiner (Paterson, NJ: Saint Anthony Guild Press, 1956), 285.

6.  Joseph H. Lynch, *The Medieval Church: A Brief History* (London: Longman, 1992), 89.

7.  Ibid., 95; Kenneth Clark, *Civilisation: A Personal View* (New York: HarperPerennial, 1969), 18.

8.  Lynch, 95.

9.  L. D. Reynolds and N. G. Wilson, *Scribes and Scholars: A Guide to the Transmission of Greek and Latin Literature*, 3rd ed. (Oxford: Clarendon Press, 1991), 95.

10. Philippe Wolff, *The Awakening of Europe* (New York: Penguin Books, 1968), 57.

11. Ibid., 77.

12. David Knowles, *The Evolution of Medieval Thought*, 2nd ed. (London: Longman, 1988), 69.

13. Wolff, 48–49.

14. Knowles, 66.

15. Wolff, 153ff.

16. Andrew Fleming West, *Alcuin and the Rise of the Christian Schools* (New York: Charles Scribner's Sons, 1892), 179.

17. Christopher Dawson, *Religion and the Rise of Western Culture* (New York: Image Books, 1991 [1950]), 66.

18. Ibid. Emphasis added.

19. Daniel-Rops, 538.

20. Wolff, 183.

21. Ibid., 177–78.

*Chapter Three*
## HOW THE MONKS SAVED CIVILIZATION

1.  Philip Hughes, *A History of the Church*, vol. 1, rev. ed. (London: Sheed and Ward, 1948), 138–39.

2. Ibid., 140.
3. A degree of centralization was introduced into the Benedictine tradition in the early tenth century with the establishment of the monastery of Cluny. The abbot of Cluny possessed authority over all monasteries that were affiliated with that venerable house and appointed priors to oversee day-to-day activity in each monastery.
4. Will Durant, *The Age of Faith* (New York: MJF Books, 1950), 519.
5. G. Cyprian Alston, "The Benedictine Order," *Catholic Encyclopedia*, 2nd ed., 1913.
6. Alexander Clarence Flick, *The Rise of the Mediaeval Church* (New York: Burt Franklin, 1909), 216.
7. Henry H. Goodell, "The Influence of the Monks in Agriculture," address delivered before the Massachusetts State Board of Agriculture, August 23, 1901, 22. Copy in the Goodell Papers at the University of Massachusetts.
8. Flick, 223.
9. See John Henry Cardinal Newman, *Essays and Sketches*, vol. 3, Charles Frederick Harrold, ed. (New York: Longmans, Green and Co., 1948), 264–65.
10. Goodell, "The Influence of the Monks in Agriculture," 11.
11. Ibid., 6.
12. Charles Montalembert, *The Monks of the West: From Saint Benedict to Saint Bernard*, vol. 5 (London: Nimmo, 1896), 208.
13. Goodell, "The Influence of the Monks in Agriculture," 7–8.
14. Ibid., 8.
15. Ibid., 8, 9.
16. Ibid., 10.
17. Montalembert, 198–99.
18. John B. O'Connor, *Monasticism and Civilization* (New York: P. J. Kennedy & Sons, 1921), 35–36.
19. Jean Gimpel, *The Medieval Machine: The Industrial Revolution of the Middle Ages* (New York: Holt, Rinehart, and Winston, 1976), 5.
20. Randall Collins, *Weberian Sociological Theory* (Cambridge: Cambridge University Press, 1986), 53–54.
21. Gimpel, 5.
22. Ibid., 3.

23. Quoted in David Luckhurst, "Monastic Watermills," Society for
    the Protection of Ancient Buildings, no. 8 (London, n.d.), 6; quoted
    in Gimpel, 5–6.

24. Gimpel, 67.

25. Ibid., 68.

26. Ibid., 1.

27. Réginald Grégoire, Léo Moulin, and Raymond Oursel, *The Monas-
    tic Realm* (New York: Rizzoli, 1985), 271.

28. Ibid., 275.

29. Stanley L. Jaki, "Medieval Creativity in Science and Technology,"
    in *Patterns and Principles and Other Essays* (Bryn Mawr, Pa.:
    Intercollegiate Studies Institute, 1995), 81; see also Lynn White
    Jr., "Eilmer of Malmesbury, an Eleventh-Century Aviator: A Case
    Study of Technological Innovation, Its Context and Tradition,"
    *Technology and Culture* 2 (1961): 97–111.

30. Joseph MacDonnell, S.J., *Jesuit Geometers* (St. Louis: Institute of
    Jesuit Sources, 1989), 21–22.

31. David Derbyshire, "Henry 'Stamped Out Industrial Revolution,'"
    *Telegraph* [U.K.], June 21, 2002; see also "Henry's Big Mistake,"
    *Discover*, February 1999.

32. Montalembert, 225, 89–90.

33. Ibid., 227.

34. Ibid., 227–28. Montalembert misspells Bishop Absalon's name.

35. O'Connor, 118.

36. Montalembert, 151–52.

37. L. D. Reynolds and N. G. Wilson, *Scribes and Scholars: A Guide to
    the Transmission of Greek and Latin Literature*, 3rd ed. (Oxford:
    Clarendon Press, 1991), 83.

38. Ibid., 81–82.

39. Montalembert, 145.

40. Ibid., 146; Raymund Webster, "Pope Blessed Victor III," *Catholic
    Encyclopedia*, 2nd ed., 1913.

41. Montalembert, 146. On this overall topic, see also Newman, 320–21.

42. Newman, 316–17.

43. Ibid., 319.

44. Ibid., 317–19.

45. Reynolds and Wilson, 109.
46. Ibid., 109–10.
47. O'Connor, 115.
48. Montalembert, 139.
49. Newman, 321.
50. Montalembert, 143.
51. Ibid., 142.
52. Ibid., 118.
53. Alston, "The Benedictine Order."
54. Thomas Cahill, *How the Irish Saved Civilization* (New York: Doubleday, 1995), 150, 158.
55. Adolf von Harnack, quoted in O'Connor, 90.
56. Flick, 222–23.

*Chapter Four*
## THE CHURCH AND THE UNIVERSITY

1. Cf. Charles Homer Haskins, *The Rise of Universities* (Ithaca: Cornell University Press, 1957 [1923]), 1; idem, *The Renaissance of the Twelfth Century* (Cleveland: Meridian, 1957 [1927]), 369; Lowrie J. Daly, *The Medieval University, 1200–1400* (New York: Sheed and Ward, 1961), 213–14.
2. Daly, 4.
3. Richard C. Dales, *The Intellectual Life of Western Europe in the Middle Ages* (Washington, D.C.: University Press of America, 1980), 208.
4. "Universities," *Catholic Encyclopedia*, 1913. The universities that lacked charters had come into being spontaneously *ex consuetudine.*
5. Ibid.
6. Gordon Leff, *Paris and Oxford Universities in the Thirteenth and Fourteenth Centuries: An Institutional and Intellectual History* (New York: John Wiley and Sons, 1968), 18.
7. Daly, 167.
8. Joseph H. Lynch, *The Medieval Church: A Brief History* (London: Longman, 1992), 250.

9. Daly, 163–64.

10. Ibid., 22.

11. A. B. Cobban, *The Medieval Universities: Their Development and Organization* (London: Methuen & Co., 1975), 82–83.

12. Daly, 168.

13. "Universities"; Cobban, 57.

14. "Universities."

15. Daly, 202.

16. Leff, 10.

17. Ibid., 8–9.

18. The classic study is Haskins, *The Renaissance of the Twelfth Century*; see also idem, *The Rise of Universities*, 4–5.

19. Daly, 132–33.

20. Ibid., 135.

21. Ibid., 136.

22. Edward Grant, *God and Reason in the Middle Ages* (Cambridge: Cambridge University Press, 2001), 184.

23. Ibid., 146.

24. This formulation of Anselm's claim belongs to Dr. William Marra (d. 1998), an old friend who for decades taught philosophy at Fordham University, and who belonged to that minority tradition of Western philosophers who believed that Saint Anselm's proof succeeded in demonstrating the necessity of God's existence.

25. Quoted in Grant, 60–61.

26. David C. Lindberg, *The Beginnings of Western Science* (Chicago: University of Chicago Press, 1992), 196.

27. On Abelard as a faithful son of the Church rather than an eighteenth-century rationalist, see David Knowles, *The Evolution of Medieval Thought*, 2nd ed. (London: Longman, 1988), 111ff.

28. Daly, 105.

29. See the excellent article by James A. Sadowsky, S.J., "Can There Be an Endless Regress of Causes?" in *Philosophy of Religion: A Guide and Anthology*, Brian Davies, ed. (New York: Oxford University Press, 2000), 239–42.

30. Henri Daniel-Rops, *Cathedral and Crusade*, trans. John Warrington (London: J. M. Dent & Sons, 1957), 311.

31. Ibid., 308.

32. Lindberg, 363.

33. Christopher Dawson, *Religion and the Rise of Western Culture* (New York: Image Books, 1991 [1950]), 190–91.

34. Grant, 356.

35. Ibid., 364.

## Chapter Five
## THE CHURCH AND SCIENCE

1. J. G. Hagen, "Nicolaus Copernicus," *Catholic Encyclopedia*, 2nd ed., 1913.

2. Jerome J. Langford, O.P., *Galileo, Science and the Church* (New York: Desclee, 1966), 35.

3. Joseph MacDonnell, S.J., *Jesuit Geometers* (St. Louis: Institute of Jesuit Sources, 1989), 19.

4. Ibid.

5. Langford, 45, 52.

6. Tycho Brahe (1546–1601) proposed an astronomical system that fell somewhere between Ptolemaic geocentrism and Copernican heliocentrism. In this system, all the planets except Earth revolved around the sun, but the sun revolved around a stationary Earth.

7. Ibid., 68–69.

8. Cf. Jacques Barzun, *From Dawn to Decadence* (New York: Harper Collins, 2001), 40; a good brief treatment of the issue appears in H. W. Crocker III, *Triumph* (Roseville, Calif.: Prima, 2001), 309–11.

9. James Brodrick, *The Life and Work of Blessed Robert Francis Cardinal Bellarmine, S.J., 1542–1621*, vol. 2 (London: Burns, Oates and Washbourne, 1928), 359.

10. James J. Walsh, *The Popes and Science* (New York: Fordham University Press, 1911), 296–97.

11. Edward Grant, "Science and Theology in the Middle Ages," in *God and Nature: Historical Essays on the Encounter Between Christianity and Science*, David C. Lindberg and Ronald L. Numbers, eds. (Berkeley: University of California Press, 1986), 63.

12. MacDonnell, Appendix 1, 6–7.

13. J. L. Heilbron, *The Sun in the Church: Cathedrals as Solar Obser-vatories* (Cambridge: Harvard University Press, 1999), 203.

14. Zdenek Kopal, "The Contribution of Boscovich to Astronomy and Geodesy," in *Roger Joseph Boscovich, S.J., F.R.S., 1711–1787,* Lancelot Law Whyte, ed. (New York: Fordham University Press, 1961), 175.

15. See Thomas E. Woods, Jr., *The Church and the Market: A Catholic Defense of the Free Economy* (Lanham, Md.: Lexington, 2005), 169–74.

16. Stanley L. Jaki, *Science and Creation: From Eternal Cycles to an Oscillating Universe* (Edinburgh: Scottish Academic Press, 1986), 150. "The coupling of the reasonability of the Creator and the con-stancy of nature is worth noting because it is there that lie the beginnings of the idea of the autonomy of nature and of its laws." Ibid. Cf. Ps. 8:4, 19:3-7, 104:9, 148:3, 6; Jer. 5:24, 31:35.

17. David Lindberg cites several instances in which Saint Augustine refers to this verse; see David C. Lindberg, "On the Applicability of Mathematics to Nature: Roger Bacon and His Predecessors," *British Journal for the History of Science* 15 (1982): 7.

18. Stanley L. Jaki, "Medieval Creativity in Science and Technology," in *Patterns or Principles and Other Essays* (Bryn Mawr, Pa.: Inter-collegiate Studies Institute, 1995), 80.

19. Rodney Stark, *For the Glory of God* (Princeton: Princeton Univer-sity Press, 2003), 125.

20. Paul Haffner, *Creation and Scientific Creativity* (Front Royal, Va.: Christendom Press, 1991), 35.

21. Ibid., 50.

22. Joseph Needham, *Science and Civilization in China*, vol. 1 (Cam-bridge: Cambridge University Press, 1954), 581; quoted in Stark, 151.

23. Stanley L. Jaki, *The Savior of Science* (Grand Rapids, Mich.: Eerd-mans, 2000), 77–78.

24. Stanley L. Jaki, "Myopia about Islam, with an Eye on Chesterbel-loc," *The Chesterton Review* 28 (winter 2002): 500.

25. Richard C. Dales, *The Intellectual Life of Western Europe in the Middle Ages* (Washington, D.C.: University Press of America, 1980), 264.

26. Richard C. Dales, "The De-Animation of the Heavens in the Middle Ages," *Journal of the History of Ideas* 41 (1980): 535.
27. Quoted in Haffner, 39; see also 42.
28. A. C. Crombie, *Medieval and Early Modern Science*, vol. 1 (Garden City, N.Y.: Doubleday, 1959), 58.
29. Haffner, 40.
30. Quoted in Ernest L. Fortin, "The Bible Made Me Do It: Christianity, Science, and the Environment," in *Ernest Fortin: Collected Essays*, vol. 3: *Human Rights, Virtue, and the Common Good: Untimely Meditations on Religion and Politics*, ed. J. Brian Benestad (Lanham, Md.: Rowman & Littlefield, 1996), 122. Emphasis in Nietzsche's original (*Genealogy of Morals* III, 23–24).
31. For a good overview of Aristotle, projectiles, and impetus, see Herbert Butterfield, *The Origins of Modern Science, 1300–1800*, rev. ed. (New York: Free Press, 1957), Chapter 1: "The Historical Importance of a Theory of Impetus."
32. On Buridan and inertial motion, see Stanley L. Jaki, "Science: Western or What?" in *Patterns or Principles and Other Essays*, 169–71.
33. Crombie, vol. 2, 72–73; on the differences between Buridan's impetus and modern ideas of inertia, see Butterfield, 25.
34. Jaki, "Science: Western or What?" 170–71.
35. Ibid., 171.
36. Jaki, "Medieval Creativity in Science and Technology," 76.
37. Ibid., 76–77.
38. Ibid., 79.
39. Crombie, vol. 2, 73.
40. E. J. Dijksterhuis, *The Mechanization of the World Picture*, trans. C. Dikshoorn (London: Oxford University Press, 1961), 106.
41. Thomas Goldstein, *Dawn of Modern Science: From the Ancient Greeks to the Renaissance* (New York: Da Capo Press, 1995 [1980]), 71, 74.
42. Raymond Klibansky, "The School of Chartres," in *Twelfth Century Europe and the Foundations of Modern Society*, eds. Marshall Clagett, Gaines Post, and Robert Reynolds (Madison: University of Wisconsin Press, 1961), 9–10.

43. Cf. David C. Lindberg, *The Beginnings of Western Science* (Chicago: University of Chicago Press, 1992), 200.

44. Goldstein, 88.

45. Edward Grant, *God and Reason in the Middle Ages* (Cambridge: Cambridge University Press, 2001).

46. Goldstein, 82.

47. Lindberg, *The Beginnings of Western Science*, 200.

48. Ibid., 201.

49. Jaki, *Science and Creation*, 220–21.

50. Goldstein, 77.

51. Ibid., 82.

52. On the Latin Averroists, see Etienne Gilson, *Reason and Revelation in the Middle Ages* (New York: Charles Scribner's Sons, 1938), 54–66.

53. Dales, *Intellectual Life*, 254.

54. Sympathetic to this argument are A. C. Crombie, *Medieval and Early Modern Science*, vol. 1, 64 and vol. 2, 35–36; Grant, *God and Reason in the Middle Ages*, 213ff., 220–21; idem, *The Foundations of Modern Science in the Middle Ages: Their Religious, Institutional, and Intellectual Contexts* (Cambridge: Cambridge University Press, 1996), 78–83, 147–48. More skeptical but conceding the essential point is Lindberg, *The Beginnings of Western Science*, 238, 365.

55. Dales, "The De-Animation of the Heavens in the Middle Ages," 550.

56. Ibid., 546.

57. Ibid.

58. Richard C. Dales, "A Twelfth Century Concept of the Natural Order," *Viator* 9 (1978): 179.

59. Ibid., 191.

60. Haffner, 41.

61. Edward Grant, "The Condemnation of 1277, God's Absolute Power, and Physical Thought in the Late Middle Ages," *Viator* 10 (1979): 242–44.

62. Walsh, 292–93.

63. A. C. Crombie and J. D. North, "Bacon, Roger," in *Dictionary of Scientific Biography*, ed. Charles C. Gillispie (New York: Charles

Scribner's Sons, 1970), 378. The *Dictionary* shall hereinafter be cited as DSB.

64. William A. Wallace, O.P., "Albertus Magnus, Saint," in DSB, 99.

65. Walsh, 297.

66. Dales, "The De-Animation of the Heavens," 540.

67. William B. Ashworth, Jr., "Catholicism and Early Modern Science," in Lindberg and Numbers, eds., *God and Nature*, 146.

68. Alan Cutler, *The Seashell on the Mountaintop* (New York: Dutton, 2003), 106.

69. Ibid., 113–14.

70. David R. Oldroyd, *Thinking About the Earth: A History of Ideas in Geology* (Cambridge: Harvard University Press, 1996), 63–67; see also A. Wolf, *A History of Science, Technology, and Philosophy in the 16th and 17th Centuries* (London: George Allen & Unwin, 1938), 359–60.

71. Cutler, 109–12.

72. Jonathan Wright, *The Jesuits: Missions, Myths and Histories* (London: HarperCollins, 2004), 189.

73. J. L. Heilbron, *Electricity in the 17th and 18th Centuries: A Study of Early Modern Physics* (Berkeley: University of California Press, 1979), 2.

74. Ashworth, "Catholicism and Early Modern Science," 154.

75. Ibid., 155.

76. MacDonnell, 71.

77. The Jesuits were suppressed in 1773 and later restored in 1814.

78. Agustín Udías, *Searching the Heavens and the Earth: The History of Jesuit Observatories* (Dordrecht, The Netherlands: Kluwer Academic Publishers, 2003), 53.

79. Ibid., 147.

80. Ibid., 125.

81. Heilbron, 88.

82. Ibid.

83. Ibid., 88–89.

84. Ashworth, "Catholicism and Early Modern Science," 155.

85. Heilbron, 180.

86. Ibid., 87–88.

87. Bruce S. Eastwood, "Grimaldi, Francesco Maria," in DSB, 542.

88. On the relationship of Grimaldi's work to Newton's, see Roger H. Stuewer, "A Critical Analysis of Newton's Work on Diffraction," *Isis* 61 (1970): 188–205.

89. For a brief discussion, with diagrams, of Grimaldi's experiments, see A. Wolf, *A History of Science, Technology, and Philosophy in the 16th and 17th Centuries* (London: George Allen & Unwin, 1938), 254–56.

90. Sir Harold Hartley, "Foreword," in Whyte, ed., *Roger Joseph Boscovich*, 8.

91. MacDonnell, 76.

92. Elizabeth Hill, "Roger Boscovich: A Biographical Essay," in Whyte, ed., *Roger Joseph Boscovich*, 34–35; Adolf Muller, "Ruggiero Giuseppe Boscovich," *Catholic Encyclopedia*, 2nd ed., 1913.

93. Hill, "Roger Boscovich: A Biographical Essay," 34.

94. Zeljko Markovic, "Boskovic, Rudjer J.," in DSB, 326.

95. Lancelot Law Whyte, "Boscovich's Atomism," in Whyte, ed., *Roger Joseph Boscovich*, 102.

96. Ibid.

97. Ibid., 103–104.

98. MacDonnell, 10–11.

99. Whyte, "Boscovich's Atomism," 105.

100. Ibid., 119.

101. For these and additional testimonies, see ibid., 121.

102. MacDonnell, 11.

103. Hill, "Roger Boscovich: A Biographical Essay," 41–42.

104. J. R. Partington, *A History of Chemistry*, vol. 2 (London: Macmillan, 1961), 328–33; MacDonnell, 13.

105. Cutler, 68.

106. MacDonnell, 12.

107. Erik Iverson, *The Myth of Egypt and its Hieroglyphs* (Copenhagen, 1961), 97–98; quoted in MacDonnell, 12.

108. Agustín Udías, S.J., and William Suauder, "Jesuits in Seismology," *Jesuits in Science Newsletter* 13 (1997); Benjamin F. Howell, Jr., *An Introduction to Seismological Research: History and Development* (Cambridge: Cambridge University Press, 1990), 31–32. For

more on Jesuit work in seismology in North America, see Udías, *Searching the Heavens and the Earth*, 103–24.

109. Udías and Suauder, "Jesuits in Seismology."
110. MacDonnell, 20, 54.
111. For a detailed and graphical explanation of Cassini's method, see Heilbron, Chapter 3, especially 102–12.
112. J. L. Heilbron, Annual Invitation Lecture to the Scientific Instrument Society, Royal Institution, London, December 6, 1995.
113. William J. Broad, "How the Church Aided 'Heretical' Astronomy," *New York Times*, October 19, 1999.
114. Heilbron, 112. Heilbron uses what in this context is the rather technical term "bisection of the eccentricity" to refer to what Cassini discovered. The phrase simply refers to elliptical planetary orbits, which are sometimes said to be "eccentric."
115. Ibid.
116. Ibid., 5.
117. Ibid., 3.

## *Chapter Six*
## ART, ARCHITECTURE, AND THE CHURCH

1. Saint John of Damascus, *Three Treatises on the Divine Images*, trans. Andrew Louth (Crestwood, N.Y.: St. Vladimir's Seminary Press, 2003), 69–70.
2. Ibid., 29.
3. Ibid., 29–30.
4. "Orthodoxy" in this case does not refer to the Orthodox Church, since the Great Schism that divided Catholics and Orthodox would not occur until 1054; the term refers instead to *traditional belief.*
5. Paul Johnson, *Art: A New History* (New York: HarperCollins, 2003), 153.
6. John W. Baldwin, *The Scholastic Culture of the Middle Ages, 1000–1300* (Lexington, Mass.: D.C. Heath, 1971), 107; Robert A. Scott, *The Gothic Enterprise* (Berkeley: University of California Press, 2003), 124–25.
7. Scott, 125.

8. Baldwin, 107.

9. Scott, 103–104.

10. Christopher Wilson, *The Gothic Cathedral: The Architecture of the Great Church, 1130–1530* (London: Thames and Hudson, 1990), 65–66.

11. Ibid., 275–76.

12. Baldwin, 107–08.

13. Ibid., 108.

14. Scott, 132.

15. Stanley L. Jaki, "Medieval Creativity in Science and Technology," in *Patterns or Principles and Other Essays* (Bryn Mawr, Pa.: Intercollegiate Studies Institute, 1995), 75.

16. The book in question is Robert Scott's *The Gothic Enterprise.*

17. Alexander Clarence Frick, *The Rise of the Mediaeval Church* (New York: Burt Franklin, 1909), 600.

18. Erwin Panofsky, *Gothic Architecture and Scholasticism* (New York: Meridian, 1985 [1951]), 69–70.

19. James Franklin, "The Renaissance Myth," *Quadrant* 26 (November 1982): 53–54.

20. Kenneth Clark, *Civilisation* (New York: HarperPerennial, 1969), 186; quoted in Joseph E. MacDonnell, *Companions of Jesuits: A Tradition of Collaboration* (Fairfield, Conn.: Humanities Institute, 1995).

21. Louis Gillet, "Raphael," *Catholic Encyclopedia,* 2nd ed., 1913.

22. Klemens Löffler, "Pope Leo X," *Catholic Encyclopedia,* 2nd ed., 1913.

23. Will Durant, *The Renaissance* (New York: MJF Books, 1953), 484.

24. Fred S. Kleiner, Christin J. Mamiya, and Richard G. Tansey, *Gardner's Art Through the Ages,* 11th ed., vol. 1 (New York: Wadsworth, 2001), 526–27.

25. Samuel Y. Edgerton, Jr., *The Heritage of Giotto's Geometry: Art and Science on the Eve of the Scientific Revolution* (Ithaca: Cornell University Press, 1991), 10.

26. Ibid., 4.

27. Ibid., 289.

*Chapter Seven*
## THE ORIGINS OF INTERNATIONAL LAW

1. Bernice Hamilton, *Political Thought in Sixteenth-Century Spain* (London: Oxford University Press, 1963), 98; J. A. Fernandez-Santamaria, *The State, War and Peace: Spanish Political Thought in the Renaissance, 1516–1559* (Cambridge: Cambridge University Press, 1977), 60–61.

2. Lewis Hanke, *The Spanish Struggle for Justice in the Conquest of America* (Boston: Little, Brown and Co., 1965 [1949]), 17.

3. Carl Watner, "'All Mankind Is One': The Libertarian Tradition in Sixteenth Century Spain," *Journal of Libertarian Studies* 8 (Summer 1987): 295–96.

4. Michael Novak, *The Universal Hunger for Liberty* (New York: Basic Books, 2004), 24. This title is also applied to the Dutch Protestant Hugo Grotius.

5. Marcelo Sánchez-Sorondo, "Vitoria: The Original Philosopher of Rights," in *Hispanic Philosophy in the Age of Discovery*, Kevin White, ed. (Washington, D.C.: Catholic University of America Press, 1997), 66.

6. Watner, "'All Mankind Is One,'" 294; Watner is quoting from Lewis Hanke, *All Mankind Is One* (De Kalb, Ill.: Northern Illinois University Press, 1974), 142.

7. James Brown Scott, *The Spanish Origin of International Law* (Washington, D.C.: School of Foreign Service, Georgetown University, 1928), 65.

8. Cf. Sánchez-Sorondo, "Vitoria: The Original Philosopher of Rights," 60.

9. Venancio D. Carro, "The Spanish Theological-Juridical Renaissance and the Ideology of Bartolome de Las Casas," in *Bartolomé de Las Casas in History: Toward an Understanding of the Man and His Work*, eds. Juan Friede and Benjamin Keen (DeKalb, Ill.: Northern Illinois University Press, 1971), 251–52.

10. Ibid., 253.

11. Ibid.

12. Fernandez-Santamaria, 79.

13. Hamilton, 61.

14. Scott, 41.

15. Ibid., 61.

16. *Summa Theologiae*, II-II, q. 10, a. 8.

17. Sánchez-Sorondo, "Vitoria: The Original Philosopher of Rights," 67.

18. Hamilton, 19.

19. Ibid., 21.

20. Ibid., 24.

21. Fernandez-Santamaria, 78.

22. Brian Tierney, *The Idea of Natural Rights: Studies on Natural Rights, Natural Law, and Church Law, 1150–1625* (Grand Rapids, Mich.: William B. Eerdmans, 2001 [1997]), 269–70.

23. Eduardo Andújar, "Bartolomé de Las Casas and Juan Ginés de Sepúlveda: Moral Theology versus Political Philosophy," in White, ed., *Hispanic Philosophy*, 76–78.

24. Ibid., 87.

25. Rafael Alvira and Alfredo Cruz, "The Controversy Between Las Casas and Sepúlveda at Valladolid," in White, ed., *Hispanic Philosophy*, 93.

26. Ibid.

27. Ibid., 95.

28. Ibid., 92–93.

29. Andújar, "Bartolomé de Las Casas and Juan Ginés de Sepúlveda," 84.

30. Carro, "The Spanish Theological-Juridical Renaissance," 275.

31. Quoted in Watner, "'All Mankind Is One,'" 303–04.

32. Lewis H. Hanke, *Bartolomé de Las Casas: An Interpretation of His Life and Writings* (The Hague: Martinus Nijhoff, 1951), 87.

33. Cf. Carlos G. Noreña, "Francisco Suárez on Democracy and International Law," in White, ed., *Hispanic Philosophy*, 271.

34. Fernandez-Santamaria, 62.

35. Samuel Eliot Morison, *The Oxford History of the American People*, vol. 1, *Prehistory to 1789* (New York: Meridian, 1994 [1965]), 40.

36. Quoted in Robert C. Royal, *Columbus On Trial: 1492 v. 1992*, 2nd ed. (Herndon, Va.: Young America's Foundation, 1993), 23–24.

37. Cf. C. Brown, "Old World v. New: Culture Shock in 1492," *Peninsula* [Harvard], Sept. 1992, 11.

38. Hanke, *The Spanish Struggle for Justice*, 178–79.

*Chapter Eight*
## THE CHURCH AND ECONOMICS

1. Joseph A. Schumpeter, *History of Economic Analysis* (New York: Oxford University Press, 1954), 97.

2. Thus see Raymond de Roover, "The Concept of the Just Price: Theory and Economic Policy," *Journal of Economic History* 18 (1958): 418–34; idem, *Business, Banking, and Economic Thought in Late Medieval and Early Modern Europe: Selected Studies of Raymond de Roover*, ed. Julius Kirshner (Chicago: University of Chicago Press, 1974), esp. 306–45; Alejandro A. Chafuen, *Faith and Liberty: The Economic Thought of the Late Scholastics* (Lanham, Md.: Lexington, 2003); Marjorie Grice-Hutchinson, *The School of Salamanca: Readings in Spanish Monetary Theory, 1544–1605* (Oxford: Clarendon Press, 1952); idem, *Early Economic Thought in Spain, 1177–1740* (London: George Allen & Unwin, 1978); Joseph Schumpeter, *History of Economic Analysis* (New York: Oxford University Press, 1954); Murray N. Rothbard, *An Austrian Perspective on the History of Economic Thought*, vol. 1, *Economic Thought Before Adam Smith* (Hants, England: Edward Elgar, 1995), 99–133.

3. Rothbard, *Economic Thought Before Adam Smith*, 73–74. Ludwig von Mises, the great twentieth-century economist, showed that money had to originate in this way.

4. Ibid., 74; see also Thomas E. Woods, Jr., *The Church and the Market: A Catholic Defense of the Free Economy* (Lanham, Md.: Lexington, 2005), 87–89, 93.

5. Jörg Guido Hülsmann, "Nicholas Oresme and the First Monetary Treatise," May 8, 2004 http://www.mises.org/fullstory.aspx?control=1516.

6.  Rothbard, *Economic Thought Before Adam Smith*, 76.

7.  Hülsmann, "Nicholas Oresme and the First Monetary Treatise."

8.  Chafuen, 62.

9.  For a good overview of key imagery in the Bible, and particularly of the oft-contested Matthew 16:18, see Stanley L. Jaki, *The Keys of the Kingdom: A Tool's Witness to Truth* (Chicago, Ill.: Franciscan Herald Press, 1986).

10. Rothbard, *Economic Thought Before Adam Smith*, 100–101.

11. Ibid., 60–61.

12. Ibid., 62.

13. Murray N. Rothbard, "New Light on the Prehistory of the Austrian School," in *The Foundations of Modern Austrian Economics*, ed. Edwin G. Dolan (Kansas City: Sheed & Ward, 1976), 55.

14. Chafuen, 84–85.

15. Ibid., 84.

16. "Carl Menger is best understood in the context of nineteenth-century Aristotelian/neo-scholasticism." Samuel Bostaph, "The *Methodenstreit*," in *The Elgar Companion to Austrian Economics*, ed. Peter J. Boettke (Cheltenham, U.K.: Edward Elgar, 1994), 460.

17. Carl Menger, *Principles of Economics*, trans. James Dingwall and Bert F. Hoselitz (Grove City, Penn.: Libertarian Press, 1994), 64–66.

18. But for a direct reply to Marx, see the neglected classic by Eugen von Böhm-Bawerk, *Karl Marx and the Close of His System* (London: TF Unwin, 1898). An even stronger and more fundamental argument, which exposes Marx's position as entirely wrongheaded (and which does not in fact rely on subjective value theory), can be found in George Reisman, *Capitalism* (Ottawa, Ill.: Jameson Books, 1996).

19. Emil Kauder, *A History of Marginal Utility Theory* (Princeton: Princeton University Press, 1965), 5.

20. Locke is frequently misunderstood on this point, so it is worth noting that he did not believe in the labor theory of value. Locke's teaching on labor had to do with the justice of initial acquisition in a world of unowned goods. Locke taught that in a state of nature, in which few if any goods belong to individuals as private property, someone may justly claim a good or a parcel of land as his own if he mixes his labor

with it—if he clears a field, for example, or simply picks an apple from a tree. The exertion of his labor gives him a moral claim to the good with which he has mixed his labor. Once a good has come to be privately owned, it is no longer necessary that anyone continue to apply labor to it in order to call it his own. Privately owned goods are the legitimate property of their owners if they have been acquired either directly from the state of nature, as we have seen, or if they have been acquired by means of purchase or a voluntary grant by someone possessing legitimate title to it. None of this has anything to do with assigning *value* to goods on the basis of the expenditure of labor; Locke is concerned instead to vindicate a *moral and legal claim to ownership* of goods acquired in the state of nature on the basis of the initial expenditure of labor upon them.

21. Kauder, 5–6.
22. Ibid., 9. Emphasis added.
23. Scholasticism had come to be despised, both by Protestants and by rationalists, and explicit reference to the work of the late Scholastics on the part of some of their successors was, for that reason, sometimes fleeting. It is still possible for historians of thought to trace the Scholastics' influence, however, particularly since even the enemies of Scholasticism nevertheless cited their work explicitly. See Rothbard, "New Light on the Prehistory of the Austrian School," 65–67.
24. On the late Scholastics' subsequent influence I am heavily indebted to Rothbard's "New Light on the Prehistory of the Austrian School."
25. Rothbard, "New Light on the Prehistory of the Austrian School," 66.
26. For my own development of late Scholastic insights, see Woods, *The Church and the Market: A Catholic Defense of the Free Economy.*
27. Rothbard, "New Light on the Prehistory of the Austrian School," 67.

*Chapter Nine*
HOW CATHOLIC CHARITY CHANGED THE WORLD

1. Alvin J. Schmidt, *Under the Influence: How Christianity Transformed Civilization* (Grand Rapids, Mich.: Zondervan, 2001), 130.

2. Michael Davies, *For Altar and Throne: The Rising in the Vendée* (St. Paul, Minn.: Remnant Press, 1997), 13.
3. Vincent Carroll and David Shiflett, *Christianity on Trial* (San Francisco: Encounter Books, 2002), 142.
4. William Edward Hartpole Lecky, *History of European Morals From Augustus to Charlemagne*, vol. 1 (New York: D. Appleton and Company, 1870), 199–200.
5. Ibid., 201.
6. Ibid., 202. For a good discussion of the absence of the Christian idea of charity in the ancient world, see Gerhard Uhlhorn, *Christian Charity in the Ancient Church* (New York: Charles Scribner's Sons, 1883), 2–44.
7. Lecky, 83.
8. John A. Ryan, "Charity and Charities," *Catholic Encyclopedia*, 2nd ed., 1913; C[harles Guillaume Adolphe] Schmidt, *The Social Results of Early Christianity* (London: Sir Isaac Pitman & Sons, 1907), 251.
9. Uhlhorn, 264.
10. Cajetan Baluffi, *The Charity of the Church*, trans. Denis Gargan (Dublin: M. H. Gill and Son, 1885), 39; Schmidt, *Under the Influence*, 157.
11. Lecky, 87; Baluffi, 14–15; Schmidt, *Social Results of Early Christianity*, 328.
12. Uhlhorn, 187–88.
13. Schmidt, *Under the Influence*, 152.
14. Baluffi, 42–43; Schmidt, *Social Results of Early Christianity*, 255–56.
15. Schmidt, *Social Results of Early Christianity*, 328.
16. Ibid.
17. Schmidt, *Under the Influence*, 153–55.
18. Ryan, "Charity and Charities"; Guenter B. Risse, *Mending Bodies, Saving Souls: A History of Hospitals* (New York: Oxford University Press, 1999), 79ff.
19. Risse, 73.

20. Fielding H. Garrison, *An Introduction of the History of Medicine* (Philadelphia: W. B. Saunders, 1914), 118; cited in Schmidt, *Under the Influence*, 131.

21. Lecky, 85.

22. Roberto Margotta, *The History of Medicine*, Paul Lewis, ed. (New York: Smithmark, 1996), 52.

23. Risse, 95.

24. Ibid., 138.

25. Ibid., 141.

26. Ibid., 141–42.

27. Ibid., 147.

28. Ibid., 149.

29. Carroll and Shiflett, 143.

30. Baluffi, 16.

31. Ibid., 185.

32. Quoted in Ryan, "Charity and Charities."

33. Baluffi, 257.

34. Neil S. Rushton, "Monastic Charitable Provision in Tudor England: Quantifying and Qualifying Poor Relief in the Early Sixteenth Century," *Continuity and Change* 16 (2001): 34. I have rendered this portion of the petition in modern English.

35. William Cobbett, *A History of the Protestant Reformation in England and Ireland* (Rockford, Ill.: TAN, 1988 [1896]), 112.

36. Philip Hughes, *A Popular History of the Reformation* (Garden City, N.Y.: Hanover House, 1957), 205.

37. Henri Daniel-Rops, *The Protestant Reformation*, trans. Audrey Butler (London: J. M. Dent & Sons, 1961), 475.

38. Rushton, "Monastic Charitable Provision in Tudor England," 10.

39. Ibid., 11.

40. Barbara Harvey, *Living and Dying in England, 1100–1540: The Monastic Experience* (Oxford: Clarendon Press, 1993), 22, 33.

41. Georg Ratzinger, quoted in Ryan, "Charity and Charities."

42. Lecky, 89.

43. Harvey, 18.
44. Ibid., 13.
45. Davies, 11.


*Chapter Ten*
The Church and Western Law

1.  Harold J. Berman, *Law and Revolution: The Formation of the Western Legal Tradition* (Cambridge: Harvard University Press, 1983), 166.
2.  Ibid., 195.
3.  Ibid., 143.
4.  Harold J. Berman, "The Influence of Christianity Upon the Development of Law," *Oklahoma Law Review* 12 (1959): 93.
5.  Harold J. Berman, *Faith and Order: The Reconciliation of Law and Religion* (Atlanta: Scholars Press, 1993), 44.
6.  Berman, "Influence of Christianity Upon the Development of Law," 93.
7.  Berman, *Law and Revolution*, 228.
8.  Berman, "Influence of Christianity Upon the Development of Law," 93.
9.  Berman, *Law and Revolution*, 188.
10. Ibid., 189.
11. Cf. ibid., 179.
12. A distillation can be found in Berman, *Law and Revolution*, 177ff.
13. This line of thought, although familiar to us, contains within it the potential danger that criminal law, in its eagerness to vindicate justice in the abstract by means of retributive punishment, may degenerate to a point at which it becomes interested *only* in retribution and abandons any attempt at restitution whatever. Thus today we have the perverse situation in which a violent criminal, instead of making at least some attempt to make restitution to his victim or to the latter's heirs, is himself supported by the tax dollars of the victim and his family. Thus the insistence that the criminal has offended *justice itself* and thus deserves punishment has completely overwhelmed the earlier sense that the criminal has offended *his victim* and owes restitution to whomever he has wronged.
14. Berman, *Law and Revolution*, 194–95.

15. Brian Tierney, *The Idea of Natural Rights: Studies on Natural Rights, Natural Law, and Church Law, 1150–1625* (Grand Rapids, Mich.: William B. Eerdmans, 2001); see also Annabel S. Brett, *Liberty, Right and Nature: Individual Rights in Later Scholastic Thought* (Cambridge: Cambridge University Press, 1997); Charles J. Reid, Jr., "The Canonistic Contribution to the Western Rights Tradition: An Historical Inquiry," *Boston College Law Review* 33 (1991): 37–92; Kenneth Pennington, "The History of Rights in Western Thought," *Emory Law Journal* 47 (1998): 237–52.

16. Brian Tierney, "The Idea of Natural Rights: Origins and Persistence," *Northwestern University Journal of International Human Rights* 2 (April 2004): 5.

17. Tierney, "The Idea of Natural Rights," 6. Emphasis added.

18. Ibid.

19. Pennington, "The History of Rights in Western Thought."

20. Tierney, "The Idea of Natural Rights," 7.

21. Ibid., 8.

## Chapter Eleven

## THE CHURCH AND WESTERN MORALITY

1. Alvin J. Schmidt, *Under the Influence: How Christianity Transformed Civilization* (Grand Rapids, Mich.: Zondervan, 2001), 128, 153.

2. Vincent Carroll and David Shiflett, *Christianity on Trial* (San Francisco: Encounter Books, 2002), 7.

3. Augustine, *The City of God*, trans. Henry Bettenson (London: Penguin Classics, 1972), Book 1, Chapter 22.

4. Ibid.

5. ST IIa-IIae, q. 64, art. 5.

6. James J. Walsh, *The World's Debt to the Catholic Church* (Boston: The Stratford Co., 1924), 227.

7. For both of these quotations, see Schmidt, 63.

8. Leo XIII, *Pastoralis Officii* (1891), 2, 4.

9. Ernest L. Fortin, "Christianity and the Just War Theory," in *Ernest Fortin: Collected Essays*, vol. 3: *Human Rights, Virtue, and the*

*Common Good: Untimely Meditations on Religion and Politics*, ed.
J. Brian Benestad (Lanham, Md.: Rowan & Littlefield, 1996),
285–86.

10. John Langan, S.J., "The Elements of St. Augustine's Just War Theory," *Journal of Religious Ethics* 12 (Spring 1984): 32.

11. ST, IIa-IIae, q. 40, art. 1. Internal references omitted.

12. Thomas A. Massaro, S.J., and Thomas A. Shannon, *Catholic Perspectives on Peace and War* (Lanham, Md.: Rowan & Littlefield, 2003), 17.

13. Ibid., 18.

14. See Roland H. Bainton, *Christian Attitudes Toward War and Peace* (New York: Abingdon Press, 1960), 123–26.

15. Ibid., 126.

16. Schmidt, 80–82.

17. Ibid., 84.

18. Ibid.

19. Robert Phillips, *Last Things First* (Fort Collins, Colo.: Roman Catholic Books, 2004), 104.

*Conclusion*
## A WORLD WITHOUT GOD

1. For this discussion of these four particular characteristics I am indebted to Marvin Perry, et al., *Western Civilization: Ideas, Politics & Society*, 6th ed. (Boston: Houghton Mifflin, 2000), 39–40.

2. Kierkegaard was a Protestant, though of course he is here describing an aspect of Christ that is shared in common with Catholics. Interestingly, moreover, Kierkegaard was very critical of Luther and deplored the suppression of the monastic tradition. See Alice von Hildebrand, "Kierkegaard: A Critic of Luther," *The Latin Mass*, spring 2004, 10–14.

3. Murray N. Rothbard, "Karl Marx as Religious Eschatologist," in *Requiem for Marx*, ed. Yuri N. Maltsev (Auburn, Ala: Ludwig von Mises Institute, 1993).

4. Murray N. Rothbard, "World War I as Fulfillment: Power and the Intellectuals," in *The Costs of War*, ed. John V. Denson (New

Brunswick, N.J.: Transaction, 1997); for more recent examples of this phenomenon, see Paul Gottfried, *Multiculturalism and the Politics of Guilt* (Columbia: University of Missouri Press, 2002).

5. David C. Lindberg, *The Beginnings of Western Science* (Chicago: University of Chicago Press, 1992), 213.

6. On the success of the Church in America, see Thomas E. Woods, Jr., *The Church Confronts Modernity: Catholic Intellectuals and the Progressive Era* (New York: Columbia University Press, 2004).

7. Frederick Copleston, S.J., *A History of Philosophy*, vol. VII: *Modern Philosophy from the Post-Kantian Idealists to Marx, Kierkegaard, and Nietzsche* (New York: Doubleday, 1994 [1963]), 419.

8. For beautiful and hideous architecture see, respectively, Michael S. Rose, *In Tiers of Glory* (Cincinnati, Ohio: Mesa Folio, 2004), and Michael S. Rose, *Ugly as Sin* (Manchester, N.H.: Sophia Institute Press, 2001).

9. "Duchamp's Urinal Tops Art Survey," BBC News World Edition, December 1, 2004. http://news.bbc.co.uk/2/hi/entertainment/4059997.stm.

# INDEX

Abbo of Fleury, 41, 42
*The Aberration of the Fixed Stars* (Boscovich), 106
Absalon, 38–39
Adelard of Bath, 87
adultery, 213–14
agriculture, monasticism and, 28–32
Alaric, 10
Albert the Great, 57, 72, 94–95, 96
Albertus Magnus. *See* Albert the Great
Alcuin, 17–21, 40, 64–65
Alexander IV, 65
Alfano, 41
Alfonso of Aragon, 179
Alhacen, 55
*Almagest* (Ptolemy), 55
*Almagestum novum* (Riccioli), 102–3, 104
Ambrose, 188
Anaxagoras, 172

Anglo-Saxons, 14, 17
animism, 12, 77
*Annals and Histories of Tacitus*, 42
Anselm, 41, 58–59; creation and, 80; existence of God and, 58–59, 62; Scholasticism and, 58–59, 62; Western law and, 194–97
Anthony of Egypt, 25–26
*The Application of the Telescope in Astronomical Studies* (Boscovich), 106
Apuleius, 41, 42
Arabs, 15, 76
archaeology, 36–37
architecture: Catholic Church and, 2, 119–24; Gothic, 119–23; modern, 223; Scholasticism and, 123–24
Arianism, 12, 15, 188
Aristotle, 40, 41, 52, 55, 57, 68, 70, 79, 86, 95, 98, 160;

Vandals, 10
Vargas Llosa, Mario, 150–51
Varro, 41, 42
*Verrines* (Cicero), 43
Victor III, 41
Vikings, 19, 21, 189
da Vinci, Leonardo, 108
de Vio, Thomas. *See* Cajetan,
  Cardinal
Virgil, 40, 41
Visigoths, 12
Vitellio, 55
Vitoria, Francisco de, 5–6;
  international law and,
  137–38, 139–44; just war
  and, 209–10
Vitruvius, 108
*Völkerwanderungen*, 10
Voltaire, 169–70
von Mises, Ludwig, 154

Waley, Arthur, 131
war, just, 207–11
Weil, Simon, 224–25

Westermarck, Edward, 212
Western civilization: Catholic
  Church and, 1–4, 7, 217–25;
  monasticism and, 25–45;
  monasticism and literacy of, 18
Western law: canon law and,
  190–94, 201–2; Catholic
  Church and, 6, 187–202;
  natural rights and, 197–202;
  separation of church and
  state and, 189–97
Widmanstadt, Johann Albert, 68
William of Conches, 87
William of Malmesbury, 31
William of Ockham, 80
Wilson, Christopher, 121
Winslow, Jacob, 99
Wisdom, book of, 76, 119
Wolff, Philippe, 18
Wolfgang, 42
World War II, 28

Zachary I, 16
Zucchi, Nicolas, 111